Jean Poulit

Connecting People While Preserving the Planet

Essays on Sustainable Development

ESRI PRESS

REDLANDS, CALIFORNIA

J. Poulit. *Connecting People While Preserving the Planet.* English-language edition edited by Michael Schwartz.

Title of the original French-laguage edition: *Le Territoire des Hommes*
Copyright © 2005 Bourin Éditeur

ESRI Press, 380 New York Street, Redlands, California 92373-8100

Copyright © 2007 ESRI

All rights reserved. First edition 2007
10 09 08 07   1 2 3 4 5 6 7 8 9 10

Printed in the United States of America

Library of Congress Cataloging-in-Publication Data
Poulit, Jean.
Connecting people while preserving the planet : essays on sustainable development / Jean Poulit.
    p. cm.
    ISBN-13: 978-1-58948-192-3 (pbk. : alk. paper) 1. Sustainable development. 2. Transportation. I. Title.
  HC79.E5P6697 2007
    338.9'27—dc   222007043839

The information contained in this document is subject to change without notice.

Ask for ESRI Press titles at your local bookstore or order by calling 1-800-447-9778. You can also shop online at www.esri.com/esripress. Outside the United States, contact your local ESRI distributor.

ESRI Press titles are distributed to the trade by the following:

In North America:
Ingram Publisher Services
Toll-free telephone: (800) 648-3104
Toll-free fax: (800) 838-1149
E-mail: customerservice@ingrampublisherservices.com

In the United Kingdom, Europe, and the Middle East:
Transatlantic Publishers Group Ltd.
Telephone: 44 20 7373 2515
Fax: 44 20 7244 1018
E-mail: richard@tpgltd.co.uk

Contents

Part III

Applications of evaluation methods for economic and natural performances of living areas   49

Part IV

A wider vision: economic and natural performances of living areas in France and Europe   71

Part V

Negative impacts caused by humans   95

Part VIII

Courses of action   155

Acknowledgments

I offer sincerest thanks to Jack Dangermond, president and founder of ESRI, who made the decision to publish this work. His urban planning training and well-known interest in environmental problems led to his immediate interest in the themes developed in this essay: positive interactions people experience daily passing through their living areas; relations with other living species that occupy our planet; the impact of nuisances stemming from human activity and the possibilities of remedying them; and courses of action for reconciling economic and ecological development. Applying these analyses calls, moreover, for the GIS techniques at the heart of activities at ESRI.

I equally express my thanks to Rony Gal, chief executive officer of ESRI France, who himself is a town planner by training, and who alerted Jack Dangermond to the interest there could be in publishing in English a work dealing with global issues of concern to many countries, especially developing nations. It is due to him that this English edition is possible. Christophe Charpentier, director of business development, actively assisted him.

Thanks also to Judy Hawkins, manager of ESRI Press, who worked diligently to ensure the best translation possible.

Finally, I thank Mike Schwartz who oversaw, with much attention, the editing of this book, and Ruth Burke, who provided the translation of a long work that included technical terms and some subtleties of the French language.

Foreword

For several decades, Jean Poulit has been studying many interrelated things—the land, people, transportation infrastructures, geography, local economies—and he's achieved a vision that many of us have been working hard to make clear for a long time. That vision is a different "picture" or design for how we can build living places that are smarter, healthier, more resource sustaining, and more robust economically than what we have now.

Jean's technical expertise was developed during 40 years as a public works and transportation specialist in France, and his know-how is coupled with a passion for woodlands, lakes, parks, and other natural surroundings where people can relax and recharge themselves—even in the middle of big cities.

Jean is a former president of EUROGI, the European Umbrella Organisation for Geographic Information, a position he held after a long and impressive civil service career with the French Ministry of Public Works, Transportation, Housing, and Planning. During that time, he developed conclusions that form the very heart of this book and apply to people everywhere—the idea that the economic well-being of a nation hinges on individuals working together within the places they live and work, and with technology making an important and vital difference.

In these pages, Jean shares a distilled wisdom that will inspire GIS users in urban design, public works, infrastructure management, and landscape and conservation planning. He gives us an innovative, complementary approach to organizing, thinking, and problem-solving that will help push our technology and spatial thinking forward. And in that process, city by city, region by region, Jean Poulit's insights will help unite, preserve, and protect our threatened but still-beautiful environment.

Jack Dangermond

Introduction

For more than 40 years, I have observed the behavior of people in living areas[1] where they reside, work, and spend their daily lives. I have studied questions related to transportation, lifestyle, environment, and urban development in these areas. And I have had the privilege, over this long period, of being in charge of very concrete and diverse responsibilities that have allowed me to confront both in theory and practice: implementation, in the 1970s, of the national program for traffic planning, which involved transforming the historical centers of our towns into pedestrian zones; development, in the 1980s, of one of the large new towns in the Île-de-France region: Marne-la-Vallée; and after this fine experience, establishment, in the 1990s, of the new master plan for Île-de-France, which affects the daily life of more than 10 million inhabitants. So, I have been immersed in national and local issues of my country for a long time.

Until the mid 1970s, I observed the enthusiasm of the French, who lived in the spirit of the 30 glorious years since 1945. Ambition was evident everywhere. It was a matter of rebuilding the nation, of relaunching the economy and reconstructing towns and cities destroyed during the last war; implementing an effective freeway system; developing modern telecommunication infrastructures; conducting an ambitious electro-nuclear program to allow France to achieve energy independence; constructing a mythic airplane, the Concorde—the first supersonic transport—which created a research dynamic that generated invaluable support for the Airbus program, whose subsequent achievements have been brilliant; and planning for high-speed trains—the famous TGVs (trains à grande vitesse).

All this creative energy testified to the exceptional vitality of our country. Then the climate changed. Large-scale investments dried up. Uncertainty took over. Economic growth petered out and unemployment rose, creating a deep sense of trauma in the social organism, especially among the young—the first victims of this slowing down of collective ambition. Debates emphasizing the dangers of intensified economic development flourished. Even the myth of zero growth prevailed for a while. For more than 20 years, the country existed in a state of moodiness, no longer confident in itself, and developed arguments that expressed real pessimism.

At the beginning of the 1970s, I was put in charge of a division responsible for studying urban problems, where I spent some thoughtful months analyzing the profound relationships that existed between transportation and urban development. These reflections led me to describe, over the course of 1973, the nature of these relations in the form of global notes, and to publish, on September 20, 1974, a reference document entitled "Town Planning and Transportation: Criteria for Accessibility and Urban Development." This volume explained the beneficial effects of quality transport services on the economic vitality of an area. These writings retain today their full freshness. They show the very strong relationship that exists between the economic performance of people working cooperatively and the number of employees (workforce) living in an area accessible within a given travel time—for example, 1 hour. The amount of time people spend going from one place to another does not change, no matter what efforts are made to facilitate movement. On the other hand, speed helps; the area accessible in a given amount of time expands; cooperative work increases, and the creation of wealth rises. The power of this phenomenon is such that almost 45 percent of the wealth produced by the country results from this type of positive interaction.

At the conclusion of these analyses, I became aware of all the benefits the country can derive from efforts to set up an area-wide development plan and how the phenomenon of urbanization is a bearer of hope. It is there—in towns and agglomerations[2]—that wealth is created through exchanges of skills and knowledge. At the same time, I demonstrated that the quality of a living area's transportation services can add value to conveniently accessible natural areas. I therefore proposed that the socioeconomic effects of transportation infrastructure be evaluated not in terms of economies in driving time—economies that no transportation survey had noted—but as a function of increasing the number of potential destinations accessible within the same time frame and of improving the socioeconomic value of the destination chosen. I proposed a precise method of calculating this creation of value, a method consistent with the observed stability in trip times, a basic phenomenon of which those in charge have not figured all the consequences. When a new transportation infrastructure—rail, road, highway—is opened, users initially take advantage of it to gain time on their usual trips. But very quickly they start to use the time gained to increase the number of potential destinations to enrich their contacts and to improve their choice of destinations—all sources of creation of value. So much so, that after just a few months, they end up still spending the same amount of time getting from one place to another. On the other hand, they create a supplementary value of economic significance identical to the travel time they could have saved.

Yet, at the time, the idea did not capture anyone's attention, and socioeconomic studies continued to address solely the time gains—fleeting in their duration—that these new infrastructures allowed at the moment of their installation, a gain that they lost in the ensuing months.

Some time afterward, I had the chance to apply the conclusions of these analyses in the process of setting up the new town of Marne-la-Vallée. Likewise, the fourth district of the new city, Val d'Europe, was conceived while carefully taking these reflections into account. This called for creating an exceptional communication hub with a bullet train station, a linked station belonging to line A of the RER (Réseau Express Régional) and a freeway bypass. The present vitality of the Val d'Europe region testifies to the wisdom of these choices.

Still later, in forming the new master plan for the Paris Île-de-France area, I applied these analyses in the framework of a working group that brought together several ministries. This allowed me to implement a policy of planning ahead in matters regarding the reservation of rights-of-way for infrastructures. But I sensed that arguments aimed at omitting transportation infrastructure were at work and that many politicians were ready to sacrifice these infrastructures without being aware of the destruction of value that would result. The planning that ensued justified these fears to a large degree, since Île-de-France lost the habit of investing at a really ambitious level and did not hesitate to adopt a rather Malthusian policy in order to protect its environment, according to those in charge. A serious illusion!

During the next five years, as part of my job as general director of the National Institute of Geography (l'Institut Géographique National), I evaluated in several European countries the economic and natural performances of living areas. The cartographic documents produced had a great evocative power. The government authorities of the time were sensitive to "creation of value" arguments and asked that concrete evaluative studies of infrastructures be carried out based on these principles. From then on, evidence began to emerge regarding the notion of a living area's economic performance. Likewise coming on strong was the idea of natural performance being linked to the quantity of easily accessible green spaces.

A final year at the General Council of Bridges and Roadways (Conseil Général des Ponts et Chaussées) provided me the opportunity to exchange, with ministerial officials, numerous notes destined to move things forward. And so they did!

On March 25, 2004, the minister of public works, transportation, lodging, tourism, and maritime affairs—absolutely convinced by the ideas I presented him—signed a directive geared to harmonizing methods of evaluating large-scale transportation infrastructures. This directive introduced the concept of creating value linked to the diversity of accessible destinations—exactly 30 years after the monograph, "Town Planning and Transportation: Criteria for Accessibility and Urban Development"!

For the time being, the concept is still limited primarily to urban areas. It is true that these represent two-thirds of travel in our country. Detailed studies are henceforth instituted. A large-scale colloquium on "living areas" has recently been organized. However, I know from experience that the debate is far from over. I think that another 10 years will go by before the notion of creation of value will become part of the everyday vocabulary of our ministry, as well as today the notion of time gain in reality does not exist after a short period following the opening of a transportation network. I am struck by the difficulty that exists in getting somebody to accept notions that rest on observed facts and results. In 1978, as general director of the Agency for Energy Saving, I was able to measure the entire gamut of environmental problems with which I am therefore well acquainted. I hope to contribute to their resolution. But I am still surprised to see how these problems are approached, very often from a perspective that is emotional, ideological and, at the end of the day, not very rational.

In this book, my purpose is to show how one can carry out policy that is respectful of the environment and attentive to the future of our planet without diminishing human mobility—that is to say, by allowing each person to exercise full and total economic action, a source of wealth and long-lasting employment, as well as to access preserved natural spaces, a source of well-being. I hope to share an optimistic vision of life on our beautiful blue planet and to fight against the despairing monotony of pessimistic ideas that surround us on a daily basis.

I also hope to share a second conviction. Every economics student knows the rules of business function—how to set up a proposed budget of receipts and expenditures; determine the factors that affect the profitability of investments; calculate tax and social security deductions; and establish the staffing level objectives to ensure the financial balance of the enterprise (unfortunately, that is how major microeconomic balance is achieved most of the time). But which teaching institution explains the determining role of geography, or brings up the relationship between the average productivity of business enterprise and the size of the employee market that business can reach within the average time individuals spend on their travels? Who explains that almost half of the wealth produced by businesses in our country comes from the amplified effects of individual productivity brought about by a large diversity of talents near these businesses? The more the market for these talents grows, the more business can find the specialist it needs to develop a new product and to institute a new fabrication method; the more it is able to produce wealth during one work hour, the more it can create employment opportunities without reducing salaries. Some will certainly call this a miracle, although there is nothing miraculous in this phenomenon, which has been at work since the beginning of time. What needs to be done is to simply teach the process in order to derive the most benefit in the interest of work, and more generally, the quality of life.

I have carefully studied this phenomenon for some 40 years. I have tried to understand the key factors involved in urbanization: what economic and environmental factors are at work? While there is modesty in my analysis of the data, there is ambition in my search for pertinent explanations. The behaviors of our fellow citizens are perfectly rational, which is reassuring. Conversely, these behaviors are hardly known and even less taught at university or in our schools of business. The government is starting to be informed and is interested in this topic. Ideas require a great deal of time to come to maturity. They are tectonic plates. Nevertheless, there is some urgency, for our country lives in a state of endemic unemployment that depresses it psychologically and depletes it of all vigor. It is for this reason that I judge it useful to bring my contribution to this need for explaining economic and environmental phenomena that govern our daily lives and widely affect our vitality and well-being.

Notes

1. Living area: roughly corresponds to the French term *le territoire*, which includes residential, employment, shopping, or recreational destinations a person can reach within a given travel time, for instance 1 hour.

2. Agglomeration: a continuous urbanized area, that is, an extended town that includes several municipalities, with a town heart (generally the heart of the main municipality) and surrounding suburbs.

Part I

Observing people's behavior in their own living area

October 4, 1996: the president of Yvelines Departmental[1] Council convenes all the departmental councillors and organizes a debate on the implementation of the master plan for Île-de-France (Paris region), approved by the government two years earlier. The master plan's elaboration and implementation represent a considerable amount of work that involves all those with political and economic responsibility in the region surrounding the French capital. The stakes are significant as much in protecting natural spaces as in developing enterprise zones or creating public transportation and highway infrastructures. The debate of the day—prolonged the following morning by efforts to synthesize a way to execute the plan contract—has to do with transportation and traffic. I am asked to introduce the discussion topics. As is my custom, I begin my talk by taking stock of the results of transportation surveys done for Île-de-France for the last 15 years. Faithfully observing human behavior is a basic principle that I don't know how to waive.

I indicate that for 15 years the surveys reveal an absolute stability in the number of trips undertaken each day by each inhabitant of Île-de-France and an equally absolute stability in the time each inhabitant spends in completing a trip by motor vehicle (29 minutes on average). I add that the percentage of trips whose length is greater than 1 hour is 9 percent and that this percentage has not varied in 15 years. I point out that the travel speed for both public and private trips increases regularly by 0.7 percent per year and that the range of the trips increases due to the stability of transportation times.

A member of the council, extremely annoyed, interrupts me: "M. Poulit, stop saying things that are contrary to the truth! Everyone knows that the situation has deteriorated considerably. Everything you're saying is wrong."

The next day, the same councillor takes up his criticism again in even harsher terms.

The regional prefect takes the floor. "Sir, you do not have the right to attack a state employee because he is reporting facts that rest on in-depth surveys. These surveys represent 16 million francs spent in outlays every seven years by the State and the region. Their results cannot be put in question."

One participant in the discussion addresses a kind word to me and asks me to excuse these inappropriate outbursts, and the president of the departmental council calms down the remarks.

Analyzing facts is thus a dangerous exercise. As Guy Béart says, "The one who tells the truth must be executed."

It is because facts are ignored that affirmations are made that are nothing more than sophisms to muddy the discussions on managing our living areas. The first of these sophisms can be labeled as follows: a new infrastructure set up in an urbanized zone is in strong demand at the outset and sometimes becomes overwhelmed; therefore, it is useless. The fact that many users wish to benefit from it is considered an incongruity. It is as if, at the end of the last world conflict, the lines of people waiting in front of bakeries bore witness to an absurdity. Lines are long and impossible to satisfy immediately; therefore, lines are useless! Let's get rid of the problem if we don't know how to resolve it. Fortunately, bakers produced more and more bread and were able to satisfy the population's demand. Understanding of the transportation phenomenon and the way in which a populated area functions remains so lacking at this point that discussions about urban and rural planning are usually unproductive.

In order to improve the situation, it is necessary to analyze the facts. To be sure, this is a stern exercise and less exciting than announcements of future catastrophes. It is, however, a necessary exercise!

Humans, like all animals, possess an important characteristic: mobility. This ability to move is at the heart of understanding the area that people occupy. For eons, humans have sought to improve this mobility by using mechanical means that amplified their natural abilities. Before the flowering of urban civilization, people primarily used their legs to move from place to place, covering 4 kilometers an hour and reaching potentially a range of 50 km^2. Taming horses allowed a tripling of speed from one place to another, covering 12 kilometers in an hour and gaining access to a potential range of 450 km^2. Then, with the advent of mechanical means—trains and cars—humans were able to cover 90 kilometers in an hour and access a potential area of 25,000 km^2. Bullet trains allowed humans to achieve average speeds of 160 kilometers an hour and to access an area of 80,000 km^2 in that time. Finally, airplanes opened a whole new stage of development: movement from one continent to another, average speeds of 300 kilometers an hour from takeoff to landing and access to an area of 280,000 km^2 in that time. This is an amazing growth curve that bears witness to mankind's ability to embrace areas that are increasingly vast by mobilizing his intellectual resources.

This progression affirms that when one speaks of a living area, it is impossible to disassociate humans from the means of transportation they use to move from one place to another. Living areas include spaces people can easily access in a realistic amount of time, but that cannot be increased due to the daily 24-hour rhythm that determines the totality of their activities. Moreover, these spaces can fit inside each other depending on the means of transportation used.

The primary mission of urban planners is to organize human living space, that is, to localize different places dedicated to living and activities; to delimit natural and recreational spaces, and to define transportation networks. But to establish good diagnostic procedures and to propose pertinent solutions, they must have a thorough understanding of how a living area functions. And for that understanding, they must not limit themselves to a simple spatial description, which is unfortunately the fate of many superficial approaches to urban planning. They need to carefully study the way in which inhabitants invest their area in their daily interpersonal exchanges: how they get to work, how they do their shopping, how their children get to school, and how they use their leisure time. What would an area look like without interpersonal exchanges, with homes and buildings designed for activities but unoccupied?

To study areas people occupy, one must look with the greatest care at the trips individuals make each day to attend to their business or leisure activities. Thus the importance that must be given in this first part of our deliberations (even if a little dry) to the observation of facts, especially of those allowing us to characterize movements from one place to another.

Transportation surveys are the only source of objective information on mobility. Some doubt that useful information can be drawn from seemingly random phenomena. Look no further than daily traffic bottlenecks. What can be gained from surveys in such a case?

As a matter of fact, surveys conducted on inhabitants are an endless source of useful information. It is not because of bottlenecks that commuters' behaviors are not observable. These follow statistical laws that are impressive in their regularity and repetitive nature. But the public at large is unaware of survey results, having only partial information often linked to exceptions that distort an understanding of the facts.

How do you conduct an exhaustive inventory of trips within a living area? Within areas that are primarily urban, well-worn techniques are available. From now on, the nature of movement from one place to another will be well understood. For 25 years, specialized surveys have been conducted periodically in the principal agglomerations of France. If you take the example of the Paris region, four global transportation surveys were conducted at the time of periodic population censuses: in 1976, 1983, 1991, and 2001. Specialized questionnaires were addressed to families selected at random from all Parisian households. These questionnaires, filled out with the assistance of survey personnel who visited households, made it possible to ascertain the daily number of trips taken by each family, the reason for each trip, the starting point and destination, the distance covered, the duration, and, consequently, the average speed. So there is, over a 25-year period, a very complete overview of all motorized and pedestrian movements conducted by residents of the Paris region. Similar surveys were carried out in the principal agglomerations of France. The available statistical base made possible very specific analysis of interpersonal exchanges between residential, economic, and recreational areas.

And in primarily rural areas? A fair number of rural areas are actually located on the fringes of urban surveys. This is how it happened that the global survey affected the eight departments comprising the Paris region. Among them are four departments of the large crescent forming the Parisian metropolitan area, of which the largest, Seine-et-Marne (6,000 km²), equals a provincial department in size. Strictly speaking, 80 percent of the living area within these four departments is in a purely rural area.

The tradition of the Ministry of Public Works Services demands nonetheless a different type of survey for rural areas. These are not done at the homes of rural residents, but rather during trips, mostly on roads, by stopping vehicles and conducting brief interviews. These methods are going to change in the near future, since road checks that involve stopping vehicles and deploying state and local police forces will no longer be feasible due to lack of labor. The solution will involve adopting a home-based survey. The same methodology employed in primarily urban areas will be implemented once more, and a unifying of census procedures will take place.

In addition, transportation surveys will be complemented by socioeconomic observations to evaluate correlations between trips and creation of economic or ergonomic value. How many persons can I meet within a given transportation time? Is there a connection with the level of distributed salary or with the wealth produced? What kind of natural spaces can I access in this same amount of time? Can a correlation be established with a sense of well-being? Trips only mean something in relation to desired destinations, that is, places people want to go that are the reason for these trips. We should be interested in trip generators, whether economic or natural. The ultimate goal of those interested in living areas at the economic level is to definitively understand the very foundation of the creation of value stemming from the exchange of knowledge humans establish when they interact. In this way, one goes beyond simple analysis of the trips themselves and the associated living areas to an evaluation of the number of interpersonal contacts made. People are, in the final analysis, the only wealth we have. The transformation may be carried out at the level of developing well-being. It is necessary to appreciate the number of natural spaces with which people can enter into close contact to relax and renew their strength. Only nature provides us well-being and renewal!

Where does one find this statistical information that goes beyond the bounds of traveling from one place to another? For employees and jobs, as well as for salaries and gross domestic product (GDP), it is at the national level—the National Institute for Statistics and Economic Studies (l'Institut National de la Statistique et des Études Économiques or INSEE). At the European level it is the Statistical Office of the European Communities (Eurostat). For natural spaces, the most reliable source at the level of each French and European city government is the geographic information database known as Corine Land Cover, established from space images covering all of Europe.

From all these sources of information follow simple results that run counter to commonly accepted ideas. I will present them and show to what degree they challenge us.

For 25 years, people spend the same amount of time moving around the area in which they live

The daily number of people's trips does not change

Over time, the number of people's daily trips has remained remarkably stable. The figures for Île-de-France (Paris region) are 3.49 in 1976, 3.47 in 1983, 3.49 in 1991, and 3.50 in 2001. You can't find a more stable result. This is one of the striking observations that came to light in periodic global transportation surveys.

This number includes trips of more than 300 meters carried out on foot and trips by motorized vehicle. *Foot traffic* (41 percent of total trips in 1976 and 34 percent in 2001) has tended to decrease slightly over time, while the use of motorized methods has increased slightly. This observation is easy to understand, for walking covers an area affected by the invariable range of this mode of getting around, while motorized methods see their performance improve regularly, making it possible to cover ever larger areas in a travel time that does not vary.

By means of transportation. An increase in use of some means of transportation and a decrease in others is noticeable, with change relating to respective performance levels. In Île-de-France, the rate of public transportation usage has hardly changed, while usage rates for individual transportation increase regularly, primarily in zones on the outskirts where this means of travel is well adapted to the light urban density being served.

By reasons for the trips. Changes are significant. It is useful, for example, to note that trips required for work only represent a small percentage of daily trips: 19 percent. Trips for the purpose of educational instruction—15 percent—and for leisure—16 percent—are growing the fastest.

Finally, *in terms of localization,* it is striking to note that the number of trips per person hardly varies, whether it is a question of someone living in Paris, the lesser Parisian crescent, or the greater crescent.

In total, the number of daily trips accomplished by motorized means or on foot in Île-de-France registered for 25 years has grown precisely in concert with population growth, that is, a little less than 1 percent per year.

The perception that there is an unlimited growth of travel within the Parisian metropolitan area is not confirmed by the facts. Rather, the total number of trips is decreasing, which is logical since the Parisian population has gone down slightly and employment opportunities are fewer today than 25 years ago. Trips in the lesser Parisian crescent have increased moderately in relation to population. It is in the greater Parisian crescent that growth is constant, matching the development of urbanization. A picture emerges of the region: the number of trips in Paris is slightly decreasing; the number of trips in the lesser crescent is slightly increasing; the greater crescent is experiencing more new travel.

The results observed in Île-de-France are also found in the *main agglomerations outside of Paris*. In particular, a significant stability in the number of trips per person is observable over the course of recent years, at the level of the urbanized area as a whole and in each part of it. This characteristic leads to a stability in the total number of trips in the center of a town, as the population there does not change, and a steady growth in the number of trips on the periphery, which is absorbing most of the new inhabitants.

As in Île-de-France, there is a regular—if moderate—decrease in walking in favor of motorized methods, and a lower percentage of trips for work reasons, which are now largely in the minority.

The amount of time spent on trips each day does not vary

Like many residents of the Paris region, I have the feeling as I listen to the radio every day that the duration of trips is doing nothing but increasing. Sometimes I hear about 2-hour trips in the morning and 2-hour trips in the evening, making the lives of Parisians tiring, stressful, and unbearable. But this is incorrect. In Île-de-France, the average time spent on a motorized trip is 29 minutes. And this time has absolutely not changed for 25 years: 29 minutes in 1976, 28 minutes in 1983, 29 minutes in 1991, and 29 minutes in 2001. This is a remarkable result, although public opinion is totally unaware of it. It's a long way from the 2 hours of travel time sometimes evoked by the media.

The time spent on trips on foot is 13 minutes, also stable (12 minutes in 1976, 12 minutes in 1983, 13 minutes in 1991, 14 minutes in 2001). In economic calculations, the amount of time spent walking is traditionally multiplied by two, in order to take into account (as suggested by behavioral surveys) the discomfort associated with this mode of travel, which is unprotected from the vagaries of weather. Thus we speak of compensated time.

Even more surprising is the observation that the percentage of trips that exceed 1 hour has remained the same for 25 years: for motorized travel it stands at 9 percent. The percentage of trips that exceed 1 hour and a quarter is equally constant—4 percent for motorized travel. The travel times seem subject to an almost perfect biological regulation.

There is equally great stability for a given means of transportation even if the times differ from one means to another. The same observation holds for reasons to travel. Finally, stability is even more noticeable depending on the place of residence.

Since the time devoted to each trip is stable throughout the years and the number of trips executed daily is also stable, it can be concluded that the amount of time an inhabitant of Île-de-France spends on travel in the course of a day is constant: compensated time (i.e., doubling the trip time on foot in order to take into account its inconvenience, a duration that consequently matches a motorized trip) stands at 94 minutes in 1976, 92 minutes in 1983, 98 minutes in 1991, and 99 minutes in 2001, an average of 1 hour and 35 minutes.

In real time, the increase of the share of motorized trips longer than pedestrian trips until 1991 led to a slight increase in total trip time per person. This was followed by stability from 1991 on. In 1976 and 1983, trip time was 76 minutes; in 1991, 82 minutes; and in 2001, 83 minutes—approximately 1 hour and 25 minutes over the course of the 10 years and holding stable since then.

A similar result is observable in principal large cities worldwide: average trip time by motor vehicle is 29 minutes in London, 27 minutes in Los Angeles, and the total time allotted to travel each day is close to 1 hour and 30 minutes. This behavior is thus very general. It characterizes human beings living in an area that offers many destination choices. It is not possible to bring up the continual worsening of travel times without contradicting observed findings.

Finally, the total travel time spent by residents of the Paris region varies exactly in the same proportions as the growth in population: an increase of 16 percent in total travel time corresponding to a 16 percent increase in the population.

What results are observable in agglomerations outside of Paris? Due to a lack of enough destinations, the travel time of a resident of a provincial agglomeration is lower than that of a Paris region resident. Depending on the size of the urbanized area, average travel times, including walking, vary from 15 to 20 minutes. But here, too, travel times remain very stable over the years. The number of daily trips is fairly close to that observable in Île-de-France: on the order of three and a half per day. Travel times within a 24-hour period stand at 50 to 65 minutes, a figure that is also stable over the course of 25 years. The stability in the number of trips and the time spent on them concretely reflect the structure of the face-to-face human interactions involved. It is only passage from a given agglomeration to one of larger size that entails a progressive growth in the length of time spent on interpersonal exchanges, a growth that stabilizes at about 1 hour and 30 minutes in large metropolises.

It is obvious, then, that over the course of a quarter century, humans have spent the same amount of time getting from one place to another, not more, not less. It's as if the chronometer of their mobility was genetically programmed.

Time measured is much shorter than time estimated by the user

What is noteworthy is seeing the significant distortion that exists between information provided by surveys and the general feeling of the population regarding how long it takes to get from one place to another. It seems as if life is taking place on two different planets. How can this situation be explained? It should probably be attributed to the influence of the media. In media terms, the most spectacular events are those that most attract the attention of readers, listeners, and viewers. News editors have little interest in traffic that is moving along smoothly. On the other hand, events like a serious accident bringing with it long-lasting road blockages, a snowfall or black ice tying up a highway, traffic snarls at the entrance or exit of towns, and traffic jams on an arterial highway become the object of major headlines. As a general rule, daily TV and radio news give credence to the idea that traffic is not flowing well; there's always a blockage somewhere! Repeating such information leads to a perception of the situation that is very different from the reality.

When people evaluate the time they spend getting from one place to another, they are fairly close to the reality. But when they provide an intuitive sense of the time fellow citizens spend on travel, they estimate twice as much as is truly the case. That is clear evidence of the news media's influence in reporting only imperfectly observed situations. Moreover, we can imagine how much the idea of a stable travel time can grate against public opinion. The widespread feeling regarding a continual worsening of transportation conditions renders this observation unacceptable. This testifies to the importance of the information effort remaining to be done to make available the most elementary facts about daily travel.

That is not to say there aren't blockages. But the reality is, on the highways of Île-de-France, motorists encounter difficulties (speeds below 30 km/hour) on a small part of their journey: 7 percent. They move 3.5 times less quickly than they would like, which leads them to spend 25 percent of their time slowing down. This means that, during this lapse of time, they cannot travel at the expected speed necessary to reach their desired destinations. Either they have to accept longer travel times or—and this is what surveys show—reduce their expectations regarding their choice of destination to remain within the time frame they have set themselves. "Saturation" is in fact the expression of a demand for pertinent destinations that cannot be totally satisfied given the way transportation networks are set up, and not, as the media suggest, a general blockage that can only get worse with time.

Distortions between reality and perception exist in other communal situations. Nonetheless, the distortion relative to transportation conditions is by far the most important. This gap equally explains the vehemence of certain positions adopted in transportation policy and the divided nature of opinions regarding their implementation in large urban centers, notably Île-de-France. Thus there is an obvious need for explanations based on survey data and observations that are as objective as possible. It is in this light that posting travel times on highways in the Île-de-France region has a universally appreciated calming effect. The announced times are almost always shorter than the times imagined. The user's stress level is reduced and the perception of reality considerably improved. The same goes for posting waiting times in subway and bus stations—the calming effect is the same.

The monetary value of travel time expressed in standard-of-living units does not vary

Time is money. Is this principle applicable to transport of people? In economic studies that allow a comparison of various solutions, how can travel time be assigned value? Are surveys available on this topic? Certainly, time holds an important place in the user's appreciation of a trip's cost. One hour spent using a means of transportation is considered by the user as equaling two-thirds of 1 hour spent working. If there is not total equivalence, it is because travel also includes monetary expenses such as the price of the ticket for public transportation, as well as the cost of fuel, maintenance costs, and amortization over time of cars and motorcycles. As we are going to see later, these expenses represent the approximate equivalent of one-third of 1 hour worked for 1 hour of travel. Thus valuing 1 hour of transportation and taking into account cash outlays during this hour clearly represent the worth of 1 hour worked.

Since the assigning of value is proportional to the worth of the hour worked, and the time spent on travel has not changed over the past 25 years, it can be deduced that the value accorded a resident's transportation time strictly falls in line with his or her standard of living. Furthermore, it can be deduced that his or her valuing is invariable if expressed in standard-of-living units, that is, units of value of the hour worked.

Thus, in Île-de-France, 1 hour of transportation is estimated in 2000 on average at EUR[2] 11.4, that is, two-thirds of the net cost of hourly wages, which rose to EUR 17.10.

An average trip lasting 35 minutes from home to work represents a time expenditure of EUR 6.65 added to EUR 2.38 in cash outlays, significantly eased by public subsidies. For an average journey of 12 kilometers, time is valued, per kilometer covered, at a value of EUR 0.55 and cash outlays at EUR 0.20. In terms of percentages, time for the resident of Paris region commuter represents 2.75 times the worth of monetary expenses. If you take into account the expenses assumed by the user and public entities, you obtain higher cash outlays of EUR 0.24 per kilometer covered. The relationship between the worth of time and monetary expenses is 2.29—closer to the relationship of 2.0 commonly accepted.

In a moderately sized agglomeration—Orléans, Angers, Saint Brieuc, Agen, or Montauban, for example—1 hour of transportation time is estimated at EUR 8.75, that is, two-thirds of a net hourly salary at EUR 13.12. An average trip from home to work, lasting 20 minutes, represents a time expenditure equivalent to EUR 2.94 added to EUR 1.90 in cash outlays. For an average journey of 6.93 kilometers, time is estimated, per kilometer covered, at a value equivalent to EUR 0.42 and cash outlays at EUR 0.27. Expressed as a percentage, time represents 1.56 times the worth of the monetary expenditures, a value slightly less than the 2.0 relationship commonly accepted.

What must be remembered above all, whether in Île-de-France or in the provinces, is that the value given to 1 hour of transportation strictly follows that of the hour worked, and therefore grows at its rate. Since time spent in travel is stable, the value attached to it, expressed in standard-of-living units, that is, as a percentage of an hour worked, also is stable.

For 25 years, people travel more quickly and go farther

The speed of travel increases when transportation improves

If the number of trips or the time spent on these trips does not change, why invest in new infrastructures? What *does* change when transportation improves? It is, in fact, travel speeds that improve, which is logical. You can go faster and farther, and you can choose more numerous and varied destinations. That is the real progress effected by improving transportation infrastructures.

Using the example of Île-de-France, in 24 years, *average speed of motorized travel*—including completed trips on foot, waiting at public transportation stations, or time spent looking for parking—has improved by 18 percent. As the crow flies, this speed was 12.4 km/h in 1976. It moved to 13.6 km/h in 1983, 13.9 km/h in 1991, and 14.6 km/h in 2001. More specifically, real speed is approximately 25 percent higher than speed as the crow flies. The path of a user is actually 25 percent longer on average than a straight-line trajectory.

Considering automotive travel speeds balanced by that of *trips completely on foot* (a portion of which is transformed each year into motorized trips), we find 10.1 km/h, 11.3 km/h, 11.7 km/h, and 12.5 km/h, respectively—in other words, an increase of 24 percent in 25 years. For trips on foot, taking under consideration compensated times, we find 8.3 km/h, 9.4 km/h, 10.2 km/h, 10.8 km/h, respectively—in other words, an increase of 31 percent over 25 years.

Nonetheless, users know little about these regular increases. Rather, they have the sense that there is a regular decrease, something that does not give them confidence in the investment policy implemented by public authorities.

Now, these speed increases are observed in all modes of transportation, private or public—for all reasons—whether it is a matter of getting to work, running errands, taking children to school, or walking in the woods—and no matter what the place of residence or work.

This is how the average speed, as the crow flies, of private vehicles has gone from 15.5 km/h in 1976 to 16.1 km/h in 1983, 16.3 km/h in 1991, and 17.3 km/h in 2001. As for the speed of public transportation, it has gone from 10.5 km/h to 11.5 km/h, 11.6 km/h, and 11.7 km/h, respectively.

From the perspective of reasons for travel, progress is very uniform: speeds for all forms of transportation increase simultaneously and proportionately with each round of surveys. So, for work, 12.7 km/h, 14.1 km/h, 14.9 km/h, and 16.1 km/h; for educational reasons, 6.2 km/h, 7.5 km/h, 8.1 km/h, and 8.3 km/h.

By place of residence, observations are similar. There is an increase in Paris—in both the lesser and greater crescents (concentric inner and outer departments surrounding the city).

For example, speed for all means of transportation is as follows: in Paris: 6.6, 7.8, 7.6, and 8.2; in the lesser crescent: 8.9, 9.7, 9.7, and 10.1; in the greater crescent: 13.8, 14.9, 15.7, and 16.7.

Note that speed is twice as high in the greater crescent as in Paris. This accrued speed makes it possible to cover in a given time a larger area, something that compensates at least in part for the low density of urbanization in the greater crescent. What counts is not speed per se, but the number of destinations that the speed makes it possible to reach in a given time. Paris, with its high density of urbanization, can afford travel means that are powerful but relatively slow, while the greater crescent must by all means call upon modes of transportation that are moderate in flow but high in speed from door to door to compensate for lower density.

In the provinces, the phenomenon is similar, although more accentuated. The increase in average travel speeds is approximately twice as rapid: 2 percent to 3 percent per year stemming from the general use of private transportation, which allows inhabitants of a traditional town to live in outlying areas and inhabitants of these outlying areas to work in the parts of the town urbanized for the longest time.

Speed leads to gains in space; living area expands

Given that motorists or the users of public transportation spend the same amount of travel time to reach their jobs and their centers of interest, the gain in speed they experience makes it possible for them to cover a larger area, a larger space. Motorists or users of public transportation increase the length of their trips in a time that does not vary, that is, without expending additional effort. They increase their range of travel. This term is more pertinent than increase of distance, for it conveys the improvement of travel efficiency within unchanged transportation times.

Thus, in Île-de-France, the average range of motorized travel has increased in the space of 25 years by about 18 percent, in other words, an increase very closely equivalent to that of the speed of travel. The annual increase is 0.7 percent. As the crow flies, the range of motorized travel has gone from 6.0 km in 1976 to 6.4 km in 1983, 6.8 km in 1991, and 7.1 km in 2001. Weighting by trips done solely on foot, the increase over 25 years is 35 percent: in effect, we must add to the increase in the range of motorized travel the consequences of transferring pedestrian travel to motorized transportation offering much wider ranges within a constant time frame. The rate of annual increase—all means of transportation merged—is 1.4 percent.

- By *means of transportation*, we notice differences that mostly translate into investment efforts dedicated to each mode.
- By *reason for travel*, there is a strong increase in travel ranges for work.

- By *place of residence*, growth is very regular: motorized travel, measured as the crow flies, shows the following results for Paris: 4.6 km in 1976, 4.9 km in 1983, 5.2 km in 1991, and 5.3 km in 2001. Lesser Parisian crescent: 5.5 km, 5.7 km, 6.0 km, 5.9 km. Greater crescent: 7.2 km. 7.6 km, 8.1 km, 8.5 km.

Accessible areas are increasing significantly. Inhabitants of Île-de-France now have at their disposal a much larger choice of destinations than 25 years ago.

That is the major characteristic of the behavioral evolution made possible by the modernization of transportation networks. An average increase in travel ranges of 1.4 percent per year means growth in the areas covered of 2.8 percent per year, or 70 percent in 25 years without changing transportation times. That means for motorized trips whose range increases by 0.7 percent per year, an increase of area covered of 1.4 percent per year, or 35 percent in 25 years.

It becomes evident to what extent improvements in transportation conditions increase the number of accessible destinations: more options when seeking out a new activity, therefore a better chance of finding an activity matching one's education, or—for the employer—a greater probability of finding an employee qualified for the specialty in question. The same observation holds for commercial or service activities: choices widen without affecting transportation times.

Looking at leisure travel, in particular green space activities, there is a rapid expansion in accessible recreational places.

Indeed, improvement in transportation networks has a double positive effect:

- It increases the number of economic, commercial, and social options, making it possible for residents to better communicate with their fellow citizens.
- It increases choices of recreational destinations, making it possible for each resident to establish better and better contact with nature.

In the provinces outside Île-de-France, travel ranges are developing even more rapidly in harmony with the increase in transportation speeds, that is, at a rate of about 3 percent per year. The areas covered—travel times remaining constant—increase by 6 percent per year, which is very significant. On top of that, there is a strong integration of town and country.

Monetary outlays for transportation, expressed in standard-of-living units, do not vary

Transportation times do not vary. On the other hand, we just saw that within this unvarying time, the distance covered increases as a function of improvements in speed. Ranges are expanding. That should imply that the monetary expenditures dedicated to trips are increasing as well. Is that the case?

Expenditures, expressed in euros, are indeed increasing. They are doing so for two reasons. First, the kilometric cost of transportation follows the general curve of prices like all other products and services in daily life. For example, from 1990 to 2000 the observed progression is on the order of 20 percent. Second, the number of kilometers covered each day is increasing. Over a long benchmark period of 25 years, travel range has grown by 1.4 percent per year on average. The daily cost of travel is increasing in proportion. Over 10 years that represents a growth of 14 percent (7 percent for the growth in the ranges of preexistent motorized trips and 7 percent for transfers from trips on foot to motorized trips, although this phenomenon is beginning to slow down). Global increase is thus on the order of 34 percent in 10 years. Note that this global increase is the same as that of the standard of living, which has risen—measured in current euros—by 34 percent in 10 years (19 percent in price increases and 15 percent in rise of purchasing power). Thus, monetary expenditures devoted to travel are stable when expressed in standard-of-living units. The increase in standard of living makes it possible to reward those means of transportation that perform better and better. Now, the increase in purchasing power, as will be seen later, is itself tied to the increase in travel range. The two results reinforce each other: better performance of transportation networks contributes to an expanding universe of economic and ergonomic choices, the bearing of economic growth and well-being, and a rise in standard of living whose results make possible spending no more than a stable portion of household revenue on travel. Each year, the system creates additional value, with the same amount of effort on the part of residents.

Since travel costs are stable in standard-of-living units and the time spent in getting from one place to another is likewise stable in standard-of-living units, the relative worth of time and monetary expenditures should not change over the years. This is in fact the case. Per survey results, users put the estimated economic worth of 1 hour of transportation, all expenses included (time and monetary expenditures), at the cost of 1 hour worked. Two-thirds of this economic worth represents, on average, the value given to the 1 hour of transportation, with one-third representing the sum of the cash monetary expenditures devoted to travel. The stability of that ratio of about two for one is perfectly understandable if one notes that time is expressed as a percentage of salary and therefore refers to the standard-of-living unit that salary represents, and that money spent on travel is stable in reference to standard-of-living units.

Another question: what role do transportation subsidies play? It is common knowledge that in Île-de-France, for instance, substantial subsidies are designated for public transportation in order to encourage their use. Do these transportation subsidies, when related to a single travel cost, represent a high percentage or a marginal one? Are private means of transportation also subsidized? To answer these questions, it is necessary to closely scrutinize all the expenditures devoted to different means of transportation and to compare them to all the expenses incurred: cost of the ticket in the case of public transportation; cost of fuel, insurance, maintenance, and amortization of the vehicle for users in the case of private transportation, and whether the vehicle is two- or four-wheeled. After performing these calculations, it turns out that the cost borne by the user in fact can be different from the costs borne by the community.

In the case of public transportation in Île-de-France, and more generally within large agglomerations, employers bear a part of the expenses, as do public entities. As a result, the expenses borne by the user are lower than those borne by the community. Thus the monetary cost borne by a user of public transportation in Île-de-France is EUR 0.07 per kilometer covered, while the cost for the community is EUR 0.23. The user is paying 30 percent of the real cost of travel.

In the case of private transportation, the user bears the cost of domestic taxes on petroleum products whose sum is more or less identical to the expenditure that public entities devote to financing construction and maintaining road infrastructure in Île-de-France. The monetary costs associated with user travel by automobile is valued at EUR 0.31 per kilometer covered. For the community, the cost is EUR 0.30. The costs for the individual and the community are almost equal.

On weighted average—all means of transportation combined—the monetary cost borne by the user of public or private transportation in Île-de-France is EUR 0.20 per kilometer covered. For the community it is EUR 0.24.

An average trip of 9.63 km from home to work as the crow flies (actually 12.04 km) represents an average expense of EUR 2.38 for an individual and EUR 2.84 for the community. The cost borne by the user is 16 percent lower than the real cost. For public transportation, the cost borne is 70 percent lower. For private transportation, the cost is about 3 percent higher.

Users who benefit from subsidies provided by their employers or by the community tend to increase their travel range to seek out more and more favored destinations and so improve their resources. In fact, subsidies benefit users either in the form of a direct reduction in transportation costs or by creating value linked to the possibility of choosing more favored destinations.

What is the situation in agglomerations outside Île-de-France? In an urbanized area of moderate size—examples being Orléans, Angers, Saint-Brieuc, Agen, or Montauban, where inhabitants do most of their travel by private transportation—the monetary cost to the user is EUR 0.28 per km covered. For the community, it is the same amount: EUR 0.28.

An average trip from home to work of 5.54 km as the crow flies (6.93 km in real distance) represents an average expense of EUR 1.95 for a resident and as much for the community.

For 25 years, living and recreational space expands; wealth and well-being increase

When the number of easily accessible jobs rises, salaries and wealth increase

In order to establish a correlation between the number of accessible jobs and wealth produced, it is necessary to have statistics available to allow measurement of both these factors.

To measure jobs that are easily accessible, it is necessary to know average travel ranges—data that global transportation surveys make possible to ascertain, as we've just seen. You find out more precisely the ranges that are exceeded by no more than 10 percent of the residents living in a given area. This criterion makes is possible to determine what constitutes an easily accessible space. Within this space, you count the number of jobs or all other significant parameters linked to the use of the area. In this way, you identify a set of accessible destinations. This set varies across time as new infrastructures are brought on line or new residences, activities, or services are set up. So, in Île-de-France, the increase in the number of accessible economic destinations stands at 2.8 percent per year for the last 25 years (if urbanization density is understood as holding steady) and at 2.1 percent per year, if we take into account—as will become apparent later on—the phenomenon of a steady 0.7 percent annual reduction in urbanization density. For a Parisian, the number of accessible jobs exceeded by no more than 10 percent of residents stood at 2,350,000 in 1976; 2,400,000 in 1983; 2,650,000 in 1991; and 2,760,000 in 2001. For a resident of Lyon center, this number is 400,000. In Guéret, it is about 5,000.

In order to estimate the wealth produced in a living area, one of the first factors to analyze is the sum of net salaries paid by employers. The second factor is the gross domestic product resulting from the economic activity of the sector under consideration. The National Institute for Statistics and Economic Studies (INSEE) does not publish salaries and gross domestic product (GDP) per worker directly, agglomeration by agglomeration. This sort of information is only available at the department level. Hypothesizing that communities not belonging to urbanized areas have a salary equal to the average of the least urbanized department in the region to which it belongs, we can determine the average net annual salary per worker for the main agglomerations of the department. This method is transposable to calculating GDP per worker.

There is a regular increase in salaries as a function of the size of the agglomeration: the larger the town, the higher the salaries. So, in 2000 net average annual salary was EUR 11,850 in a scattered rural area; EUR 15,115 in a small market town of 1,000 inhabitants; EUR 17,365 in an agglomeration of 10,000 inhabitants; EUR 20,325 in one of 100,0000 inhabitants; EUR 23,900 in an urbanized area of 1 million; and EUR 28,805 in Île-de-France.

Île-de-France pays salaries 20.5 percent higher than those paid by an agglomeration of 1 million and 42 percent higher than those of an urbanized area of 100,000 inhabitants.

If you look at the wealth produced by a worker (GDP), the picture is the same: the larger the agglomeration, the greater the wealth produced. In 2000, wealth produced per worker stood at EUR 28,600 in a scattered rural area; EUR 35,545 in a market town of 1,000 inhabitants; EUR 46,650 in a town of 10,000 inhabitants; EUR 48,110 in an agglomeration of 100,000 inhabitants; EUR 58,835 in an urban area of 1 million; and EUR 74,765 in one of 10 million inhabitants. The relationship between GDP per worker and net average annual salary per worker is on the order of 2.44. It ranges from 2.34 in towns of 10,000 inhabitants and 2.37 in towns of 100,000 inhabitants to 2.46 in cities of 1 million and 2.60 in Île-de-France. Considering only the additional GDP per worker and the additional net average annual salary per worker, and employing the values noted in scattered rural areas as reference points, the average is 2.43. Starting with towns of 10,000 inhabitants, the respective data is as follows: 2.19, 2.30, 2.51, and 2.72.

In sum, then, GDP per worker increases as a function of the size of the agglomeration a little more rapidly than net average salary per worker.

When the number of easily accessible jobs increases, work and jobs improve

It is clearly evident that unit salaries and GDP per worker go up with the size of agglomerations. Can the same be said of work rates, that is, the number of workers who have a job in relation to the number of inhabitants in an urban area? It is important to know if there is a correlation between the number of easily accessible jobs and the rate of activity. When unemployment is endemic, this query is of central importance.

Active employment increases with the size of the agglomeration. The larger the town, the more workers per household are on the job. INSEE statistics support this statement. In 1994, the Île-de-France regional urban planning administration carried out a study in 12 agglomerations classified by increasing size. The study, on the basis of the 1990 census, shows that the rate of active employment is 42 percent in an agglomeration of 208,000 inhabitants, such as Angers; 45 percent in urbanized areas of 650,000 inhabitants or more, such as Bordeaux and Toulouse; and 48.3 percent in an agglomeration of 9,320,000 inhabitants, such as the Paris area. Extrapolating and interpolating these references produce the following results: 32 workers per 100 inhabitants in a scattered rural areas; 35 in a small village of 100 inhabitants; 37 in a market town of 1,000 inhabitants; 39 in a town of 10,000 inhabitants; 42 in an agglomeration of 100,000 inhabitants; 45 in an urbanized area of 1 million inhabitants; and 49 in one of 10 million inhabitants. The growth is quite significant, since the active employment rate in the Paris area is 50 percent higher than that in scattered rural areas.

Which criterion is ultimately the most important? The number of inhabitants who actually have a job or those who say that they are seeking one? Glancing at this simple statistic, it immediately becomes evident that the phenomenon of urbanization has a very beneficial effect on the employment activity of residents.

This influence is particularly significant in rural communities located on the edge of agglomerations. The active employment rate of residents there matches that of the entire agglomeration, not the rate that applies to extremely rural areas outside urban influence. INSEE and the INRA (Institut National de la Recherche Agronomique) published a joint study in March 1998 entitled "Country-sides and their towns." This study shows that one-quarter of these peripheral rural communities consist of workers engaged in strictly agricultural activities, and three quarters engaged in technical, industrial, or tertiary activities. Workers are active in the different communities of the agglomeration easily accessible by motorized transportation, especially automobiles.

In reality, the inhabitants of these rural communities benefit from the diversity of jobs in the neighboring urban area. At the same time, they benefit from the open spaces in these negligibly urbanized areas. This observation explains the large-scale osmosis that is gradually developing between urbanized areas and rural areas in their vicinity. On the other hand, rural communities that are not within reasonable distance of urbanized zones depend only on their own jobs or on those of neighboring rural communities. The rate of active employment is low and can hardly increase in these localities due to the lack of enough job opportunities at an easily accessible distance of 1 hour from home.

So, it is in the large agglomerations that the largest diversity of jobs and the best rates of active employment are to be found. It is also in these urban areas that unemployment tends to be more moderate.

Nonetheless, unemployment is a factor that is more difficult to analyze than the employment rate. Three main components are at work: the change in the number of jobs; the demographic effect that determines the population of working age; and residential mobility, that is, the propensity of inhabitants to gravitate to one residential area over another to live. An INSEE study from July 2003 describes the growth of local employment markets from 1962 to 1999. This study shows four classes of job areas:

- Areas exhibiting dynamic demographics and jobs, and favorable migrations. These zones bring together most of the areas situated around the periphery of the Parisian basin, the Rhône-Alpes region, Alsace, and the Atlantic Coast. For the most part, these areas are urbanized.

- Areas with strong demographic patterns, often affected by economic mutations, situated in a crescent going from the eastern Pays de la Loire region to Lorraine, by way of Normandy and the northern part of the country. On average, unemployment has gone up more quickly here than in France as a whole. But the regional capitals, important urban centers (for example, Amiens, Lille, Rouen, Nancy) have benefited from a better job climate and have resisted unemployment trends.

- Areas exhibiting demographic depression, from Morvan to the Pyrenees. These encompass almost every job area in the center of France and the Southwest. These areas show weakening demographics and job growth that is below the national average. Large cities like Bordeaux, Toulouse, and Clermont-Ferrand are excluded from this pattern and continue to see job growth.
- Finally, a number of attractive areas located in the south of the country and in the large Parisian crescent. Jobs are increasing rapidly in these areas. However, large influxes of population cannot be satisfied by local employment opportunities, which means that unemployment rises significantly.

In the final analysis, urbanized areas have a very positive effect on the unemployment rate, either serving as the location for a significant reduction in unemployment when demographics and residential mobility remain reasonable, or limiting unemployment where demographics and residential mobility have considerable impact, as in the south of France, or when economic mutations are at work, as in the north or east of the country.

When the number of easily accessible green spaces increases, well-being increases

For all that, quality of life does not just consist of employment rates, salaries, and GDP! Inhabitants are more and more sensitive to the attractiveness of their place of residence and of their workplace. They want to have access to open spaces where they can recoup their strength, eliminate stress, and keep themselves in good health. Do we know how to measure these benefits? This is an important question that the national accounting office does not handle in a satisfactory way.

Today, it is a priority to have a roof over one's head, to have a place to live, to do what one can to make it as comfortable as possible—that's the first step in improving one's standard of living. And people devote considerable means to this endeavor; the national accounting office actually takes note of this. The expenses that individuals allocate to lodging, those that businesses spend in constructing factories, warehouses, offices, are indeed part of the GDP.

But what about the worth of a riverbank's coolness, the pleasure of a walk in the woods, the feeling experienced when watching a magnificent sunset in a peaceful landscape? The national accounting office does not pay any attention to these, and yet the worth attached to everything regarding quality of open spaces, quality of the countryside, and quality of the air is of supreme significance. It is almost always a question of nature's "gifts" being viewed as acquired in rural areas and whose absence in poorly planned urbanized areas is profoundly resented by those so deprived.

There is a real inequality of access to open spaces. Even if no balance sheets account for this type of wealth, it is obvious that access to these goods has a real value. It will shortly become clear how an analysis of the behaviors of residents who spend part of their transportation time going to places where they take part in absolutely no economic, social, or cultural activity can make it possible to evaluate the worth of these spaces.

Are there concrete statistical means of evaluating the worth of open spaces linked to residential or professional standard of life? The answer is yes. Just as residents are aware of the choices available economically and socially in the form of job opportunities or services accessible within a given transit time, they are aware of the lifestyle choices available in the form of variety and extent of open spaces accessible in a given amount of transit time.

France has a surface area of 55 million hectares. Built-up areas cover about 5 percent of the total. Each of the 60 million French have at their disposal on average 0.875 hectare of open space, almost 1 hectare per inhabitant. What really matters is the number of hectares of open space that an inhabitant can actually access in a reasonable amount of transit time, a figure that depends on the transportation network that serves the place of residence or place of work. Likewise, one can take as a point of reference the surface area of a 100 m^2 dwelling, and express the result in the form of ares (hundreds of square meters) of open spaces that are easily accessible. As in the case of economic activities, with the help of transportation surveys we determine travel ranges for open-air activities, ranges that are only exceeded by 10 percent of the residents living in a given area—or the workers employed in a given area. We count within this area the number of ares of existing open spaces. In this way, we obtain an indicator that illustrates in summary (but already pertinent) form the presence of open spaces in the vicinity of a residential area or a place of work. In Île-de-France, for example, the number of ares of open space that meet this criterion rises to 10 million in the central portion and to 60 million in the peripheral areas, big figures that testify to the presence of numerous protected green spaces in the records of urban planning, and also to the vitality and diversity of the transportation networks that make access to them possible. The growth in the number of these easily accessible green spaces for leisure activities stands at 2.8 percent per year, based on a stable density of urbanization, and at 3.5 percent per year, taking into account a steady reduction of this density (0.7 percent per year). Such a rate is quite remarkable. In agglomerations outside of the Paris region, easily/readily accessible open spaces are on the order of 60 million ares. If built-up areas are much fewer than in Île-de-France, transportation networks are equally less powerful, which explains an indicator just like the one obtained in the peripheral areas of Île-de-France.

A living area behaves like a living organism

One gets the feeling that a living area is really a living organism that reacts to the demands made of it.

Indeed, that is the case. Adaptations are of two types, corresponding to two paces of adaptation. One—rapid—employs a process of flexibly occupying existing residential or work spaces as a function of possible interactions offered by the transportation infrastructures serving the area. The other type of slower adaptation puts to work a process of adaptation of the built-up space itself, a process that may take decades.

The adaptation that grabs the most attention is the one of the choice of destinations offered inhabitants within an area. We could believe that improvements in the performance of transportation networks automatically lead to a reduction in travel times. If this observation is true during the very first months that follow placement of new infrastructures in service, it is no longer so after a certain time lapse: workers change their place of employment as they take advantage of new opportunities. Employers call on the services of specialists whom they could not access before. Consumers patronize other retailers, and retailers prospect for new clientele. And inhabitants change their place of residence. Through it all, transportation times hardly vary at all in spite of the often-considerable efforts made to improve the infrastructures. Humans adapt perfectly.

Note that the adaptation in question here is totally independent of the creation of new residences or of new industrial parks, that is, independent of the creation of urban networks designed to absorb new inhabitants, workers, or employers. It really is a matter of adapting to better travel conditions without modifying all existing dwellings, stores, offices, and other structures. By sticking to this factor alone, one realizes that the residents of a town show a great deal of reactivity. The choice of new destinations induces better productivity or greater environmental satisfaction. There is a profound transformation in the ways an area functions without a single new inhabitant or job appearing on site. One already can sense that the time residents could have gained at the initial placing of new infrastructures in service is transformed into new productivity, that is to say, into wealth produced or—yet again—into additional forms of environmental satisfaction. This point will be discussed in more detail and will prove to be absolutely on target.

A living area adapts in equal measure to accommodate new inhabitants or simply to provide its current inhabitants more life comforts. In this case, it is definitely construction of buildings that did not exist before. An area refurbishes its aging structures or builds new ones to accommodate new populations and new jobs. Thus, in Île-de-France, population and employment have grown on average by 0.54 percent per year over the past 25 years. Residential and construction space attributed to existing structures reached a growth of 1.5 percent per year, that is, about three times the rate of growth observed for population and employment. Part of this growth can be attributed to renovation of aging structures;

another part provides additional comfort to inhabitants and to current workers; a third part accommodates the additional population and new employment opportunities. The existing urban network has absorbed a small part of the construction agenda, on the order of one-sixth, the main portion being provided by new urbanization areas that have increased the annual average of urban space by 1.28 percent. The existing urban network has not been able to make up for aging structures that need to be rebuilt, and even less for providing life comforts to current inhabitants and workers. Population and employment density in urbanized areas has fallen on average by 0.74 percent per year.

This change is observable in all metropolises. It signals the desire of residents to have more comfort each time the improvement of transportation system performance allows them to maintain or increase their range of economic choices.

This change interferes—without modifying it very much—with the evolution of economic and recreational spaces accessible within a given transit time. Annual growth in the number of accessible economic destinations must in reality be attenuated by the rate of annual reduction in the population and employment density, which leads to an annual growth of 2.1 percent instead of 2.8 percent. On the other hand, the annual growth in the number of recreational destinations must be increased by reduced population density of the land, which leads to an annual growth of 3.5 percent rather than 2.8 percent. In any case, we can clearly see from this example the difference that exists between adaptations involving destination choices based on reactions to improvements in travel conditions without modifying buildings, and much slower adaptations of built-up space destined to compensate for aging structures, to offer more comforts of life and work, and to accommodate new population and jobs.

In each of the scenarios previously presented, a living area illustrates a remarkable capacity for adaptation—similar to a true organism endowed with great intelligence.

Notes

1. Department: an administrative unit in France and many former French colonies, roughly analogous to counties in England. There are 100 departments grouped into 22 metropolitan (and four overseas) regions—all integral parts of France.

2. In December 2000, US$1 equaled EUR 1.1561.

Part II

Interpretation of observations: the economic and natural performances of living areas

December 5, 2003: I visit the director of the staff of the Minister of Public Works and Transportation (Ministre de l'Équipement et des Transports). The director of the staff of a ministry as enormous as that of Public Works and Transportation carries heavy responsibilities. As he himself often says, one only balances such responsibilities, continuously fascinating as they are, if the human organism is willing to do without its share of sleep. Five-hour nights are commonplace.

At the beginning of the meeting, I sense that yesterday's files must have been stacked high and the night short. So I have some reticence about bringing up the subject of the discussion: the economic and natural performance levels of living areas. How can a well-serviced living area create value by improving cooperative work between people?

Being familiar, nonetheless, with the director's attachment to serious, well-argued technical approaches, I do not hesitate to plunge into my demonstration. I provide running commentary, graphic by graphic, on traffic models that detail how residents move around the space surrounding their home to seek—at a distance—desired goods or services they cannot find on the spot. I explain to him the way in which these models have a reassuring aspect: that of demonstrating unchanging travel times noted in surveys. You can spend as many billions of euros as you wish on roads, highways, bullet trains, and airports, but you won't change the amount of time residents devote to traveling from one place to another. Average travel time will always be on the order of half an hour, and the time that is exceeded by no more than 10 percent of the users will be twice that. In the course of a day, travel time attributable to 1 person will not exceed on average 1 hour, 30 minutes. I show him how the number of desired goods, whether jobs, goods, or services, determines the probability of going to a given area. I also show him that the worth of these goods and services is dependent on their availability on the spot and the time it takes to obtain them (10, 20, 30 minutes). Each time that access time increases by 10 minutes, the worth of the desired good goes down by 2.7 and the probability of going to the area where it is located also goes down by 2.7. I immediately point out that if I offer a quantity of goods that is 2.7 times higher in the desired area, I obtain the same result—in terms of the probability of going there—as if I reduce access time by 10 minutes. So I create a positive economic value equivalent to a time gain of 10 minutes. Thus the number of desired goods among which I can make a choice has a value—that of making possible a more efficient selection than the one that I must make in the case where I do not have a choice. Time is certainly money, but the efficient choice I can make among a rich array of various goods is also money.

In spite of his fatigue, I see his eyes beginning to sparkle.

I continue by showing that the number of goods among which a choice can be made has a property that manifests quite frequently in the laws that govern human organisms: its value must be multiplied in order to obtain a linear progression of the expected effect. So, each time, I have to multiply by 2.7 the number of desired goods among which I can make a focused choice in order to make up for the effect of increasing access time by 10, then 20, then 30 minutes, that is, a linear progression of 10 minutes. It's a phenomenon similar to one observed in music. You have to double the frequency of sounds in order to move up an octave.

I continue my line of reasoning, skipping some steps because of time, which is moving along rapidly. If I am interested in the totality of desired goods that surround the place where I live, I can determine the value of the potential choices afforded me by reckoning the goods that exist within the identified living area delimited by twice the average travel time, that is, 1 hour, a limit that seems intuitively reasonable for determining an easily accessible area. As I proceed, stage by stage, to a multiplication by 2.7, I find that the relative increase in the number of these goods reckoned inside that area expresses the value of the choice that I will be able to make as I poke around in this breeding ground of goods and services. As for travel time needed to make the choice, it will always be half an hour on average, and 10 percent of residents will exceed twice the average time, that is, 1 hour. All I need to do, if I want to place a value on the worth of a well-serviced area, is identify the number of goods accessible in 1 hour from where I am located and to establish the relative value equivalent to a cash value.

I finish up my remarks by explaining that in 1 hour of travel I cover a distance equal to my speed, which seems evident to my listener. I cover an area proportional to the square of the radius, thus to the speed squared, which he finds equally simple to understand. And I can encounter a number of persons equal to the surface area of the living area accessible in the hour multiplied by the occupation density of this area, d, thus a number equal to $d.V^2$.

"But that's the energy of the area, the energy of human cooperative effort!" he exclaims.

"Yes, it is indeed a question of cognitive energy, economic energy, the energy that humans expend in their face-to-face encounters during which exchanges of information reach an extraordinary intensity, far higher than what new information technologies can offer. And it is the relative value of this energy that determines the productivity of human cooperative effort. That's what illustrates the creation of value.

His eyes are twinkling. The short night is forgotten.

So I show that if I calculate the value linked to the number of jobs in Guéret, Marseille, Lyon, and Paris, and if I multiply this value by the number of annual trips to work, I find exactly the salary differential observed in deeply rural areas and Guéret, then Marseille and Lyon, and finally Paris.

If I take into account all the trips that have an economic function—work, purchases, schooling, business—I find exactly the differential of GDP between deeply rural areas and the various types of agglomeration.

Then I share with him the results obtained by going on to calculate the value of choices within living areas accessible in 1 hour, starting with all the municipalities in France and then on to municipalities in nine neighboring European countries. The cartographic representation is gripping. Areas come alive. Value abounds in the place where humans live and in the place where they communicate with each other by means of high-performing transportation routes.

The director is hypnotized by these maps, which correspond exactly to his intuition about human activity in a well-serviced area.

"I would like for this method to be used for evaluating two competing projects for linking Grenoble to Sisteron via the Alps," he says. "One variant goes by way of Gap. The minister and local elected officials prefer it. The other bypasses Gap. The technicians prefer that one. I would be curious to know how it would turn out."

He adds, "This method ought to be incorporated into the administrative order that the minister is about to sign in order to standardize methods for evaluating large-scale infrastructure projects under the umbrella of the Ministry of Public Works and Transportation. This method is universal. On top of that, it fits in with what elected officials are thinking. That's a fortunate situation when the point of view of elected officials coincides with that of the technicians; let's take advantage of it!"

And that's how the administrative order of March 25, 2004, introducing the creation-of-value method into evaluation of large-scale transportation infrastructures was born.

In the space of a weekend, at the request of the president of the economic studies section of the General Council of Bridges and Roadways, I had to write up the directives that put into place the method's principles, and the document was signed the following week.

To be thorough, I had held monthly meetings throughout the previous year with this same president, along with the Council's economic specialist, the person responsible for socioeconomic evaluations within the roadway technical services, and finally, a young engineer still at the National School of Bridges and Roadways. Serving as an honest broker, he provided his independent opinion on projects going back 30 years. The convergence of points of view became apparent, which made it possible for the president of the Council's economic studies section to add his favorable recommendation and to pass on the draft administrative order requested by the ministry in a matter of days. The minister himself had already become aware of the cartographic results illustrating the economic performance of areas in France and in various European countries and was in complete agreement with the conclusions of these studies. What's more, the maps were prominently displayed on his desk and had already piqued the curiosity of journalists.

Finally, the study regarding how to cross the Alps has been published recently. The director had the satisfaction of noting that the minister's intuition was validated by the creation-of-value approach. The solution that goes through Gap is much more efficient than the one that bypasses it. People rule!

Let's attempt, like our dear director, to look deeper and to interpret the observations made during the surveys carried out for more than a quarter century: stability in the number of trips per person; stability in daily travel time regardless of efforts exerted by public entities to improve transportation infrastructures; constant increase in travel speeds and, consequently—within an invariable travel time, an increase in travel ranges, an extension of accessible areas, a diversification of potential destinations, and more pertinent destinations chosen. Possible relationship with rising salaries and with rising GDP. Increasing well-being. Can one give a rational explanation for all these observations or these correlations? Can one arm oneself with tools that, after faithfully reproducing the facts observed, could be used to make projections in the future and make it possible to create coherent scenarios?

As always, one must be humble in the face of facts rather than try to distort the truth in order to obtain predetermined results. So, be reminded how hundreds and hundreds of transportation engineers and economists the world over mathematically represent—model, as we say—human behavior in daily travel. They only translate by means of the simplest formulas the results they have observed during transportation surveys, whose main conclusions I reiterated above. The modeling that they do is much less complex than that undertaken, for example, by aerodynamic engineers when they plot the laws they use for calculating the wing of an airplane like the Airbus that is making our country's reputation. Human behavior in daily travels can indeed be put into a formula, a solution that permits not only the reconstruction of situations observed in the present but also to predict with a fair amount of certainty situations that will be observed in the future.

To reconstruct or predict the movements of an area's residents does not detract at all from their freedom of choice. It is a matter of applying reconstructions or predictions to the totality of residents living in a neighborhood. It is possible to reconstitute or determine the percentage of those who will go to a vicinity for a given reason, but it is not possible to say who will go to work in such-and-such a firm or to buy goods in such-and-such a shopping center. Reconstruction and prediction are statistical means that are pertinent, for example, in estimating the size of transportation systems, adapting them to the needs of inhabitants, and evaluating their collective behavior. It is not possible to reconstruct or predict each individual behavior, but each is certainly included in a totality that is itself perfectly determined. Some people are surprised that such models of behavior can be produced, but that is the case. Economists do not contest these behaviors. They observe them and seek to evaluate how the totality of users reacts, for example, to different collective investment hypotheses. So, no a priori judgments, but faithfulness to facts observed.

For all that, these behaviors are universal. Similar formulas apply to the inhabitants of the Paris area, New York, Los Angeles, Tokyo, Hong Kong, or Shanghai, and even to those living in a favela in South America. *Homo sapiens* has a universal way of behaving in relation to the surrounding area. Of course, he has not the possibility to use the same means of transportation for movement from place to place in Paris or Tokyo versus a developing metropolis where certain neighborhoods with few resources only offer movement on foot or by bicycle as means of transportation. His travel range is vastly different according to the area he occupies and the means of transportation he is using. But there is a constant that he shares with all inhabitants of our planet. He has 24 hours per day in which to live, whether he is rich or poor, whether he lives in a developed metropolis or in an isolated rural area of a developing country. The time that he spends on physical transactions with all his fellow humans for the purpose of creating wealth, exchanging wealth, relaxing, taking care of health needs is the same: about 1 hour and 30 minutes per day out of the 24 that set the rhythm of life on earth. And this travel time is used to obtain materials that make it possible to produce high-level goods; encounter fellow humans and learn from them how to produce these goods; use machines that make production more efficient; sell goods produced or buy goods produced by others; obtain food and feed others; entertain oneself; find one's soul mate and start a family; relax; take care of those in one's sphere of influence who also occupy a living area and make a reality of everything *Homo sapiens* is capable of manifesting on the planet as a link in the great chain of being.

It all comes back to our faithfully reconstructing this behavior in order to be better able to interpret it, and to determine the levers we can tweak to emphasize positive aspects of this behavior and restrain certain negative ones—without becoming sorcerer's apprentices to be sure!

The results of transportation surveys can be modeled

Humans travel to seek desired goods and services unavailable on the spot

If humans travel, it is certainly in order to seek elsewhere what cannot be found on the spot. Let us suppose that the area in which a person lives is of homogenous density, with as many workers per square kilometer as jobs, somewhat like Los Angeles. Simple reasoning, what some would call "good sense," would lead to this statement: "Since there are as many jobs as there are workers all over the area, there is no need to travel. All that is necessary is that each worker take the work available right there on the spot. The perfect solution has been found."

In reality, that is not how it works. It would be too good to be true! In Los Angeles, just as in all the large cities of the world that resemble it, residents persist in choosing a job different from the one available right there. And in order to find a job, they do not hesitate to travel. Simply because all jobs are not equal.

If I have a degree in aeronautics, it will be hard for me to take a job as a teacher of literature, even if it is right at my door. I will want to use my knowledge and expertise as an engineer. Travel will become the inescapable means of seeing to it that my education and experience find optimum use by an employer who does not offer this type of job at my doorstep. And in a way, my desire to seek satisfaction will be virtuous. The job of literature professor that I have let go will be highly attractive for a worker who does not live in the same place as I do, since this worker is a professor of literature and has all the desired references to practice this profession. As it is, the two trips that cross each other make it possible to optimize the match between the qualifications required by the jobs and the expertise of the workers.

The additional satisfaction that both will gain from these trips will be, from all appearances, higher than the cost of travel. If this were not the case, the transactions would not take place.

What is true for work and jobs is equally true for feelings. If I am an attractive young man in search of a soul mate (please rest assured that I respect equality!) and there are as many representatives of the masculine gender as there are of the feminine in the space of one square kilometer, simple reasoning would say I should set my heart on the stunning young lady who lives downstairs from me. But in reality there is a rather small chance, in spite of her attractive points, that this charming girl will meet all my specifications. And it is highly unlikely that I will please her either. The one who will please me and who will find me attractive probably lives somewhere else. To meet her and fall under her spell, I will have to travel. The opposite will of course be true. The charming young girl who is looking about for her future will only be able to find happiness by going elsewhere to discover what she has little chance of finding right there on the spot.

Using these two examples—you can multiply them at will—it becomes clear that travel is engendered by the diversity of ends desired. If all jobs were identical, no one would have a reason to go looking elsewhere for what was available right there. If all suitors were the same, there would be every reason to choose the one who lives in one's neighborhood. To be sure, in the first case, everyone would have work and, in the second, everyone would be able to marry and have children, but the situation would be far from satisfactory: everyone would have lost all the value of a judicious choice. On-the-job effectiveness would be a joke and the future household without doubt rather boring. It's been established that travel and a universe of destination choices are inextricably linked. And this universe of choice is linked to specific needs to be satisfied.

Is it possible, despite their complexity, to reconstruct the totality of these transactions? Can their evolution in the future be predicted?

This can be done without deception or sleight of hand. There are, beyond appearances, a few simple rules.

First of all, one must determine the number of daily trips—during the week or on the weekend, starting from home—that each person carries out in order to respond to different needs, to satisfy travel needs. In general, the following reasons for traveling are observed: home to work, home to school/university, home to personal appointments (visiting friends, going to doctor's office, moving for administrative matters, searching for a soul mate), professional business with transactions between places of activity, home to places of leisure and entertainment, home to places for outdoor activities.

One knows exactly for each of these reasons, at a given time period, the number of trips carried out on a workday or on a weekend, and total number of trips in a year.

Future trends are equally well reported. The number of trips from home to work, for example, is diminishing steadily, the number for school/university or for leisure activities is increasing steadily. On the other hand, as was demonstrated earlier, the number of trips for all reasons combined is stable. It stands at an average of 3.5 trips per inhabitant per workday.

The traffic engendered by these reasons of all types is thus linked to the number of inhabitants (or workers) in a living area by a simple rule of proportionality. All you have to do is to multiply the number of inhabitants, today or tomorrow, of a residential zone by the average number of trips executed daily for a given reason. It couldn't be simpler.

However, the number of trips generated by a zone tells us nothing about the destinations themselves. For example, it says nothing about the job areas toward which residents are headed, or about the commercial zones to which they go to make their purchases. It says nothing, in fact, about the close relationship that links residents and their living area. And that is exactly what provides the key to the paradoxes revealed by transportation surveys.

The more desired goods and services there are in a zone, the more reasons exist to go there

How are trips distributed in relation to the zones that surround their starting point?

If one considers work as the reason, surveys indicate that trips that start in a given residential zone are spread among surrounding neighborhoods, including the neighborhood where one lives, on a pro rata basis to the jobs available in each of these locales. The more jobs there are in a zone, the more opportunities one has of finding a suitable job in this zone, and the higher the probability of traveling there. There is proportionality between the number of jobs offered and the probability of accessing this place. The number of jobs thus qualifies the attractiveness of the zone in terms of travel for work reasons. In the final analysis, that corresponds to criteria for good sense.

If one considers travel motivated by purchases, surveys indicate that trips starting in a given residential zone are spread among the neighborhood where one lives and surrounding neighborhoods on a pro rata basis of sales jobs, or—because of a proportionality—what amounts to the same thing: the number of square meters of sales space.

On the other hand, if one looks at trips motivated by a search for a soul mate, surveys are mute on the subject. But I am more or less certain that trips that start from a given residential zone are distributed among surrounding neighborhoods, including the neighborhood where one lives, in relationship to the number of males and females living in these neighborhoods.

As for business trips, they are distributed on a pro rata basis to the number of tertiary (service sector) jobs in the destination zones. Moreover, it's a matter of trips that do not generally originate from home and that are usually called trips on the rebound.

Finally, for trips that have no other function than that of satisfying needs for relaxation and personal renewal, surveys show that they are distributed pro rata across the expanse of accessible natural areas.

From these examples one can extrapolate two types of trips characterized by the nature of the desired goods:

- Trips of the economic kind that place humans in relation to each other for work, business, education, trade, and services.
- Trips of the rest and relaxation kind that place humans in relationship with nature.

These trips are distributed in space in relation to the number of desired goods or services such as jobs of different kinds—or equivalent indicators related to travel of an economic nature or—yet again—to expanses of natural spaces for travel, rest, and recreation.

The probability of accessing an attractive zone from your trip's starting point is in direct relation to a primary factor: the number of desired goods or services present in the zone of attraction.

The more time the trip takes, the more expensive it is and the less attractive the destination

The probability of accessing a zone of attraction from an origination point does not depend solely on the number of desired goods or services present in that zone. A good available on the spot has more attraction than a distant good that requires spending time and money to take possession of it. And this attraction decreases very quickly with the time and cost that must be spent on travel.

The concept of "transportation generalized cost" is used to denote the value attributed to transit time ("time is money") and the money (ticket, fuel, insurance, tolls) actually spent for travel.

Surveys show that the user equates 1 hour of travel to about 1 hour of work. It is also noteworthy that the money spent during this hour of transit represents about one-third of an hour of work. This is what explains why the hour of travel itself is valued at two thirds of an hour worked.

The generalized cost of the trip is obtained simply by multiplying the time it takes expressed in hours or fractions of an hour by the generalized cost of 1 hour of transit (that is, remember, equivalent to the value of an hour worked). As a rough estimate, then, one can speak interchangeably of the generalized cost of travel, or travel time, multiplied by a constant coefficient.

Surveys indicate in detail how the generalized cost of travel time, or what boils down to the same thing, travel time, comes into play in the loss of attractiveness of a desired good. The higher this cost (or this time), the less attractive the good. This, too, is a simple rule of good sense!

To take the example of travel from home to work, a job possesses a different level of attractiveness for a resident depending on whether it is right there on the spot with zero travel time, or far away with a long travel time. Attractiveness drops sharply as travel time increases. An increase in travel time of 10 minutes is enough to reduce the attractiveness of a job by more than one-half (2.71 to be exact, which is the value of the mathematical number e). An increase of 20 minutes reduces by more than five times the attractiveness of a job (7.34 to be exact, 2.71 x 2.71). This type of very rapid decrease is of the "decreasing exponential of travel time" variety. For those who dislike decreasing exponentials, we could speak of the "out of sight, out of mind" effect.

In all the countries of the world and in all parts of these countries, this is the law that characterizes the effect of travel time on the attractiveness of a job and, more generally, of a desired good that is distant from the place where the resident interested in this good is located. More precisely, the decreasing exponential, in the case of traveling to work, applies to a number equal to six times the travel time, expressed in hours. This coefficient of six explains that each time that travel time increases by one-sixth of an hour, that is, by 10 minutes, the attractiveness of the desired good goes down by the mathematical value e, that is, 2.71.

In this way, trips for the purpose of work that are distributed, within the different zones surrounding the residential zone of reference, in pro rata relation to jobs E located in each zone, are also distributed in pro rata relation to "decreasing exponentials of travel times" between the residential reference zone and work destinations. It is the phrase "jobs weighted by the decreasing exponential of travel time" that determines for a resident the probability of access to a zone containing E jobs or—what amounts to the same thing—that determines the frequency of using, for work reasons, the connection between the zone where the resident lives and the one where E jobs are located. This complex is also designated as E^*.

The exponential has the property of being equal to one when it is applied to a term equal to zero. Note that when travel time is zero, that is, when one is focused on local activities, accessible employment is weighted by a factor of one. As—and when—jobs being considered move farther away, their attractiveness goes down and gradually reduces to zero by a division of a factor of 2.71 each time the travel time increases by 10 minutes.

What has been said about travel for the purpose of work can be transposed to other reasons for travel. For example, for travel to school/university, the element of attraction is the number of teachers; for personal affairs, it is the tertiary jobs; for outdoor leisure activities, it is the surfaces of accessible open spaces. Traditionally Q represents the quantity of goods desired by the users in a given zone for a particular reason. Trips are distributed between the different zones that surround a residential zone in a pro rata relation to the quantities of desired goods weighted by "the decreasing exponential of travel time between this zone and the desired zone." This quantity of goods desired weighted by "the decreasing exponential of time" is written as Q^*. Thus one can say that the probability of accessing a given zone, or what amounts to the same thing, the frequency of using the connection between the zone of residence and the desired zone, will be proportional to Q^*.

Such is the universal formula that governs the behavior of humans in relation to the living area to which they belong, that is to say, the one that they can easily access by means of transportation, including walking on foot. It is the space-time relation that links humans to the soil with which they live in intimate osmosis.

This universal relation has a remarkable property. When it is applied to an indefinite homogenous urban area, it leads to an average motorized travel time of two-sixths of an hour, that is, 20 minutes, or of 30 minutes, including final parts of the trip completed on foot, a result that transportation surveys confirm.

The number of goods or services among which a pertinent choice can be made has an economic or ergonomic value

The diversity of goods or services accessible at the time of a trip is a source of value

The underlying rules that surveys have made it possible for us to identify for the reconstruction of trips by residents desiring goods or services in zones surrounding their residences are going to allow us to precisely identify the value that they attribute to being able to access these desired goods and services. We thus will be able to measure the worth they attach to their economic and natural environment.

Let us first analyze what is happening in a transportation link between the residential reference zone and one of the neighboring vicinities. The number of trips issuing from the residential zone in the direction of this adjoining neighborhood, that is, using the link (for work reasons, for example) is proportional to E*, the number of jobs available in the neighborhood (let's say there are 1,000), weighted by the decreasing exponential of the transportation time between the two zones (the "out of sight, out of mind" function). When travel time increases by 10 minutes, use of the link (due to the fact that jobs at the destination decrease in attractiveness) drops by 2.71 (*e* in mathematical terms). If the time increases by 20 minutes, usage drops by a new factor of 2.71, or 7.34, and so on. Each time that 10 more minutes are added, usage decreases by an additional coefficient of 2.71.

Let us now go on to the following experiment: on the link between the two neighborhoods in question, I establish a toll weighted to equal the equivalent of 10 minutes of transportation, that is, one-sixth of an hour worked, approximately two euros in a city of 100,000 inhabitants. The attractiveness of jobs in the destination neighborhood is going to go down by 2.71. Question: can I, by increasing the number of jobs offered in the neighborhood, make use of the link go back up to its previous level; in other words, can I find a level of satisfaction for those residents who desire jobs in that neighborhood that is identical to what they experienced before the toll was introduced? The answer is yes: it only requires that I offer in the neighborhood a number of jobs equal to 2.71 times the number of jobs offered before the toll was introduced. It only requires that I bring the number of jobs up to 2,710. Use is actually proportional to the number of jobs offered. And if I raise the toll to four euros, I can maintain use of the link by raising the number of jobs to 7,345, or 2.71 times more. At six euros, the number must be multiplied by 2.71 once again, that is, reach the figure of 19,900.

I deduce from this that offering a choice among growing numbers of jobs has a real economic value, since the resident is ready to pay a higher and higher toll in order to access this choice. If the initial choice is moderate (1,000 jobs), a slight increase in *absolute* value (choice brought up to 2,710 jobs) but quite an appreciable one in *relative* value (multiplying coefficient of 2.71) will be perceived with interest by the commuter (gain equivalent to two euros per trip). On the other hand, if the initial choice is larger (for example, 7,345 jobs), a much larger increase in absolute value (choice brought up to 19,900 jobs) but identical in relative value (multiplying coefficient of 2.71) will be necessary in order for the increase in worth to remain the same (new gain equivalent to two euros).

This type of relation is common in the biological realm, notably in the area of sensory perceptions (Weber–Fechner Law)[1].

For example, only a multiplying increase of sound energy makes a linear increase in auditory perception possible. This is the reason why the unit of sound measurement (the decibel) is proportional to the "logarithm" of acoustic energy. It is not necessary to fear the logarithm. The logarithm simply makes it possible to have an additive increase corresponding to a multiplying increase. When you go from 1,000 jobs to 2,710, then to 7,345, and finally to 19,900 and—at the same time—indicate that the economic value attached to the possibility of making a choice between this increasing number of jobs increases by two, four, and six euros per trip executed, you are only saying that the economic worth attached to this growing choice of jobs is proportional to the logarithm of the number of jobs offered at the destination. To reassure yourself once and for all, think of the octaves of your piano, which are quite simply the logarithm of the frequencies of strings hit by the hammer. You go up one octave when the frequency doubles.

The coefficient of proportionality that makes it possible to pass from the logarithm of the number of jobs—a value without dimensions—to euros, is equal to the generalized cost of 1 hour of transportation, expressed in euros (equivalent to the value of an hour worked), divided by the coefficient six that fixes the rate of decrease of the decreasing exponential of travel time, in the case of travel from home to work.

Economic worth ("utility" as economists call it) linked to the possibility of being able to choose between E jobs, compared to a limited choice, is thus equal to the value of 1 hour worked, divided by six, multiplied by the logarithm of the number of jobs, E.

This notion is significant. It explains the reason why residents are willing to head for the destination neighborhood for work reasons. It is simply because the possibility of choosing among many jobs in this zone affords them a benefit greater than that of taking a job right there on the spot. The added worth is greater than the generalized cost of traveling between the residential zone and the destination. This is what justifies traveling. We discover the basic coherence of the world of mobility.

What applies for work travel is transposable under the same conditions to other reasons for travel. In the case of purchases for example, the utility of destinations is of the following form: value of 1 hour worked, divided by a constant coefficient equal to nine, multiplied by the logarithm of the quantity Q of salespeople in the desired zone of destination. In the case of travel for business, the quantity of desired goods is that of tertiary jobs. In the case of outdoor leisure travel, it is the quantity of open spaces.

The concept of the utility of accessible destinations really ought to be declared useful to the public good, or rather the creation of gross value associated with a pertinent choice made within a number of potential destinations, Q. How much time would be saved in explaining trips and evaluating their worth! How many errors would be avoided, such as the well-known one: "an infrastructure, upon being put into place, is saturated, therefore it is useless." It is true if one reasons solely in terms of transportation costs, but it is not true if one takes into account the utility of the accessible destinations, the creation of value associated with choice of a pertinent destination.

If one subtracts the transportation generalized cost from the gross utility of accessible destinations, one obtains the net utility of the trip.

If the net utility is positive, there is a trip. In the opposite case, the trip does not take place. One cannot find a simpler conclusion.

If Q^* represents the number of goods desired for a particular reason, weighted by the decreasing exponential of travel time, one can easily verify that net utility is equal, apart from a multiplying factor (value of the hour worked, divided by a constant coefficient), to the logarithm of Q^*, an extremely simple expression. Net utility is directly proportional to the logarithm of the goods weighted by the decreasing exponential of travel time.

The diversity of the totality of goods or services accessible from a given zone represents the creation of value of the living area surrounding this zone

Following the extensive study of a transportation link between a reference zone and one of the neighboring vicinities, let us extend our analysis to all the links issuing from the reference zone. Let's limit ourselves first of all to travel from home to work and proceed step by step.

Let's begin by taking the case of two adjacent links: the first one connects the residential zone to the neighborhood we just studied; the second connects the same residential zone to a second neighborhood that we are going to study simultaneously from now on. Let us proceed to the following experiment that is more sophisticated than the preceding one.

I establish a toll on the transportation link on the way to the first neighborhood, for example, in the amount of two euros, corresponding to an increase in the total cost of transportation equivalent to an increase in trip duration of 10 minutes. I establish a second toll on the link heading toward the second neighborhood, say four euros, corresponding to an increase in the total cost of transportation equivalent to an increase in travel time of 20 minutes. In the first case, use decreases by a 2.71 coefficient. In the second case, use decreases by a 7.34 coefficient (2.71 x 2.71).

Question: can I, by increasing the number of jobs offered in the two neighborhoods, make it so that use of the sum of the two transportation links does not vary, that is, can I make it so that there is no change in the global satisfaction of the residents who live in the reference area and who have an interest in the two neighborhoods, and if so, under what conditions?

In order to find a solution to this question, it is merely necessary that the sum of uses of the two neighborhoods not vary. All that is necessary is that the sum of jobs weighted by the attenuating effect of transportation, "E_1* + E_2*", be stable.

The value of an hour worked, divided by a constant coefficient equal to six in the case of travel from home to work, multiplied by the logarithm of "E_1* + E_2*" is the only quantity equal to a cost that is, like "E_1* + E_2*", invariable when the sum of the uses of the two neighborhoods does not vary. It represents, therefore, the net utility that the residents of the reference zone attach to jobs accessible in the two neighborhoods.

We can pursue the experiment by focusing step by step on all the links that issue from the reference zone and that head toward all the neighborhoods that surround this residential zone. In order that global use not vary, it is only necessary that the total number of jobs accessible in each destination neighborhood—each one multiplied by its own decreasing exponential of transportation, that is, the "sum of all E*"—be stable.

The value of an hour worked, divided by a constant coefficient equal to six, multiplied by the logarithm of the "sum of all E*" is the only expression equal to a cost that is, like the "sum of all E,*" invariable when the sum of uses of all the neighborhoods that surround the zone of reference is stable. It represents the net utility that residents of the reference zone attach to jobs accessible in all the neighborhoods surrounding this zone to which they want to travel from home to work.

What has been said regarding trips from home to work is clearly transposable to other reasons for travel by adopting, for each of them, the appropriate attraction factors, Q, such as sales jobs for purchases, tertiary jobs for business, the number of ares of open space for outdoor leisure activities. If one takes into account the sum of attraction factors, Q, each multiplied by "the corresponding decreasing exponential of travel time" for a given reason, the net utility that the residents of the reference area attach to accessible goods in all the neighborhoods surrounding this area, for this reason, is equal, apart from a multiplying factor (value of the hour worked, divided by a constant coefficient valid for the reason in question), to the logarithm of the "sum of the Q*."

What has just been explained is rigorous but makes it possible to avoid misinterpretations that are so widespread. However, this presentation, I must confess, is scarcely intuitive. That's why I have attempted to find a presentation that is almost as rigorous and that is a good teaching tool as well. I've tried to break down global net utility of trips issuing from a reference zone into two terms, one illustrating the gross utility of easily accessible destinations (the reason for the trip), the other showing the average transportation generalized cost issuing from the reference zone (the resistive aspect of the trip). Since public authorities are used to the idea of transportation generalized costs, that makes it possible to show how the gross utility of destinations constitutes the missing link in the argument.

I made this attempt a reality from the moment I first thought about the economic utility of destinations. The results were published in summary notes dated January and November 1973.

The gross utility of easily accessible destinations is connected to the quantity of goods available within a certain perimeter surrounding the reference zone. The simplest perimeters that we can imagine are curves described as "isochronal" (or iso-costs), adopting as reference the gravitational center of the zone studied. These curves are defined by the percentage of users, originating from the zone, who exceed them. For example, the Iso 50 curve is defined by the perimeter that is exceeded by no more than 50 percent of users. The Iso R curve is the one whose perimeter is exceeded by R percent of users.

I have shown that net utility can be broken down into a gross utility and an average transportation generalized cost, net utility being the difference between these two terms.

Gross utility is equal, in this case, to a multiplying factor (value of the hour worked, divided by a constant coefficient valid for the reason in question) equal to the logarithm of Q^{90}, an expression in which Q^{90} represents the number of goods counted inside isochronal curve 90, that is, the curve that is exceeded by no more than 10 percent of users issuing from the zone of reference. Why isochronal 90? Essentially because it delimits a perimeter beyond which the probability of reaching a destination becomes small. It is a question, therefore, of a probabilistic definition delimiting an easily accessible living area. Isochronal 90 corresponds, in fact, more or less to twice the average time of travel trips issuing from the reference zone. When the average trip time is 30 minutes, which is the case of trips in large metropolises, isochronal 90 corresponds to an hour of travel. That is the reason why, as a preliminary approximation, the gross utility of easily accessible destinations can be determined by counting the desired goods within a living area accessible within an hour's time. The teaching aspect of the presentation derives from that fact.

In an hour, the distance covered by a resident is in fact equal to the average travel speed, V, the living area covered is equal to the square of the speed, V^2, and the number of desired goods Q that the resident can access in an hour is equal to d.V^2, d being the average occupation density of the living area.

The expression d.V^2 symbolizes a form of energy, that of the diversity of goods that a living area irrigated by a transportation system offers to its residents. The logarithm of this energy translates the value that the resident attaches to the choice of a desired good within the living area served. When the occupation density of the living area in terms of desired goods goes up, or when the speed of means of transportation making it possible to access these goods goes up, the value of the destination chosen by the resident increases. That is where the reason for the trip is to be found.

The generalized cost is, for its part, the average generalized cost of trips issuing from the reference zone. In large metropolises, the generalized cost is that associated with an average travel time of 30 minutes. It is almost invariable, regardless of the efforts put forth to increase the performance levels of transportation systems supplying the living area. Only the worth of the destination increases.

The net utility of an average trip issuing from a zone of reference appears composed of two terms:

- A positive term, the gross utility of the destination chosen within a totality of desired goods that are easily accessible, Q^{90}, symbolized by the logarithm of $d.V^2$, which is the reason for the trip and which constitutes its justification.[2]
- A negative term, one that is traditional in transportation studies, the average transportation generalized cost, that represents the difficulties the resident encounters going from the zone of reference in order to access the desired goods.

This presentation has the merit of being evocative. I will use this format for the rest of the book. It will allow us to clear up all the contradictions that we are used to, taking into account only the concept of transportation generalized costs.

We have defined the net utility associated with a trip issuing from the reference zone. To obtain the net utility associated with all trips taken in the course of a given time, it is simply necessary to multiply the net utility connected with a trip by the number of trips taken during the period under consideration. When you look at annual trips, you obtain the net utility of trips issuing from the reference zone over a period of one year. It is the same, of course, for gross utility and for transportation generalized costs.

Net utility of trips in the course of a given period is calculated by looking at the difference between the gross utility of goods and services chosen in the course of the trips executed during this period (within a totality of desired goods and services in an easily accessible space) and the transportation generalized costs paid out during this same period in order to make the actual choices within the totality of these desired goods and services. We are finally in possession of the reference formula.

In the case of heterogeneous urbanized areas, the formulation elaborated for homogenous urbanized areas provides a very good approximation of the creation of value

What has just been worked through is perfectly applicable in the case of homogenous urbanized areas, for example the city of Los Angeles, comprising a relatively stable density, with inhabitants and workers spread uniformly throughout the living area and jobs also spread out in a homogenous fashion. But is the analysis still valid in the case of urban areas that are very heterogeneous, such as the kind you encounter in Europe, with significant differences in density between the center and the periphery, or between the center, intermediate urban hubs, and residential outskirts? The question is worth studying carefully.

In the case of homogenous urbanized areas, the models for generating and distributing trips have the property of determining totally isotropic trips whose distribution of ranges is the same all over the area. For example, Isochronal 50, which is exceeded by no more 50 percent of the residents issuing from the zone of reference, is located at a constant distance from the zone of origination, regardless of the zone under consideration. It is the same for isochronal 90, the isochronal that is exceeded by no more than 10 percent of the residents of the reference zone. The average travel time is the same all over the area. Leaving out the part completed on foot, it is equal to two-sixths of 1 hour, which is 20 minutes, or—including the part completed on foot (two times 5 minutes)—on the order of 30 minutes. The time exceeded by no more than 10 percent of residents is equal to 0.64^{e} of an hour; without the last part on foot, that is 38 minutes, close to 40 minutes. With the part completed on foot that is often a portion of long distance public transportation (two times 10 minutes), you get close to 60 minutes. The probability of an actively employed worker of the area occupying a job is equal to one, regardless of the business zone considered. Likewise, each actively employed worker is certain to find a job, regardless of the residential zone considered. There are no marginal constraints—as the specialists say—to impose so that every job is occupied by an actively employed worker or that every actively employed worker has a job. The large cities born in the century of the automobile are very close to this configuration. Evaluations of net utility attached to work destinations take into consideration jobs weighted by the attenuation factors of distance of the decreasing exponential of travel time without modifying these factors. The net utility of an average trip issuing from the zone of origination can be broken down into a gross utility, equal to the value of an hour work, divided—in the case of trips from home to work—by a coefficient six, multiplied by the logarithm of E^{90}, and an average transportation generalized cost. Isochronal 90 clearly delimits the domain within which jobs, E, must be counted.

In the case of heterogeneous urban areas, the effects of competition between zones become apparent. These effects can be illustrated in the following way by using analysis of trips from home to work as the context.

If a zone of activity, denoted as a zone of destination, is located near extremely large residential zones, the jobs that this zone can offer actively employed workers are small in number. Choice is reduced. By applying the general law of distribution of trips, one would find that the number of actively employed workers who wish to go to the destination zone is higher than the number of jobs that it offers. To obtain the identity, it is necessary to assign to the zone's jobs a coefficient of reduced attractiveness.

On the other hand, if the zone of activity is very extensive and is surrounded by rather small residential areas, the actively employed workers desiring to go to the destination zone are fewer in number than the jobs offered there. To obtain the identity, it is necessary to assign to the zone's jobs a coefficient of increased attractiveness.

The same premises apply inversely to a residential zone surrounded by job zones.

If the residential zone, called the zone of origination, is located near extremely large zones of activity, the actively employed workers it provides is small. Choice is reduced. By applying the general law of distribution of trips, one would find that the employed workers of the origination zone are destined to occupy more jobs than they can hold. To obtain the identity, it is necessary to assign to the zone's employed workers a coefficient reducing their qualification, which would have the effect of attenuating the value that they would present to an employer.

On the other hand, if the residential zone is very extensive and is surrounded by rather small zones of activity, the totality of actively employed workers of the zone of origination cannot find a job. To find one, it is necessary to assign to the zone's employed workers a coefficient of increase of their qualification, which would have the effect of increasing the interest they would hold for an employer.

The coefficients of increase or reduction in the attractiveness of jobs or of the qualification of the employed workers according to the zones under consideration are in effect calculated by models of generation, trip distribution.

These coefficients must be taken into account in calculations of net utilities for destinations accessible from different zones of the living area studied. The results of calculations carried out in the course of simulations express the reality of the interest paid by the user to each of the destinations or origins identified.

Nonetheless, we observe, after completing the calculations, that in the case of heterogeneous urban areas, the different corrective coefficients that are applicable to trips from home to work do not go much beyond one, because jobs are always present in the residential zones, even if only in the form of service jobs, and zones of activity always remain near residential zones. This observation therefore limits taking into account corrective coefficients linked to the reason of traveling from home to work in the case of heterogeneous urban areas. We can, as a general rule, use the formulation of net utility of the elements of attraction of trips, without appealing to corrective factors, and use, for example, for net utility of work trips, the logarithm of the "sum of all E*" weighted by the multiplying factor representing the value of an hour worked, divided by the constant coefficient equal to six.

Moreover, it is necessary to note that the corrections introduced in the case of trips for work reasons no longer have any point in the case of other reasons for traveling. If one takes the example of purchases, the number of trips is not dictated by the size of the sales areas. The level of sales depends on another regulating factor, the intensity of sales activity per square meter. The marginal constraints of the type "one job, one worker" no longer exist. The corrective coefficients are no longer calculated. Now, trips for work reasons are mostly in the minority, since they only represent henceforth 19 percent of all trips.

It still remains to be determined how precise the calculation of gross utility is when referring to isochronal 90 in the case of heterogeneous urbanized areas.

I set about making that determination by calculating gross utility in two extreme cases: an urban area that rapidly decreases from the center of town outward (the case, for example, of a moderately-sized town when one leaves downtown), and an opposite case, one of a rapidly expanding urban area of the type observed when a resident is installed on the outskirts of a large metropolis and heads toward the center of town. I adopted as a definition of net utility of reference the logarithm of the "sum of all E^*" multiplied by the value of an hour worked and divided by the constant coefficient equal to six, without assigning to each E (since their value is almost 1) the corrective coefficients linked to the heterogeneity of the urban area (taking these elements into consideration would have, by the way, improved the results). I sought to determine the isochronal that, in each of the two cases, made it possible to calculate a gross utility that would give back the net utility of reference, after subtracting the average travel generalized cost starting from the zone of origination.

In the case of a rapidly decreasing urban area, the isochronal making it possible to attain this result is isochronal 0.94. In the case of a rapidly growing urban area, the isochronal making it possible to attain this result is 0.88. One notes that these results are very close to isochronal 0.90. Since corrective coefficients are for their part close to one, we can concede for the time being that the adoption—for gross utility of work destinations in a heterogeneous environment—of the formula value of an hour worked, divided by the coefficient equal to six, multiplied by the logarithm of E^{90}, is a perfectly satisfactory solution. In this case, for gross utility, the logarithm of jobs accessible in an hour, or the logarithm of $d.V^2$, will turn up again, with d being equal to average job density within the living area studied.

It is this formulation that will be used in the examples that follow. But at any time net utility experienced by each worker can be calculated directly by using the logarithm of the "Sum of Jobs*", multiplied by the value of an hour worked, and divided by the constant coefficient equal to six, or, even better, the logarithm of the "Sum of Jobs*", assigning to each job the corrective coefficient linked to the heterogeneity of the urban area. In symmetrical fashion, for the employer, it is the logarithm of the "Sum of Workers*" that must be considered, by assigning to each worker the corrective coefficient linked to the heterogeneity of the urban area.

All the same, in general diagnostics that are largely sufficient at the outset, simplified approaches will be quite pertinent, including within heterogeneous areas. The error will be far less significant than the one resulting from not taking into account the gross utility of easily accessible destinations!

This approximation will also be quite satisfactory in the case of other reasons for traveling, the ones, we're reminded, that are widely in the majority. In these cases, moreover, since there are no marginal constraints, there will be no need to take corrective coefficients into account.

Urban and rural areas constitute a single living space

A grand continuity from town to country

Urban spaces, rural spaces. French administrative tradition, coupled with a history in which rural spaces play a determining role in a low density country, leads to clearly dissociating rural spaces from urban spaces. But recent growth in the living areas, as well as the appearance—and then the accelerated development—of private transportation, has profoundly changed the French landscape.

A joint study of INSEE and of l'Institut National de la Recherche Agronomique (INRA) (the National Institute of Agronomy Research), published in March 1998 and entitled "Countrysides and their towns," shows that the distinction between town and country is becoming more and more artificial. There is increasing overlap between towns and countryside. One notes, for example, three times more laborers than farm workers in a primarily rural area. Industrial employment holds its own better in the rural than in the urban. Every day, 2.6 million periurban and rural residents leave their rural communities to go to work in town. Today, 90 percent of households that live in rural areas contain no agricultural workers. Less than 20 percent of rural jobs are agricultural ones. Due to increasing mobility, lifestyles are rapidly becoming the same everywhere.

The traditional separation between urban travel and rural travel does not resist objective analysis.

Many surveys providing an exhaustive description of humans traveling in their area have been conducted in urban environments. The very thorough technique used results quite simply from the impossibility—a fortunate one in my opinion—of conducting surveys along roads and avenues, due to their being crowded with traffic and people. The surveys were conducted at people's homes. They made it possible to identify all the trips executed by all of the household's members, regardless of the reason mentioned and the means of transportation employed.

In the middle of the countryside, the techniques used have been different. They have been focused mainly on stopping vehicles and putting questions to the drivers. The approach has remained attached to a particular means of transportation, each type using its own observation techniques. Analyses and predictions have remained marked by this piecemeal approach.

Therefore, is it necessary to deduce that there is, when it comes to travel, a world of the city and another world of the country. I think not. At the beginning of my active years, I worked primarily with urban spaces and I applied generative models of traffic distribution (known as gravitary models) that faithfully reproduce the trips executed in this type of space. But as I thought about it, I realized that the traditional distinction between urban and rural areas no longer had validity. The only pertinent notion is that of living area, whether this area is established in an urban or a rural environment.

What validates this analysis is, first of all, the fact that gravitary models applied to the Île-de-France region make it possible to faithfully reconstruct trips executed in the heart of Paris as well as on the farthest fringes of Seine-et-Marne, where the population is decreasing under the influence of neighboring urban hubs. These models are equally well adapted to the reconstruction of traffic patterns within new towns that are often organized into multipolar and multispatial structures, with open spaces of large dimensions and highly organized hubs.

Unfortunately, predictive studies of traffic in the countryside do not traditionally resort to gravitary models. They rest on counts made along screen lines and on the adoption of extrapolation coefficients. So there are few correlation studies with data on the use of the living area, such as resident population, workers, and jobs.

To illustrate the difference between urban and rural spaces, the persons in charge of these studies present the argument that traffic in the country is increasing rapidly, while in urban areas there is stability in the number of trips per person. In reality, the arguments advanced are exactly those that make it possible to demonstrate the continuity between the urban world and the rural.

In effect, interurban trips are conventionally defined as being trips of more than 100 km in length. In an urban system, travel is defined—in a completely orthodox way—as the link between a point of origin and a destination, for a particular reason. Travel is attached to a person and not to a distance to be covered. In the context of this definition, the number of trips per person is, in fact, stable. On the other hand, the range of trips increases in proportion to unitary gains in speed. If we considered travel speed prior to bringing a new public works project on line and travel speed after completion, we will note that the range of travel varies in strict relation to these speeds. There is indeed an increase in the kilometers covered without an increase in the number of travel trips. The increase has to do with the number of kilometers covered, not with the number of trips. The relation between the rate of increase in kilometers covered by a person and the rate of increase in travel speed is strictly equal to one.

In actuality, this is the same phenomenon observable out in the country. The number of kilometers covered grows annually in proportion to the increase in unitary travel speeds. That means that the rise in kilometers covered is not linked to a possible increase in the number of trips but in an increase in their range. Studies carried out on large-scale roads and highways (Lyon, Marseille, Lisbon, Quebec) show that the relation between the rate of increase in the number of kilometers covered and the rate of increase in travel speed observed at the opening of these facilities stands between 0.6 and 1.0. In general, when the coefficient is close to 0.6, the observation perimeter of the growth in traffic is defined in terms that are too limited. Besides, a coefficient below one would mean that the number of trips dropped, which would be a paradox. In the case of the Quebec project, the coefficient is indeed one, confirming that the increase in travel range, the number of trips remaining invariable, accounts for the total increase in the number of kilometers covered. Thus the growth in trips of more than 100 km, along with the increase in unitary speeds in the projects brought on line, is proof that generative models of traffic distribution used in urban areas are perfectly capable of reconstructing traffic patterns in country environments. The proposals formulated when using these models in an urban context are entirely transposable to rural living areas. Moreover, there is no real break between the rural and the urban. A third of French rural spaces whose demography is stagnant or decreasing is being revitalized nowadays by neighboring urban spaces, as the 1998 joint study by INSEE and INRA shows.

In effect, the economic and ergonomic performance evaluations that I undertook for 36,000 municipalities in France and for 46,000 municipalities in nine neighboring EU countries, accompanied by particularly instructive cartographic illustrations (see maps pages 85–86) make no distinction between the urban and the rural.

It is the creation of economic or ergonomic value that matters, not the time gained

How does one briefly but definitively characterize the fundamental elements of the way humans behave in their relation to the living area that they occupy on a daily basis?

Humans do not seek to gain time; they seek to enlarge their range of choices within the unvarying amount of time they spend traveling from one place to another. They desire to establish more and more professional, social, cultural, spiritual relations within this given amount of time. This phenomenon most profoundly characterizes *Homo sapiens*. It is a matter of establishing ever more numerous, ever more effective relations, a form of economic energy that renders today's humans so efficient in their constructive, as well as their destructive, undertakings.

The appearance of motorized means of transportation has given people the capacity to multiply contacts tenfold compared with possibilities at the beginning of the Christian era. Humans, once integrated into the vegetable and animal kingdom and living within its rhythms, took on a dimension, in the space of a few hundred years, that they did not possess before—that of mastering more and more of their know-how exchange space—their cognitive space—a source of exceptional effectiveness.

The ranges of choice revealed by studies of human travel within living areas highlight the power and richness of this approach, which responds to all the criticisms that can be leveled against traditional traffic studies.

In a very concrete way, when one brings a new infrastructure to serve a living area, there is no time gain nor transportation cost, but rather an increase in the ranges of travel and opportunities for wider contact, all expressed in monetary terms by the concept of gross benefit of easily accessible destinations. This gross benefit increases, and—as travel costs do not vary—the net benefits obtained by subtracting transportation costs from gross benefits increase in parallel fashion. We will see later that this growth is expressed very concretely by increases in remuneration and a rise in GDP. In the same way, access to open spaces multiplies. Well-being increases. The living area thrives.

In an equally concrete way, the simple act of making a vicinity denser by adding activities, along with efforts to increase transactions leading to a stabilization of travel times, constitutes undeniable progress. The possibilities for contact increase, since jobs are more numerous than before while travel speeds are stable. It is the number of individuals with whom one can enter into contact in a given time that is the determining factor of efficiency in the community. It is obvious that it is a form of the living area's energy that is at work.

The number of colleagues with whom one can come into contact in 1 hour is, as we have seen, in the form of $d.V^2$, with d equal to density of human occupation of the living area, and V equal to average travel speed.

The expression $d.V^2$, which stands for the energy expended by the community to establish effective contacts, is at the heart of the relations between *Homo sapiens* and his living area. Economic energy grows when the density of the area's human occupation increases or when the travel speed of the residents goes up.

It is the relative value of this energy, the logarithm of this energy, which characterizes the economic performance of human cooperative work. It is this value that illustrates the benefit of easily accessible destinations. The numerous applications of the concept of a living area's economic performance and the benefit of easily accessible destinations that I am going to present in the pages that follow will demonstrate the richness of this approach.

People are just as sensitive to conditions of access to open spaces that they need for renewal and relaxation. The surface area of open spaces accessible in an hour is expressed in the form of $s.V^2$. The value s represents the density of open spaces, and V is the average speed of means of travel.

The expression $s.V^2$ is a form of "ergonomic" energy, that which favors access to open spaces and makes it possible for humans to preserve health and vitality.

The relative value of this energy—the logarithm of this energy—represents the well-being experienced by people in their contacts with nature.

Preserving these open spaces by law is the first act of well-thought-out urban policy. Serving them by efficient means of transportation is a way of providing residents beneficial spaces. It's a way of providing conditions for people to really thrive.

It is certain that bringing together economic vitality and ergonomic well-being in a living area, exempt from negative influences on a healthy planet, is not only desirable, but actually possible. The pages that follow are meant to demonstrate this possibility by resorting to the most objective interpretation possible of human behavior and the cooperative relations that humans can establish with the animal and vegetable kingdoms.

Notes

1. Weber–Fechner Law: The Weber–Fechner Law describes the relationship between the physical magnitudes of stimuli and the intensity of the stimuli perceived by humans. Gustav Theodor Fechner (1801–1887) in 1860 provided a detailed theoretical interpretation of earlier findings by Ernst Heinrich Weber, one of the first scientists to try to quantify the human response to physical stimuli.

2. The term d in the formulation $d.V^2$ expresses the occupation density of the living area in the form of desired goods. These goods can be jobs or workers of different kinds. They also can be open spaces. In the case of open spaces, the term s would be preferred to represent the density of desired goods and the energy that goes with it $(s.V^2)$.

Part III

Applications of evaluation methods for economic and natural performances of living areas

January 28, 2004: I am the guest of the president of the RATP (Régie Autonome des Transports Parisiens, or Paris City Transport Authority). On the top floor of the glass building that houses the authority's headquarters, I am afforded a magnificent view of the River Seine. Paris sprawls at my feet and I think of all the economic energy that such a collection of skills and talents is capable of producing.

Sitting next to the president is the director of the authority's studies who is in charge of giving life to projects included in the master plan for Île-de-France.

The president and I are longtime friends, and our professional paths have often crossed: she was director general of the New Town Development Public Authority in Cergy-Pontoise when I was her counterpart for the New Town of Marne-la-Vallée; director of surface transportation at the Ministry of Public Works and Transportation, then secretary of state for transportation when I was prefect, regional director of Public Works and Transportation for Île-de-France, in charge of rewriting the master plan for the Paris region.

The purpose of this meeting is to discuss the work that I have conducted on the economic and natural performance of living areas.

She tells me, "I have a real problem getting the point across to the elected officials whose municipalities are due for an extension of subway lines or the establishment of public transportation belt routes. Would you have in your bag some arguments they can easily understand?"

I briefly share with her the basics of economic and natural performance of living areas. I show her that there is no way for her to make her clients gain time, but that she can make it possible for them to reach new, more pertinent destinations, which are sources for creating value.

I talk to her about $d.V^2$, a form of economic energy that characterizes the number of workers an employer can access in 1 hour or the number of jobs a worker can access in 1 hour. The higher this number, the better the match between jobs offered and workers adequately prepared, and the more wealth created via focused use of the skills of each one. It is the variation of the logarithm of this quantity that makes it possible to calculate the creation of wealth produced. As a result, one can easily predict how much additional wealth can be created by each extension of a subway line or by the public transportation belt route destined to connect the starts of the lines thus extended. According to correlation studies to which I have devoted myself, it is indeed a question of wealth produced, expressed as additional salaries paid to residents of each community, social security contributions made by businesses, or taxes paid to the state, the region, the departments, or the municipalities. The growth of wealth can be pinpointed municipality by municipality and can be the object of cartographic representations that are particularly instructive.

I then show her calculations done to determine the value produced by people working, buying, or conducting business within the living areas surrounding each French municipality and—more generally—each municipality of nine neighboring European countries. The maps that illustrate these results are a true revelation. They win her complete support.

"I understand. This is exactly what I was looking for," she says. "To show that transportation networks—and in particular public transportation in the dense areas of Paris and its neighboring suburbs—contribute enrichment to the municipalities served and also to the local authorities who collect the taxes. Perfect!"

She asks the director of studies, "Do you think that you can, with the modeling instruments you use, determine the opening up of accessible living areas when the projects you have under study come on line, and determine the creation of wealth that results from it, worker by worker, within each community under consideration?"

"I'm afraid our models are not complete and do not make it possible to determine the opening up of accessible territories when travel speeds increase. But we're going to study the matter."

"Do it in such a way that the instruments faithfully reproduce the behavior of the users and go on to evaluate the creation of wealth brought about by the projects that we have to defend in front of elected officials. For us, it will be a strategic way to proceed."

She turns to me and says, "Thank you, Jean. I suggest that you and the director of studies meet with the people in charge of travel simulation instruments and that you advise us regarding the putting in place of evaluation instruments in our projects."

So, a few weeks later, I meet the RATP officials in charge of studies. I bring them the ministerial directive, signed in the meantime by the minister of public works and transportation. Unfortunately, the RATP's model cannot be used unmodified since this model, like many others, does not modify destinations when transportation conditions improve. It is limited to apportioning the flux of travel between different projects. It will be necessary, as a result, to adapt the instrument in order to make it match the behavior of users and to make possible calculating the creation of value induced by the new public works projects envisaged.

However, I have confidence in the result because I know the president's determination and I know that the simulations will be conducted according to the rules of the game.

Moreover, in the meantime, I have met with the director of surface transportation at the Ministry of Public Works and Transportation who has decided to put together a working group comprising the SNCF (Société des Chemins de Fer Français, or French National Railway Company), the RATP (Régie Autonome des Transports Parisiens), the Île-de-France Public Transportation Authority (le Syndicat des Transports d'Île-de-France), and the regional administration of Public Works and Transportation for Île-de-France (la Direction Régionale de l'Équipement d'Île-de-France). Its purpose: laying out the instruments that will make possible implementing instructions in the ministerial directive of March 25, 2004. My job in this working group will be to facilitate understanding of the directive and to assist in putting the best instruments in place.

It is clear to see, from the example of RATP projects, all the practical interest in the notions of living areas performance and the creation of value that goes with it.

Examples of applications are numerous and concern all means of transportation, public or private, as well as all living areas, be they rural or urban. We are going to describe a few of them in order to show the pertinence and the coherence of the concepts derived. We are also going to show how one can, thanks to appropriate cartographic representations, illustrate the results obtained with force and instructive value.

It is necessary to clearly distinguish two phases in the applications: calibrating the models based on the result of surveys, and proceeding to actual simulations. There is a clear-cut difference between interpreting the result of a transportation survey that only expresses the behavior observed in residents of a living area and proceeding to travel simulations using predictive models whose object is to forecast the trips that inhabitants of a living area will make in 5, 15, or 20 years, as a function of factors related to habitat, employment, and transportation at these different points in time.

Surveys are traditionally conducted at intervals of 5 to 7 years. All members of a family are questioned regarding the trips made on the day before the survey, including the starting point, destination, purpose, time of departure, time of arrival, and means of transportation used. In this way, if we examine a significant sample of inhabitants, we can reconstruct with a good deal of accuracy all the trips made by the living area's inhabitants. In addition, at the time of the survey we are familiar with the composition of the population and jobs in the different vicinities of the living area thanks to data of the National Institute of Statistics and Economic Studies (l'Institut National de la Statistique et des Études Économiques or INSEE). Finally, we are familiar with the structure of transportation networks, be they private or public. From there on out, we are in possession of all the objective data that makes it possible to determine the gross benefits of accessible destinations, the transportation costs, and the net benefits—everything that makes it possible to evaluate a posteriori the efficiency of the complex entity made up of inhabitants, activities, community facilities, and transportation systems within a given living area.

In addition, surveys play a role in calibrating simulation instruments that make it possible—starting with data on population, employment, and the nature of transportation systems—to reconstruct as accurately as possible the different trips made by inhabitants of the study area. We go on to calibrating generations of trips and travel attractions, neighborhood by neighborhood, and the division of trips between each of the neighborhoods considered as starting points, as well as attractions. That comes back to checking if these divisions actually take place as a function of a "very rapidly decreasing exponential of the transportation generalized cost" and determining the coefficient a that calculates the rapidity of this decrease. These tests are carried out for one travel purpose at a time. Then we evaluate the instruments making it possible, on a given transportation link, to determine the different portions of trips that use walking, public transportation, two-wheeled vehicles, or private transportation. Finally, for individual transportation (cars and two wheelers), we test the simulation instruments that make it possible to determine, on a given link, how users are spread among different possible itineraries, keeping in mind the levels of saturation attained. In this way, the gamut of instruments that make it possible to reconstruct the movements of a living area's residents in their diverse characteristics is mastered fairly well.

These instruments are subsequently used to simulate the trips that can be predicted in a given living area at different intervals in the future, for example, 5, 10, or 20 years, using as components the number of inhabitants and jobs, the surface area of open spaces, and the characteristics of transportation systems anticipated at these various time periods. Thanks to these instruments, we can estimate the dimensions of transportation infrastructures in urban planning documents.

Nonetheless, these surveys or simulation instruments say nothing about the value of such-and-such transportation system applied to such-and-such living area, or the value of a given urban structure associated with a transportation system. These are automata that express no valuation of the why of things. They only deal with the how. In fact, using the data they collect as a starting point or the perspectives they trace, they make it possible by using pertinent methods of evaluation or those applicable for determining gross or net benefits of accessible destinations to make a judgment. It is actually the object of the methods I propose to apply. That is where we get into the area of the why, and that is what is exciting. Thanks to such approaches, public authorities can make decisions about urban planning projects and transportation. That is where public debate is established and opinions confront each other.

An important point to underline: evaluations must always be done by adopting a baseline situation from which we can determine the evolution of benefits. If a choice is to be made between two options, we will determine the evolution of benefits in one option and the other by starting from this reference point. This will be, for example, the situation observed today. By comparing the evolution of benefits in each case we will be able to debate the comparative value of each solution.

The examples presented in this chapter respect this criterion. They emphasize an entirely orthodox approach of evaluation methods.

The next chapter will be devoted to a broader approach that will seek to determine over time the cumulative benefits of area-wide structures associated with transportation systems in France and in nine neighboring countries belonging to the European Union. The results are amazing and particularly interesting. But they belong to a specific structure of evaluation and appreciation whose characteristics and limits will be pointed out clearly.

The benefits of accessible destinations are easy to calculate and represent

It is simple to calculate the benefits of easily accessible destinations

How do we proceed concretely in order to evaluate the benefits of accessible destinations? It seems, a priori, that not everyone is able to do so.

It is specifically in trying to put this notion at everyone's disposal that I recommend adopting the method of clearly separating calculation of the gross benefit of easily accessible destinations from the transportation generalized cost, a well-known traditional idea. The difference between them constitutes the net benefit of the destinations.[1]

The average generalized cost of a trip issuing from the reference zone or the average time associated with it, through the medium of the complete cost of an hour of transportation, both are practically invariable when the characteristics of transportation infrastructures change. That is the first result that transportation surveys demonstrate. It is also the one faithfully reconstructed by travel distribution models whose object is to simulate these survey results. In the case of a homogenous urbanized area, this average time is on the order of 30 minutes, consisting of a motorized portion of about 20 minutes, and a final portion on foot of about 10 minutes. The net benefit of the trip is not influenced much by the average generalized cost (or the time) of the trip, which is stable. It is the variation in the gross benefit that is the determining element of the evaluation. The travel range expands when infrastructures improve. And the quantity of goods accessible within a given time increases, causing the corresponding destinations to increase their benefit. So that is the term that needs to be examined.

The gross benefit of easily accessible destinations is expressed by the logarithmic value of the number of goods, Q^{90}, countable in the domain delimited by a perimeter exceeded by no more than 10 percent of the users issuing from the reference zone, result multiplied by the value of an hour worked and divided by the constant coefficient a (six in the case of work and nine for other travel reasons), making it possible to transform this result into euros. Travel simulation models that are easily able to classify trips issuing from the reference zone by increasing order of time or cost can determine the perimeter exceeded by no more than 10 percent of users. Once the perimeter is known, these same models can count the number of goods (the same figure that served to calculate the trips) inside the area delimited. The calculation of the gross benefit of easily accessible destinations follows from this procedure. This is a relatively simple process. This approach, rigorous in the case of a homogenous urbanized area, constitutes a fairly accurate approximation in the case of large metropolises, each comprising a heterogeneous urbanized area.

During preliminary calculations, we can proceed even more quickly. In the case of a homogenous urbanized area, average travel time is 30 minutes, as we have seen. We also know how to determine the travel time applicable to isochronal 90, which is composed of a motorized portion of about 40 minutes (38 minutes) and foot travel at the end amounting to about 20 minutes. Isochronal 90 thus is situated at about 1 hour of transportation time. We can, from here on out, proceed to a preliminary evaluation of gross benefit of easily accessible destinations by determining the number of identifiable goods within the area delimited by an hour of travel originating in the reference zone. The logarithm of this number, multiplied by the value of an hour worked, divided by the constant coefficient a, provides a very good idea of the gross benefit of easily accessible destinations issuing from this area.[2]

Henceforth, calculating benefits and costs becomes easy to memorize and put into practice. For costs, the basis is an average travel time of 30 minutes, practically invariable, that is assigned a value in preliminary approximation, of a half hour worked. For gross benefits, it is an isochronal of 60 minutes, which delimits an area within which we count the goods desired by the resident. We take the logarithm of this number, apply to it the value of 1 hour worked and divide the result by the constant coefficient a, which is six for work reasons and nine for other purposes. Net benefit is obtained by subtracting from gross benefit the total cost of travel.

The result obtained for one trip can be multiplied by the number of trips in the chosen study period. In this way, one can evaluate the annual gross benefit of easily accessible destinations issuing from the reference zone, total annual transportation cost issuing from this zone and annual net benefit of these same destinations by multiplying the respective values—associated with an average trip issuing from the zone—by the number of trips made during the year for the reason in question.

The representation of the values of easily accessible destinations is instructive

Both gross and net values of easily accessible destinations lend themselves well to high-quality cartographic representations. Each neighborhood studied can receive a growing density frame as a function of the benefit obtained by each inhabitant or worker. In the case of color maps, one can use sequenced chromatic palettes that have big impact. This type of exhibit makes it possible to immediately highlight the areas that are well served and those that are less so.

This type of cartography allows us to illustrate the value of each reason for travel, make evident the values associated with economic activities and those with relaxation and renewal. For economic activities, we can arrange in hierarchical order those that reveal productive work, business, sales, and education.

We can illustrate the creation of value by socioprofessional category and make evident any geographical disparities.

We also can show the structural differences associated with different means of transportation, such as public and private.

Displays can also be used to point out the effects of a projected transportation infrastructure, municipality by municipality. We portray in absolute value the results of the reference situation, without the infrastructure. Then we proceed in the same way to illustrate results obtained after bringing the project on line. The differences are extremely instructive. It will immediately become obvious which municipalities will benefit and which will not. Sometimes, the municipalities that will benefit can be located several kilometers away from the public works project. The localization of benefits varies according to whether one considers travel for economic reasons or travel for green space activities. Visualizing effects that can be obtained in each municipality makes possible fruitful debates and a much greater objectivity with local inhabitants and local authorities.

Used to compare two competing projects (for example, going through or bypassing an area), the placement of gross and net benefits—as well as differences—into visual form can illustrate the effects of each project on all neighborhoods in the urbanized area, whether they are far away or close, as well as the advantages and disadvantages one may present to the other.

The benefits of easily accessible destinations definitively constitute instruments of work, reflection, and decision making. They are relatively simple to handle, easy to represent cartographically, and are highly effective methods of instruction.

The annual generalized travel costs per worker or inhabitant are hardly significant because they scarcely vary upon the opening of new infrastructures. Nonetheless, we can represent them by attaching to each worker or inhabitant the expenditures in travel generalized costs associated with them. In absolute value the results will be very homogenous, and in relative value they will not be very apparent.

The benefits of easily accessible destinations adapt to use

Benefits adapt to the reason for travel

The methods of evaluating benefits make it possible to clearly distinguish the reasons for trips, in fact, the nature of desired goods and services at different destinations.

In general, we may differentiate trips with an economic and social purpose from those with a relaxation and renewal purpose.

In the first category, three types of travel are usually identified:

- Travel from home to work and back
- Travel from and to home for other reasons (purchases, visits, personal business)
- Travel that has no connection to home

In each case, we can take the resident's perspective, but we can also take the perspective of the economic agent offering the service.

For work reasons, from the worker's perspective, the gross benefit of destinations is characterized by the logarithmic value of the number of jobs E^{90} accessible in 1 hour after leaving home, multiplied by the factor that makes possible transforming this result into monetary value: value of an hour worked, divided by the constant coefficient equal to six, and multiplied by the number of annual trips if one wishes to obtain an annual result. Some doubt the effect exerted on the trip's benefit by the number of jobs and the notion of choice that is coupled with it. They point out that in a period of unemployment choice is forcibly limited. Actually, it is necessary to note that even in a period of serious unemployment workers change jobs every four years on average. There is a rapid turnover in jobholders. There is real choice. Moreover, there are many advertisements for jobs, even in periods of job market difficulties. It must not be forgotten that in times of unemployment, positions do not find takers. The concept of vacant positions is just as much a reality.

For work reasons, from the employer's perspective, the gross benefit of destinations is represented by the logarithmic value of the number of workers T^{90}, accessible in about 1 hour from the zone where the business is located, multiplied by the factor that makes it possible to transform this result into monetary value: value of an hour worked, divided by the constant coefficient equal to six, then multiplied by the number of annual trips if we want an annual result. The more numerous the choices, the better chance the employer has of finding the worker who corresponds to the desired profile. One can note that in moderately sized urbanized areas, some large enterprises cannot develop for lack of finding workers corresponding to the specialties sought.

For other reasons, primarily purchases or personal affairs, the resident's satisfaction is represented by the logarithmic value of the number of tertiary jobs, E'''^{90}, such as sales and service jobs, that the resident can access in a time corresponding to boundaries exceeded by no more than 10 percent of users, multiplied by the factor making it possible to transform this result into monetary value: value of an hour worked, divided by the constant coefficient a applicable to "other reasons," and multiplied by the number of annual trips for other purposes, if we want an annual result. For the other purposes, the coefficient a that comes into the travel time calculation is equal to nine (instead of six for work reasons). Average travel time, as well as isochronal time 90, for this sort of reason is thus reduced by a third in relation to times applicable to work reasons. As a result, isochronal 90 stands at about 40 minutes, and average travel time is approximately 20 minutes. The value of tertiary jobs countable within isochronal 40 minutes, E'''^{90}, expresses the scope of choices offered the resident, particularly in the retail sector. For an equal expenditure, the resident is able to satisfy needs better if the number of tertiary jobs is high.

For other purposes, the perspective of the retailer or the service provider can be expressed by the logarithmic value of the extent of the potential clientele, $P'''90$, that he or she can expect to access in a given time (about 40 minutes), multiplied by the factor making possible a transformation of this result into monetary value: value of an hour worked, divided by the constant coefficient a applicable to "other purposes," that is nine, and multiplied by the number of annual trips for an annual result. This is how the establishment of commercial centers is studied. The size of the residential population located less than x minutes away represents one of the essential placement criteria.

In the case of trips that do not originate at home (rebound trips), one encounters considerations that are fairly close to those developed to characterize the perspective of retailers. Those in charge of retail businesses have an interest in seeing to it that benefits corresponding to the logarithm of tertiary jobs E'''^{90}, weighted by the multiplying factor representing the value of 1 hour worked, divided by the constant coefficient a and multiplied by the number of annual trips are as high as possible. Trips are usually executed on the rebound, from one service to another. The higher the concentration of services, the easier it is to travel on the rebound.

Let's remember, by the way, that in addition to trips for economic and social reasons that we have just described, there are trips whose only purpose is to access open spaces for relaxation and renewal. The benefits of these trips are expressed by the logarithmic value of the surface area of open spaces, Q^{90}, that residents can access within an area delimited by the isochronal exceeded by no more than 10 percent of users (about 45 minutes for this purpose), multiplied by the factor that makes it possible to transform this result into monetary value: value of an hour worked, divided by the constant coefficient a, and multiplied by the number of annual trips if we seek an annual result.

Thanks to transportation networks, residents live in osmosis with the area that surrounds them. From the series of examples above, it becomes apparent to what extent benefits of accessible destinations correspond to the expectations of residents living on a given site and wishing to access different services offered by that living area.

Values/benefits adapt to the socioprofessional category of the residents

As we already have noticed, the given most widely shared by humans is the 24 hours that constitute their day. In this regard, no inequality exists. This observation turns up again at the level of time devoted to travel. Daily times spent on physical travel within a living area are the same regardless of the socioprofessional category in question. Whether you are a blue-collar worker, a white-collar worker, or a CEO, you spend on average an hour and a half in travel daily. There is no difference with regard to time. As for transportation costs, the worth of 1 hour of travel time is calculated on the basis of two-thirds of the value of 1 hour worked. From this point of view, the hour and 30 minutes of the CEO would not be valued at the same level as the hour and 30 minutes of the blue-collar worker. In our economic approach, there is, of course, a differentiation according to socioprofessional category. In practice, it is found at the level of monetary expenditures associated with travel. On average, they represent—per hour of travel—one-third of the hour worked, or half of the time spent. If we consider trips by private transportation, we note that the users, very intelligently, choose types of vehicles corresponding to their economic capacities (size and horsepower chosen). But all vehicles have practically equivalent performances in terms of travel within a living area. The average speed is the same. Travel ranges are, for all practical purposes, indifferent to the socioprofessional category, and the performance of the transportation system is very homogenous from one category to the other. Only the comfort of the trip can vary. All the same! Today's cars have a very good level of comfort regardless of type. So performances are very much identical.

At the level of economic value, these performances take into account the value of the hour worked. For travel costs, an hour of travel time is valued at two-thirds of an hour worked. Monetary expenditures represent in practice the remaining third, with a real adaptation of motorized transport depending on socioprofessional category. This observation alone makes one think that if we wished to establish tolls to support the setting up of urban infrastructures, for example, and if we had available very flexible ways of collecting tolls (like those that authorities in the Federal Republic of Germany have recently introduced for heavy-duty trucks), it would be necessary that the toll be proportional to the horsepower of the vehicle so that the weight of monetary expenditures overall would not exceed a third of the total travel cost.

In the case of the benefits of easily accessible destinations, it must be remembered that the logarithmic form of the number of goods accessible is valorized by the factor: value of an hour worked, divided by the constant coefficient a. If, on one hand, a is independent of the socioprofessional category (six for work reasons, nine for other purposes), on the other, the value of an hour worked depends directly on the socioprofessional category.

Should it be deduced that more should be invested in favor of the highest socioprofessional categories? A formidable question. Let us take note, however, that in the area of motor vehicles, drivers and automakers have resolved the problem. Manufacturers have brought to market a large variety of models ranging from the most powerful to the least powerful, from the largest to the smallest, with very different sales prices and costs of upkeep, but all offering the possibility of transportation at more or less equivalent speeds under normal circumstances. For highway investments, on the other hand, it is not clear how we could differentiate infrastructure usage by means of construction techniques. A vehicle, regardless of type, occupies about the same surface area as it moves on a roadway. Yet, if a flexible toll could be introduced for financing this infrastructure, nothing would prevent adapting the toll level to the horsepower of the vehicle or to any characteristic that makes differentiating the socioprofessional category of the user possible.

For public transportation, partial reimbursement by the employers plays a role. For the least favored socioprofessional categories, specific reimbursements are in place. The community owes it to itself to provide a good level of mobility for everyone.

But that does not prevent it from considering the specific needs of the highest categories, those whose valuing of time and of the benefits of easily accessible destinations is the strongest. Remember, for example, that air transportation owed its first expansion to satisfying the needs of a limited category of users—those for whom travel time was extremely valuable and for whom the benefits of accessible destinations thanks to this rapid means of transportation were highly valued. But since then the range of users has expanded considerably.

This type of problem is posed when those in charge of large agglomerations decide to allocate a certain priority to providing service to airports, so that the terminal portion of the trip does not impinge too much on the total travel time, door to door, of users of air transportation.

These examples clearly show the interest that lies in evaluations of travel benefits by distinguishing, for example, three socioprofessional categories (low income, moderate income, high income) and in discussing strategies to implement in order to satisfy their needs.

Benefits adapt to the means of transportation

Benefits of easily accessible destinations clearly reveal the levels of service offered by different means of transportation. They bring to light the strengths and weaknesses of each system. For example, for public transportation, as soon as we move away from the lines and their stations, the number of goods accessible in a given time, whether it be jobs or workers, salespeople or consumers, tends to fall rapidly. If, moreover, the density of the neighborhoods served drops, the range of choices peters out and the attractiveness of the network evaporates. We understand clearly the influence of the density factor. It is not the speed of travel that is the principle criterion for measuring the efficiency of a public transportation network, but the linking of speed to the density of sites served, that is, the potential of goods accessible within a given travel time.

For private transportation, the benefits of easily accessible destinations are spread out much more evenly. Private transportation includes short trips on foot at the end. When urbanization density remains moderate, users don't run into problems of infrastructure saturation, and the number of goods accessible in a given travel time stabilizes at a very satisfactory level. It is only when densities become high that saturation problems appear. Travel speeds stabilize or drop, and the number of goods accessible in a given time reaches a ceiling. On the other hand, it is in these high-density areas that public transportation can offer a large number of stations and increasing frequency of passage. The number of accessible destinations grows. Here, the complementarity between public and private transportation becomes transparent, the former taking over from the latter when it reaches saturation.

Under these conditions, how does one put a value on the services offered by a rapid public transportation system when the system itself is fed by cars that drivers leave parked in station parking lots?

This is a difficult question, but it is not an exception. What the benefits of easily accessible destinations make it possible to put a value on is the satisfaction felt by the user who uses all transportation systems available and seeks to make the best possible use of them. The user can use several means of transportation in succession, such as walking, driving, then taking public transportation, and—finally—walking once more. The number of destinations accessible in a given travel time will express the performance of the complete chain of means used. In this way, we realize that the different means of transportation are as closely linked to each other as to the activities they serve. A network of roads and public transportation serving a living area constitutes a whole that must be evaluated globally.

In reality, transportation surveys show that cases of mixed use of systems are relatively rare. Transhipments are disadvantageous, and the average length of a trip is—must it be repeated?—30 minutes, including time spent walking at the end. Trips that exceed an hour are only 10 percent of the total. By taking certain precautions, we can, in general, assign a dominant means of transportation to a trip. In fact, that is how we can determine usage rates for the different means of transportation.

But the benefits of accessible destinations are perfectly able to accommodate complex trips using several transportation systems, which illustrates, once again, their universality.

Applications illustrate the coherence of the approach

The case of the Francilienne freeway in the west of Île-de-France

The Francilienne (the outermost of three ring freeways surrounding Paris) in the west of Île-de-France, between freeway A16 to the northeast of Cergy-Pontoise and freeway A13 level with Orgeval, is the perfect illustration of conflicts of interest between the community as a whole and directly affected local residents. It is a very important project whose cost is estimated 775 million euros[3]. This urban freeway, included in the master plan for Île-de-France, lengthens the Francilienne already completed to the north of Île-de-France between Roissy and freeway A16. Its principal functions are to take care of urban short-range trips (10–20 kilometers) that stretch out along this itinerary and use traditional roads that are not conceived for this type of rapidly increasing traffic. It should also provide a smooth exit for freeway 16 coming from Amiens.

This project was the object of preliminary public debates at the moment when its awarding to a private firm was considered in 1990. Local residents mobilized to prevent the completion of the project. They grouped themselves into local associations that were united in a federation of associations, the COPRA (Collectif pour la Protection des Riverains[4] de l'Autoroute), which took a very active part in the criticisms launched against those who had conceived the project. Voices pleading on behalf of the global interest of the operation, in particular from the point of view of accessibility to different areas of activity, did not succeed in expressing themselves with equal force. The project file reached the stage of elaborating a preliminary plan that can become the object of a public notice if the government decides to pursue completion of the freeway

A considerable number of studies justifying the project were conducted from 1990 to 1995, years that saw the main stages of the public debate play out. More recently, an evaluation study of the improvement of economic and natural benefits that this project would be capable of supplying, adopting as reference the option of doing nothing, was ordered from IGN (Institut Géographique National), which was conducting elsewhere the evaluation study of economic and natural performances in the living areas of France, as well as in nine neighboring countries belonging to the European Union. The simplified method used leads to evaluation of gross benefits of destinations within isochronals of 1 hour around the different points studied. These were the centers of the municipalities comprising the rather large area affected by the project. First, the evaluation hypothesized a start-up date in 2005, then extrapolated to the year 2015 as a probable start-up date. Travel costs were not directly evaluated since their value will remain stable from the moment the infrastructure is put into service. Only the gross benefits will increase, as will the net benefits that result by subtracting the travel costs (which don't change).

The results obtained are extremely interesting. Globally, with a 2005 start-up date, the gross benefits and net benefits increase by 230 million euros per year: 184 million for economic destinations and 46 million for natural destinations. With a 2015 start-up date, the results measured in 2005 euros are, respectively, 470 million euros, 376 million euros, and 94 million euros.[5]

Compared to the cost of the project, estimated at 775 million in 2005 euros, after all the improvements that were brought to it, these gains in benefit lead to a return on investment time of about three years for a 2005 start-up date, and two years for a 2015 start-up date, which is very positive. Even if the cost increases by another 50 percent, the turn around time will remain highly satisfactory. Every year, the project should increase the resources of the living area's inhabitants by 185 million euros (2005 start-up date) and by 375 million euros (2015 start-up date).

The municipalities that gain the greatest advantage from this project are situated on the northwest and southwest edges of Île-de-France, as well as in neighboring regions located in the Parisian basin, at distances that are sometimes several tens of kilometers from the project site. From now on, these municipalities can access clusters of jobs that were previously inaccessible. The following benefits can be achieved:

- 2005 = 2,300 euros per year per worker
- 2015 = 4,700 euros per year per worker (including 40 percent in net salary)

Local residents in the project area, on the other hand, only obtain more modest improvements because they already have a fairly powerful economic environment at their disposal.

As far as natural benefits are concerned, the municipalities that gain the greatest advantage from the project are located in the area close to the freeway site. That's understandable because these municipalities, lacking large natural spaces, can now access the forests on the outskirts of Île-de-France and the Parisian basin. The municipalities on the outskirts of Île-de-France, in contrast, are only lightly affected.

Techniques for evaluating gross and net benefits of accessible destinations thus prove to be particularly effective for illustrating the impact of a project as important as the Francilienne in the west of Île-de-France. The information is not only quantitative, making it possible to justify the proposed investments, but it also gives a very precise spatial vision of the project's effect. The municipalities affected are often situated tens of kilometers away. In light of this example, the value of such an approach becomes evident.

The government should doubtless launch a dialogue procedure again in the near future. But discussions have not yet started up again. Consequently, it is not clear if this type of result can have a positive effect on the progress of procedures preliminary to a public notice. At any rate, it is evident that it does make it possible to clearly explain the economic and natural benefit of such a project and to show to what measure it contributes significant services to the ensemble of residents living in the western section of Île-de-France. It also makes it possible to explain why the project is beneficial, even though it does not provide any gain in travel time, the main counterargument advanced by opponents of the project. The technical improvements brought to the project (the original cost has gone up three times) eliminate all negative aspects from the viewpoint of visual and sound nuisances. The public will be exposed to fewer nuisances than before. Everyone stands to gain. But demonstration doesn't automatically elicit belief! The road is still a long one before a consensus will arise, if it does indeed arise some day. In the meanwhile, nuisances are becoming more and more serious, and every three years the residents as a community are losing the equivalent of the unrealized investment in terms of economic wealth. Moreover, unemployment is on the rise. These are the negative effects that issue from an absence of constructive discussions!

Le Mans: do we go through town or around it?

Let's move on to the example of studies carried out a long time ago in Le Mans when it was necessary to conceive a new master plan. Two projects were in competition: one cut through from the north in order to serve the center of the town and another bypassed the town on the west, making it possible to free up the center and—in the minds of defenders of this version—to greatly improve access conditions to this center. The two sides advanced contradictory arguments.

Evaluation of gross and net benefits of the two projects makes it possible to shed some light on the discussion and to clearly advise the adoption of one solution over the other.

First of all, the two projects yield travel times and total costs that are almost identical, even though they are of fundamentally different types. We observe, once again, that travel times and costs do not constitute a definitive criterion. Any argument advanced that relies on travel times can only lead to dangerous, not to say incorrect, conclusions. Discussion is at a dead end.

On the other hand, by looking at the two projects and considering the difference in gross travel benefits and, consequently, net benefits obtained by subtracting unvarying travel costs from gross benefits, the analysis becomes transparent.

The two projects bring with them increases in benefits, not only to places where the projects are installed, but also very often to places that are a long distance away. Indeed, all the neighborhoods of the urbanized area have a stake in the results.

The bypass solution affords greater improvement of conditions for accessing the center than the solution that cuts through town. A priori, this can seem a paradox. In reality, the bypass removes from the center a large number of trips that have nothing to do with it: peripheral trips between neighborhoods that go through the center of town because there is no way around. The central avenues, relieved of this traffic, become efficient again and perfectly carry out their role of serving central administrative and commercial areas.

A comparison of gross benefits neighborhood by neighborhood in the case of each project shows that we obtain the best results in all the areas, including the town center, by adopting the bypass solution over the one that cuts through town. Of course, neighborhoods in the west of the town are much better served by this solution. In fact, the bypass solution leads to a treatment of the town's various neighborhoods that is more harmonious and evenly distributed among them. This is what we generally observe in urban areas. This is the reason local authorities prefer this type of solution. It can be seen that the choice of such solutions tends to favor urbanizations of relatively homogenous density and to call into question the efficiency of the hierarchical structure of agglomerations founded on walking and public transportation that are organized in a radial fashion.

In comparison with the solution that cuts through town, the bypass solution yields additional benefit on the order of 1,150 euros per worker per year (in 2005 euros). In some neighborhoods that are well served by the bypass, the additional benefit can reach 1,700 euros per worker per year. Obviously, choices made by public entities have significant consequences for the economic vitality of the area in which the effects of public investments play out.

As it happened, it was the bypass solution that was chosen, correctly, by the local authority. The general equilibrium of the agglomeration of Le Mans was reinforced by this decision.

Nancy and Rouen: private transportation and public transportation

Much discussion today centers on the comparative worth of public transportation and private transportation. People attribute negative effects to private transportation, as far as nuisances are concerned, without assigning any real positive effects as far as service rendered. What is the truth of the matter?

For the moment, I will withhold responses on the problem of nuisances, which I will address later. I am going to give my opinion on the services rendered, in terms of travel benefit, for both means of transportation. To begin with, I will study the case of a moderately sized city like Nancy, composed of about 400,000 inhabitants. I will then present the case of an extremely large metropolis such as Île-de-France that comprises exceptionally large densities at its center.

First of all, comparison of travel times gives Nancy a slight advantage in having private transportation that allows residents to avoid significant final parts of their trips on foot. But that is not the main difference.

Studies of travel benefit in the case of private transportation reveal results that are satisfactory and relatively homogenous from one neighborhood to another. Peripheral areas attain values that are hardly different from those noted in the center. The reason is that the decreasing density of destinations as—and when—you move away from the center is compensated for by an improvement in travel speeds, since private vehicles only encounter insignificant obstacles to their progress on the periphery. The number of destinations accessible in a given time varies only slightly in relation to distance from the center. Consequently, there is maintenance of a good range of destination choices. This is what constitutes the strength of private transportation and its success in areas of moderate density such as those encountered in urbanized areas of several hundreds of thousands of inhabitants. This type of result is, in fact, observed in Nancy and Rouen.

Travel benefit studies in the case of public transportation reveal, on the other hand, differing results depending on whether one is in the center or on the periphery. In the center and in neighborhoods near the center, the density of destinations to be served is high. Frequency of bus or tram services is high and terminal trips on foot are moderate. The benefits of accessible destinations for residents living in these areas are totally satisfactory. But as soon as you leave the center, the limitations inherent in public transportation become increasingly apparent and the benefits of accessible destinations for the residents of these areas progressively fade. It is difficult to do anything about these well-known situations.

It's a good idea to think about novel solutions that make it possible to respond to personalized travel requests in areas of average-to-low density. We can well imagine that users without vehicles might provide themselves, or be provided with, portable telephones armed with GPS localization. All calls coming from this type of user would be recorded by the transportation management center responsible and conveyances set aside for this purpose would optimize their routes to respond as quickly as possible to the needs of users who had called.

It is, of course, necessary that everyone in an agglomeration has at his or her disposal a means of transportation that provides good access. But it is not certain that it is traditional public transportation on fixed routes that will make it possible to respond to this objective in the least dense peripheral areas. We ought not hesitate to call upon all the resources of modern technology to succeed in providing access to a broad range of choices for all.

Île-de-France: Paris and Marne-la-Vallée

How about very large metropolises whose centers have high densities and whose outskirts have less dense areas? How does one evaluate the situation of central Paris and that of Marne-la-Vallée in Île-de-France?

These two examples will allow me to compare two very different urban structures. The first, central Paris, comprises job densities on the order of 200 per hectare. It is served primarily by the Paris metro that provides average travel speeds, door to door, of 9 kilometers an hour. These speeds may seem modest at first glance. The second, Marne-la-Vallée, has a job density about 20 times lower, on the order of 10 jobs per hectare. It is served, within its different urbanization hubs, by the RER (Réseau Express Régional, the express rail network serving Paris and its suburbs), but it is essentially private transportation, using a network of rapid, large freeways that, outside of the RER axis, ensures the transactions of daily life. This is the dominant means of transportation. Travel speeds are on the order of 36 kilometers an hour, door to door.

What do evaluations of benefits of easily accessible destinations tell us in either case?

First of all, as in all the other examples cited, travel times, despite differing travel speeds, are approximately the same: 30 minutes of average travel time and 1 hour for the isochronal exceeded by no more than 10 percent of users.

Gross benefits of destinations accessible in this 1 hour's time are not very different either, since the number of jobs accessible in the hour is fairly close in the two cases. The number of jobs per hectare in Marne-la-Vallée is 20 times less than in Paris. But the area covered in 1 hour in Marne-la-Vallée, with private transportation, is 16 times greater than that covered in 1 hour in Paris with the metro. Door-to-door speed compensates for the lower occupation density of the area, and the results obtained are fairly comparable. In reality, central Paris yields results that are a little better than Marne-la-Vallée. Precise calculations place the number of jobs accessible in 1 hour in Paris at exactly 2.5 million, despite relatively slow average speeds on the metro. The figure is 1.5 million in Marne-la-Vallée, a result that is quite considerable.

One realizes then that it is not just the speed of a mode of transportation that determines its performance, but its ability to offer a number of destinations within the urbanized structure it serves. A transportation system is indissolubly linked to the places of residence and activity that it connects. The method of evaluating the benefit of easily accessible destinations appears totally neutral with regard to the system of transportation serving a living area. A fairly slow public transportation system that serves a very dense living area can obtain better results than a private system of transportation that offers higher door-to-door speeds but serves a less dense area.

As we've already noted, the number of goods accessible in the hour that qualifies the performance of a transportation system serving a living area—in terms of benefit of easily accessible destinations—is obtained, as a preliminary approximation, very simply. We multiply the density d of the goods served by the surface area of the land covered in 1 hour, which is proportional to the square of speed V of the transportation system. The product $d.V^2$ applies to urban structures that differ greatly from one another. What is actually identified by this concept is the quality of transactions among people. The logarithmic form of the energy of a living area, of this quality of exchanges of expertise, illustrates the performance of the community as a whole. We will see shortly that there are strong relationships with the actual creation of wealth. The intelligence of a living area occupied by people is a reality that is a key element of a society's organization.

Notes

1. In its normal definition, the net benefit of desired goods that surround a residential zone of reference is obtained by considering all the goods that surround this zone, weighting each of the goods by its decreasing exponential of travel time, adding together and taking the logarithm of the whole, and finally by multiplying by the factor that makes it possible to express this result in euros, that is, by multiplying by the value of an hour worked, itself divided by the constant coefficient a (which equals six for work reasons and nine for other travel purposes). You have to agree that even if it's normal, it's not very user-friendly!

2. In extremely unusual cases, the travel average time and access time at isochronal 90 deviate from the 30 and 60 minutes just mentioned. For example, in the case of urbanized areas whose density is decreasing rapidly, as is the case in moderately sized agglomerations possessing a historical center and peripheral areas that have not extended very far, the average travel time stands at a lower value than that obtained within a homogenous urbanized area. This time is on the order of 10 minutes, to which the time on foot has to be added (an additional 10 minutes), bringing the total average time to 20 minutes. Isochronal 90 stands at 27 minutes, to which must be added time on foot in the wake of public transportation (20 additional minutes), bringing the total time of isochronal 90 to 47 minutes. In the opposite case of areas situated on the outskirts of large metropolises and near significant hubs that lead to a rapid increase in urbanization density, the average travel time stands at a value higher than that obtained within a homogenous urbanized area. This time is on the order of 30 minutes, to which must be added foot travel (an additional 10 minutes), bringing the total average time to 40 minutes. Isochronal 90 is located at the value of 49 minutes of motorized travel, a value to which must be added time on foot in the wake of public transportation (20 additional minutes), bringing the total time of isochronal 90 to 69 minutes. But we should note that moderately sized agglomerations whose urbanization density is decreasing very rapidly, as well as residential areas located near large hubs, represent exceptional situations. In the large majority of cases, an average travel time of 30 minutes and 1 hour for isochronal 90 will produce entirely satisfactory results. In unusual cases of very heterogeneous urbanizations, it will be necessary to call upon actual delimitation of isochronal 90 and to substitute this delimitation for rapid evaluation methods.

3. One euro equaled 1.35 U.S. dollars as of the April 12, 2007, exchange rate.

4. Riverains are residents of municipalities alongside streets or motorways, or more generally, transport networks in France.

5. The original simulation, carried out for the year 2000, yields 150 million euros per year in growth of gross and net benefits, of which 120 million is for economic destinations and 30 million for natural destinations.

Results from 2005 take into account the following: a 10.6 percent slide in prices between 2000 and 2005, an increase of 3.2 percent in the standard of living, and accelerated expansion of easily accessible territories linked to freeing existing networks that have become increasingly saturated in the absence of the Francilienne. This expansion is expressed by a multiplying coefficient of 1.35.

With a start-up date of 2015 and results expressed in terms of 2005 euros, the "standard of living" element leads to a new increase of 20 percent (hypothesis of 2 percent per year in volume) and the "expansion of easily accessible territories" element, linked to freeing up existing networks, to a new multiplying coefficient of 1.70.

Part IV

A wider vision: economic and natural performances of living areas in France and Europe

January 14, 2003: I am received in Brussels by a high official from the staff of the commissioner for regional action and the expansion of the European Union, a former minister in the French government.

This meeting is a follow-up to one with the commissioner himself, a few weeks earlier. I share the comments of the commissioner upon viewing the maps showing the economic performances of different European countries, created with the assistance of geographic information systems of the National Geographical Institute.

"Impressive, M. Poulit, I plan to make full use of these maps for the totality of the countries that comprise the European Union, as well as those that are soon to join it. In effect, they show everything that well-served living areas can contribute to countries' economic vitality. I couldn't have imagined that one could evaluate so clearly the effect of the quality of transport services on a region's salaries and GDP. The illustrations that I've seen show very well how the outstanding biological vitality of the Brittany region and the quality of transport services explain the economic dynamism of this region that was formerly so disadvantaged. I also understand how urban metropolises are the locus of an economic force that favors the global vitality of a country, and how the region of the capital produces 28 percent of the country's GDP with just 19 percent of the population. If we have to support regions that comprise very few inhabitants, it has to be done with a portion of the wealth produced by the areas where people develop goods and services in large quantities thanks to the exchange of their expertise. I will take these maps with me as I travel. I will comment on them during working meetings with those whom I engage in discussions. This is excellent."

"So go and see the person in charge of studies in my office. He is going to assist you in pursuing your ideas at the level of the different European countries."

So I present the official in charge of studies the result of my thoughts on the economic and natural performances of living areas. I explain that the times spent on travel by residents does not change when new efficient routes are inaugurated and that only the extent of the areas that each resident can access in a given travel time will vary. The increase in the number of accessible destinations, among which an ever-more pertinent choice can be made, is the source of creation of value. Moreover, an impressive correlation exists between the value associated with home-to-work trips in agglomerations of growing size and the additional salary observable when we move from deeply rural areas to increasingly urbanized ones. The same correlation is observed between the value associated with the totality of trips for economic reasons and the additional GDP observed when we move from deeply rural areas to increasingly urbanized ones. The living areas account for about 45 percent of the country's GDP. Bringing on line high-quality infrastructures inside the areas that accommodate a numerous and diversified population is extremely beneficial for the economic vitality of countries.

"M. Poulit, I don't understand you very well. You probably know that when we bring expressways on line in populated areas, they automatically become saturated. They aren't good for much, except for creating more and more bottlenecks and pollution."

In that instant, I realize that sophisms have struck once again and I don't have much hope of getting the person with whom I am speaking to change his mind. I can talk to him about creation of value, and job support. I think that in spite of his cordiality he's not really listening and won't listen any more closely tomorrow. He's not ready to abandon his beliefs, an attitude that is honorable in the long run. After all, we live in a democracy! However, as far as I am concerned, it is pointless to talk to him about carrying out studies on creation of value in the countries soon to join the European Union. The idea of serving an area doesn't provide him any evidence as a determining factor of progress. I realize that the discussion will require some time.

It is at this juncture that the white paper on transportation in the European Union was published. This report picks up again all the topics dear to destroyers of economic development: stall mobility by disconnecting it from the creation of wealth, which is impossible. Slow down the installation of the means of transportation that are in highest demand in favor of those that are not desired.

Fortunately, 12 months later, the commissioner of transportation and energy asks that the report be taken up again. M. Van Miert finds himself in charge of proposing a program for setting up international infrastructures in Europe. However, there is still a great deal of wariness about serving metropolitan areas, even though these are the ones that create the basis of the wealth of countries and sustain their vitality.

I leave the official in charge of studies with the feeling that I will hardly receive any encouragement to go forward with subjects that the commissioner would consider essential. I will have to turn to other authorities in order to provide financing for case studies with cartographic illustrations. I understand better the reason why different countries in the EU have so much difficulty defining successful strategies regarding economic development and the support of employment. In order to move forward, it is necessary to first win the battle of ideas and relentlessly chase down the sophisms that muddy the thinking of some decision makers.

Fortunately, other people in charge of studies in other Directorates General, such as the one in charge of European statistics or the one in charge of transportation and energy, prove to be extremely sensitive to the idea of creation of value and wish to become spokespeople for it. Once again I am to help them improve their methodological understanding.

The first action aims to make absolutely clear how a living area creates value and how this value actually correlates with increases in salaries and GDP. This attests to the importance of the studies with which I proceeded, comparing the benefits created by workers in sixteen agglomerations of growing size in France with salaries paid within these urbanized areas and with the GDP produced. It likewise demonstrated the importance of the calculations of benefits with which I also proceeded within living areas centered in the 36,000 municipalities of France and 46,000 municipalities in nine neighboring European countries (see maps pages 85–86).

All the same, attention must be paid to the pertinence of the studies carried out. From now on, comparison will bear on living areas that have, over time, accumulated goods and services, often with complex progressions that differ from one area to the other.

In all the examples described until now, I have made a point of comparing situations bearing on a single living area, on a single reference period: for example, the situation with or without the west Francilienne in Île-de-France; comparison of a project running through town or bypassing it in Le Mans, both feasible by the same date; comparison of a public and a private transportation system in Nancy; comparison in Île-de-France of the urban fabric of Paris, served by the metro, and that of Marne-la-Vallée, served primarily by private means of transportation.

Economists are, in effect, very attentive to reference solutions taken into consideration when proceeding to comparative studies that bring public investments into operation. They do not want projects to stray too far from a common benchmark situation. In this case, we can clearly specify the investments to be made in order to move from the reference solution to each of the projects recommended, as well as judge the change in the service rendered by each of these projects by adopting the benchmark as the basis. Comparing the improvement in benefit obtained with the foreseen investment in order to implement each project makes it possible to prioritize the solutions. In the last case that I discussed, that of Paris and its metro versus Marne-la-Vallée with its predominantly private transportation, I placed myself at the outer limits of what economists can accept. I would have found it hard to specify the investments necessary to implement one or another of the solutions. Therefore, the commentary remained general in nature. A strict economic comparison would require a study of the urbanization of the Marne-le-Vallée area on the same model as Paris, as well as a comparison of this situation with what was actually adopted for the development of the eastern portion of Île-de-France. In the two cases, it would have been necessary to specify the investments required to move from the solution without any urbanization to the Parisian type or the new town type. This kind of analysis is difficult because the reference situation is far removed from the situation being evaluated, and it is not easy to determine all the investments it would take to implement the entire project.

I wanted to show with the examples that I discussed—in particular those that pit alternative projects against each other—that gross or net benefits of easily accessible destinations are totally adapted to this type of analysis and that they are consistent with extremely rigorous economic approaches.

That does not prevent us from exploring all the potential contained in notions of benefits of easily accessible destinations to characterize the efficiency of organization in different living areas. It will be enough in these cases to avoid comparing these benefits with public investments that have been necessary in order to achieve the results observed. On the other hand, evaluating the efficiency of a public organization is of great value, especially when there is evidence of strong correlations with wealth produced.

Gross and net benefits of destinations easily accessible for economic or natural reasons lend themselves to evaluation in living areas as diverse as rural locales, small or medium-sized agglomerations, or—ultimately—a global metropolis such as Île-de-France.

I am surprised to note that studies are underway regarding average travel costs in these types of living areas without any notice being taken of the orthodoxy of the methods used. The Department of Budget Forecasting (la Direction de la Prévision)—and I find this initiative very useful—proceeded to conduct an analysis of this kind in spring 2003 while preparing a seminar on "transportation and setting taxes on urban space." Since economic traditions bear on the analysis of transportation costs, the perspective of this approach appears natural. It seems to me that study of the benefits constituting this other quadrant of transportation research should benefit from the same perspective.

It is extremely important to introduce the benefits of accessible destinations into these global studies because they make possible avoiding diagnostic errors that can have serious repercussions in the realm of investment strategies or national development policy.

In this way, the Department of Budget Forecasting study, serving as preparation for the discussion of setting area taxes, establishes—what I had already observed in the course of studies I had conducted—that average transportation costs increase with the size of agglomerations. It's a reasonable observation. Only very large urban areas offer wide choices of destinations. These are the agglomerations in which average travel times stabilize at 30 minutes and where isochronal 90 reaches about 1 hour. In smaller agglomerations, the choice of destinations is smaller. Because of a lack of accessible destinations, the average travel time is less than 30 minutes and isochronal 90 is also less than 1 hour. The Department of Budget Forecasting concluded that it was legitimate to consider a specific tax on inhabitants of large agglomerations that would penalize them and encourage them to relocate to moderately sized ones. Of course, I shared my doubts, and after discussion the administration accepted my input.

It was to forget that the gross economic benefits of these same trips, as we will see shortly, are on average three times higher than the travel costs and increase at a rate three times higher than transportation costs when the size of the agglomeration increases. Net economic benefits therefore grow very rapidly along with the size of the urbanized area. The conclusions are thus exactly inverse to those established by considering transportation costs alone. And so there is the need to take into account the benefits of an accessible destinations approach when one wishes to evaluate the global efficiency of a living area.

As it is, the "benefits of easily accessible destinations" approach is consistent with the collective behavior of residents, and explains why the urban area develops. On the other hand, to avoid any misunderstanding, the preceding results do not justify a priori that large agglomerations be supported at the expense of small ones. It would be necessary, in order to make a judgment of this sort, to compare increases in the benefits in the different agglomerations studied with investments of all kinds (not solely for transportation) necessary for implementing these different developments. The agglomerations that yield the best relationship between benefits and costs would be the ones to be particularly supported. But economists, guardians of the temple, would doubtless remind us that this type of comparison is subject to caution since the reference solution is not clearly identified and investments of all kinds needed for the success of such-and-such type of development are difficult to list.

It is no less true that the absence of all consideration for the benefits of accessible destinations would lead to an erroneous strategic diagnostic. After discussion, the Department of Budget Forecasting willingly recognized this and admitted the pertinence of the "benefits of accessible destinations" approach. It seems to me that the legitimacy of a global approach to benefits in living areas of different kinds is as secure as that of evaluating transportation costs. Be reminded, however, that it is necessary to be very aware of the limits of applying such global methods.

Global evaluation of the benefits of accessible destinations in fact leads to taking into account the time factor. They make it possible to judge the overall efficiency of an urban area served by a given transportation system, an organization that was put in place only gradually—often thanks to the efforts of several generations of residents. Do we need to be reminded that medieval towns had a radius on the order of 4 kilometers, the distance covered on foot in an hour? Doubtless the inhabitants of these towns respected the constants of travel time and considered the hour as the limit of access to desired destinations! Today, the residents of these same towns that have grown into agglomerations cover in 1 hour living areas that are 20 times as large.

In the pages that follow, we are going to present the results of studies bearing on the comparison of benefits observed in different living areas:

- First of all, a study carried out in 1994, whose goal was to compare economic and natural performance of 16 French reference agglomerations, growing in size and extending from Guéret to Île-de-France, and to compare them with the salaries and GDP produced in these urbanized areas.

Indeed, as soon as the first studies conducted in 1973 were published, I hoped to see whether or not the concepts of "range of choice" and "benefits of accessible destinations" were connected to salaries and GDP. The rather theoretical notion of benefit would certainly be more suggestive if it were correlated to more common notions such as those of salary or GDP, with which both economists and the public at large are familiar.

In reality, I noted that benefits of travel from home to work and work to home, such as could be determined in agglomerations of increasing size by using the results of transportation surveys, fell on a curve that is strictly parallel to that of salaries paid in these agglomerations.

I kept checking this data for many years. On September 13, 1994, I turned in to the Council General of Bridges and Roadways a report summarizing all the tests conducted in 16 French reference agglomerations: Guéret, Le-Puy-en-Velay, Annonay, Alençon,

Montauban, Agen, Saint-Brieuc, Angers, Le Havre, Brest, Nancy, Toulouse, Bordeaux, Marseille, Lyon, and Paris. Transportation surveys had been conducted in these cities, making possible the calculation of benefits for the different travel reasons indicated by residents. What's more, we had at our disposal data coming from the National Institute for Statistics and Economics Studies (Institut National de la Statistique et des Études Économiques or INSEE), making it possible to determine the salaries distributed in these agglomerations and to find out the GDP generated. The field of comparison was wide open, and extremely interesting results came to light. There were indeed correlations present and they showed remarkable precision.

- Next, a very extensive study, conducted in 2003, aimed at evaluating the economic performance of living areas surrounding the 36,000 municipalities of France and the 46,000 municipalities of nine neighboring European countries. This study was complemented by a first evaluation of natural performances of the living areas surrounding French municipalities.

In effect, during the course of my 5 years as the head of the National Geographical Institute, I had put to use the capacities of geographic information instruments in order to think about accessibility to all municipalities in France, as well as those of several neighboring European countries. It is a considerable asset to be able to render as cartographical maps the results of evaluating economic performance of living areas both in France and Europe. As a matter of fact, maps possess great suggestive power. With a single glance, we can appraise significant phenomena that mathematical formulas cannot convey by themselves. The bulk of the work was done during my last year at the Institute as well as during my year of activity at the Council General of Bridges and Roadways.

For natural performance, I did not have time to go on to analyze all European municipalities. It required having at my disposal, municipality by municipality, the surface areas of the open spaces, a task that required not a small amount of work. As a result, I concentrated my efforts on the 36,000 French municipalities, putting off until later studies on municipalities in the other European Union countries.

The results obtained have great suggestive power and are highly instructive.

Comparison of economic and natural performances in 16 reference agglomerations

Salaries are correlated with economic benefits of work destinations

For a worker, the economic benefit represented by the choice of a job within a living area containing accessible employment opportunities has a quality demonstrated by all previous analyses: the benefit increases with the number of jobs from which to choose. It does not increase in a linear manner, but in a relative one; that is to say, the number of jobs among which a choice can be made must be multiplied in order to obtain a linear increase in the economic benefit of the choice made. Actually, it changes as the logarithm of the number of easily accessible jobs, that is, the jobs that can be counted within the living area delimited by a boundary exceeded by no more than 10 percent of residents in the zone studied—in practice, this boundary corresponds to 1 hour of travel. This is called the logarithm of E^{90}. If you compare the results of this observation at the level of salaries paid in agglomerations of increasing size (1,000; 10,000; 100,000; 1,000,000; 10,000,000 inhabitants), you find that salaries do, indeed, increase as a function of the agglomeration's size, starting with the level of salary paid in deeply rural areas that constitute the reference in situations where choice is reduced, in the same manner as the logarithm of E^{90}, *but at an even faster pace.*

This difference is simple to explain: economic benefit that a choice of job represents for a worker is connected not only to the relative value of the number of jobs from which to choose, but also to the value of 1 hour worked, divided by a constant coefficient equal to six and finally to the number of trips made annually for the purpose of getting to work and back. The number of trips made annually for work is stable from one agglomeration to another. On the other hand, the value of the hour worked is itself a function of the number of easily accessible jobs among which a job choice can be made. The efficiency of human cooperative labor increases with the number of jobs among which a choice is possible. It is natural that the price of the hour worked increases with this number. The economic benefit represented by the choice of a job in an easily accessible area thus grows faster than the logarithm of E^{90}. It increases as the product of the salary paid in deeply rural areas (R_0) by a numerical factor that is a development in series of the expression "logarithm of E^{90} divided by a constant factor equal to 25 (the factor 25 being the relation between the number of hours worked annually multiplied by six and the number of annual trips to work)." The development in series means that the rise in gross benefit of easily accessible jobs in relation to the situation of reduced choices observed in deeply rural areas is the result of an increase in the range of choices connected with urbanization and also an increase in average salary, which results from the growing range of choices as a function of a rising number of accessible jobs. Thus we obtain the series of converging terms that make it possible to determine the economic benefit of job choice within a given area.

When we take into account this cumulative phenomenon[1], we find that the increase in salaries between deeply rural areas where choice is almost nonexistent and increasingly more urbanized living areas is strictly identical to the economic benefit, itself growing rapidly, represented for the worker by the choice of a job within a living area that offers increasing numbers of easily accessible jobs. The correlation is impressive in its precision.

It is observed in particular in the 16 sample agglomerations that I studied intensively[2].

The correlation had already clearly appeared in 1973. when INSEE indicated that a worker's average net salary was (measured in year 2000 euros):

- EUR 11,850 in deeply rural zones
- EUR 16,350 in Guéret
- EUR 28,600 in Île-de-France,

the benefit of an average trip from home to work or back, multiplied by the number of annual trips for this purpose, yields at Guéret a value of 4,500 euros, or exactly the difference between net salaries paid in Guéret and those distributed in deeply rural areas; in Île-de-France, it yields a value of 16,750 euros, or exactly the difference between net salaries paid in Île-de-France and those paid in profoundly rural areas. Since this correlation expresses a phenomenon of value creation connected to pertinent choices, it suggests the existence of a cause-and-effect relationship, not just an accidental correlation.

To establish definitively this cause-and-effect relationship, it would be necessary to go on to an a posteriori evaluation of the efficiency of one—or of several—large transportation infrastructures recently brought on line, then calculate the discounted effect of this infrastructure with respect to creation of salary value and verify that the observed increase in salaries is indeed that predicted by the calculations.

This kind of check will soon go into effect, adopting as a reference freeway A75, famous for the Millau viaduct that spans the Tarn Valley. Evaluation of the impact of this infrastructure on the increase in salaries and—more generally—on the GDP in the municipalities served is in progress. Checks on the reality of economic growth predictions will be carried out by comparing the changes observed by INSEE before implementation of the infrastructure and after its installation. If the results of the calculations and observations agree, the cause-and-effect relationship will be confirmed. I need to note that in November 2003, the president of the section of economic studies of the Council General of Bridges and Roadways asked the research director of the Ministry of Public Works and Transportation to proceed to this type of evaluative check of transportation infrastructures large enough to measure a posteriori the existence of such a causal relationship. The case of freeway A75 is the first test conducted on the basis of this directive.

Gross domestic products are correlated with the benefits of all economic destinations

Does the correlation exist with gross domestic products?

Of course, I followed my curiosity to the point of asking myself if there was a correlation (a cause-and-effect relationship?) between the benefits of all destinations having an economic value such as work, business, purchases, instruction, administrative matters, and GDP increases observed in the areas studied and deeply rural areas. To my surprise, the correlation does indeed exist. It is as precise as the relationship that connects additions of net salary and the benefits of destinations for the sole purpose of work.

The relation that exists between travel benefits for all economic reasons and for work reasons stands at

2.26 in agglomerations of 10,000 inhabitants

2.37 in agglomerations of 100,000 inhabitants

2.47 in agglomerations of 1,000,000 inhabitants

2.62 in Île-de-France

The relationship between increases in GDP and net salary, taking deeply rural areas as the reference for determining these increases, is on the order of

2.19 in agglomerations of 10,000 inhabitants

2.30 in agglomerations of 100,000 inhabitants

2.51 in agglomerations of 1,000,000 inhabitants

2.72 in Île-de-France

(If you consider the GDPs and salaries themselves, the figures are respectively 2.34, 2.37, 2.46 and 2.60.)

The relationships are almost identical. Since there is a correlation between salaries and benefits for work reasons, there is likewise a correlation between the GDP and the benefits for all economic reasons.

In the same way as for salaries, we can establish a formula that makes possible evaluating the GDP in a given urbanized area by referring to the GDP observed in deeply rural areas (GDP_0) and adding the travel benefit for all economic reasons, evaluated by taking into account only the number of jobs countable in the area exceeded by no more than 10 percent of users.[3] The results published by INSEE follow this formulation with remarkable precision.

Transportation infrastructures are responsible for an improvement in the benefits of accessible destinations for all economic reasons. Thus, the way in which these infrastructures can participate in the creation of national wealth becomes obvious. It would make sense to teach this type of result in business schools to show the deep solidarity existing between private investments—improvement factors that belong to business productivity per se—and public investments that make possible a match between the array of educational and professional preparations possessed by workers and the array of jobs offered by business owners.

The study undertaken in the living areas served by freeway A75 should make it possible to verify the reality of GDP increases at the level of increased value estimations for all travel for economic reasons. Other studies of the same kind will be launched to complete and perfect a posteriori evaluation checks.

Well-being is correlated with the ergonomic benefit of destinations for open-air activities

In the case of trips that have no economic purpose, for example, trips for open-air leisure activities, to what can the result of evaluations of "ergonomic" benefit be compared? The national accounting office says nothing about the subject. Couldn't there be room for a GDE, gross domestic environment, in the same way that there is a GDP, gross domestic product?

Actually, everything that emphasizes "ergonomic" satisfaction does not figure in national accounting. To begin with, we can approach the satisfaction we feel being in a comfortable house, sheltered from cold and inclement weather, by identifying the expenses we're willing to devote to establish, maintain, and run our home. Yet for identical expenses, certain homes provide considerably more comfort than others. Nothing in our accounting makes it really possible to identify our deep satisfaction.

When we look at the topic of open-air leisure activities, that is, those that bring a sense of well-being without having to put anything out for expenses, such as strolling in free public places open to all, we have no monetary indicators at our disposal to identify the level of satisfaction. And yet there is indeed satisfaction. This type of leisure is even a fundamental element of the pleasure of life. But just because monetary identifiers are absent does not mean that we have to give up evaluating the "ergonomic" benefit of open spaces.

We note today that about 15 percent of trips have no economic function. These trips are almost always linked to frequenting open spaces for relaxation and renewal. There is nothing to make, nothing to buy. All we have to do is breathe and appreciate the environment. The distribution of trips for this purpose is calculated in proportion to the surface area of easily accessible open spaces, while the distribution of trips for work is calculated in proportion to the number of easily accessible jobs.

In this area, what attracts residents is the extent of open spaces expressed in ares, or units near an average lodging. The ergonomic benefit of open spaces surrounding a place of residence is the logarithmic value of the surface of countable open spaces in a living area exceeded by no more than 10 percent of residents multiplied by the value of an hour worked, divided by the constant coefficient a (which makes it possible to transform this value into euros), as well as by the number of annual trips for the purpose of "open-air leisure activities."

This ergonomic benefit is truly felt by the resident and corresponds to a real benefit of use, even if it has no monetary expression. It is a way of evaluating a part of the GDE, the gross domestic environment.

Note that ergonomic benefit depends not only on the surface area of easily accessible open spaces, but also on the value of an hour worked. Now the value of this hour worked is itself linked to the economic performance of the zones under consideration. Thus, in strict economic orthodoxy, the ergonomic benefit of a given number of easily accessible open spaces is all the higher as the standard of living of the residents who benefit from it goes up. The value of parks and forests in urbanized areas will be more sustained, for a given quantity, than the value of forests and open spaces in deeply rural areas. In practice, it will be reasonable to evaluate, first of all, the strict effect of the "quantity of easily accessible open spaces" factor by adopting for the value of the hour worked a national average, and by not proceeding to a complete evaluation of the benefit until later, taking into consideration the value of the hour worked, which varies from one zone to another.

What is the result of the calculations performed in the 16 reference agglomerations studied?

I expected to obtain very satisfactory results in deeply rural areas and mediocre results in metropolitan areas, where the urbanization density is the highest. In reality, the situation is relatively stable from one point to another of the country. Rural areas offer ergonomic benefits at a good level, but urbanized areas are not far behind. They yield values equivalent to—and sometimes above—those obtained in nonurbanized locales. In fact, the master plans of large metropolises contain vast open areas that are protected. Moreover, transportation infrastructures are well developed in large cities and make it possible to cover more extensive living areas than in rural areas, thus compensating for a more moderate density of open spaces with the rapidity of traveling. Cities are not irretrievably places of major environmental limitations. Urban development plans have a primary function of delimiting and protecting spaces not to be built on, spaces whose purpose is to allow the city to breathe, and the inhabitants to experience renewal and well-being. The first basic act of urban planning is to delimit "empty" spaces. It is between the empty spaces that residential and business spaces will develop with transportation networks that make connecting them possible. By respecting this kind of balance, the townsperson can find environmental and at the same time economic satisfaction. Indeed, this is a double conquest that explains the success of the urban phenomenon.

Some will say that this is incorrigible optimism! Perhaps. But why not accept good news with the same enthusiasm as bad news?

Economic and natural performances of living areas in France and Europe

Study of living areas in France and nine neighboring European countries demonstrates the economic strength of urban areas

Evaluating the economic performance of living areas in France and nine neighboring European countries represents an objective that is ambitious and—at the same time—relatively simple to achieve.

All it takes is the following procedure: determine the living area accessible in 1 hour starting from the center of each municipality in our country and in the nine neighboring European countries. Then count the number of jobs E^{90} located within each of these living areas, determine the logarithmic value of this number, multiply the result by the value of 1 hour worked, divided by the constant coefficient a, and finally multiply the whole by the number of annual trips for economic reasons. This tally makes it possible to determine the gross benefit of easily accessible destinations in relation to situations where choices are reduced. If we adopt the GDP of deeply rural areas, GDP_0, as the reference base and add to this base the gross utility thus determined, we obtain the equivalent of a calculated GDP.

Nonetheless, there is one difficulty we have already identified. It follows from the fact that the value of 1 hour worked is not constant from one place to another in the country. It is itself a function of the range of choice E^{90}. Thus we get the advantage of applying a formula that does not need revealing hourly wage in each living area studied.

This formula exists. As we have seen, the gross benefit of easily accessible economic destinations, in relation to a situation of reduced choices, can be directly determined by calculating the product of GDP in deeply rural areas (GDP_0) by a numerical factor that is a development in series of the logarithmic expression of E^{90} divided by 25.[4] The development in series means that the growth in gross benefit of easily accessible economic destinations in relation to the situation of reduced choices in deeply rural areas results from the increased ranges of choices linked to urbanization, logarithm of E^{90} divided by 25. It results at the same time from the increase in average salary level that is, itself, a result of the growing range of choices linked to the rise in the number of accessible jobs. Thus we get the series of neatly converging terms.

If instead of observing from the point of view of workers seeking jobs, we observe from the point of view of employers seeking workers, it is necessary to consider the number of workers, T^{90}, identifiable in the area exceeded by no more than 10 percent of users. The development in series must be applied in conditions similar to those practiced for benefits relative to jobs.[5]

Counting workers rather than jobs yields a statistically identical average when we consider areas large enough that the number of jobs and the number of workers is equivalent. In practice, statistical data on workers are more easily accessible than data on jobs. This is what explains the choice made in the context of the study bearing on the different municipalities of France and Europe: the viewpoint taken is that of the employer seeking workers, not that of workers looking for employment.

The geographic base used to determine living areas accessible in an hour is the roadway navigation system of Navigation Technologies Inc., which respects homogenous specifications in all European countries and makes possible calculation of travel speeds. In urban areas, speeds from the Navigation Technologies base take into account the presence of public transportation. In the absence of these collective means of transportation, living areas accessible in 1 hour would be significantly different. The approach is—in this way—truly multimodal, even if it might seem that only highway data is taken into account. In France, this base is of the same consistency as l'Institut Geographique National (IGN) Géoroute navigation base. To identify the workers within each living area thus determined, we employ data from Eurostat, the European statistical organization. The results that pertain to each municipality are attributed to it. Thus 36,000 points of information were obtained for France and about 46,000 for the nine other European countries studied.[6] The results are converted into visual form using a sequenced chromatic scale that goes from blue for zones where the choice of workers is very small all the way to red for the densest urban zones where the choice of workers is most numerous.

The results obtained are extremely impressive. When you read the maps, the first thing you feel is a sense of beauty and reasonableness. Regions come alive with their areas of economic intensity or places of less vitality, and their relations to neighboring regions.

The GDPs of France's 22 regions are correlated to the economic performance rates of living areas

Of course, I took advantage of the multitudinous calculations made regarding the living areas surrounding the different municipalities of the regions of France in order to compare, region by region, economic performance rates and the data published by INSEE.

I added up the economic performance rates of the different municipalities composing a region. In this way, I obtained 22 values representing in equivalent GDP the economic performance rates of these regions. Then, region by region, I compared these values with the GDP published by INSEE. The correlation is excellent. It confirms in every respect results obtained in the 16 reference agglomerations previously cited.

So, in Île-de-France, the calculated economic performance in equivalent GDP for the year 2000, stands at 400 billion euros; the one noted by INSEE reaches 395 billion euros.

Economic Performance of European Living Areas

Additional value created by workers annually
(based on the value of euros in the year 2000 per job occupied)

Value based on accessibility to workers located less than one hour away
(starting at the center of each municipality)

Additional value created	Equivalent GDP	Municipalities
R = 28,600 X [Logworkers60mn/ (25–Logworkers60mn)]	GDP = 28,600 + R	Number of municipalities affected
43 400 - 49 500	72 000 - 78 100	4798
35 400 - 43 400	64 000 - 72 000	9453
31 400 - 35 400	60 000 - 64 000	8352
29 900 - 31 400	58 500 - 60 000	5758
28 400 - 29 900	57 000 - 58 500	6416
27 400 - 28 400	56 000 - 57 000	4542
26 400 - 27 400	55 000 - 56 000	4747
25 700 - 26 400	54 300 - 55 000	3044
24 900 - 25 700	53 500 - 54 300	3291
23 900 - 24 900	52 500 - 53 500	4373
22 900 - 23 900	51 500 - 52 500	4335
21 400 - 22 900	50 000 - 51 500	5033
19 900 - 21 400	48 500 - 50 000	4129
18 400 - 19 900	47 000 - 48 500	2959
15 400 - 18 400	44 000 - 47 000	3393
0 - 15 400	28 600 - 44 000	2334

Données: NAVTEQ® et Eurostat®
©IGN 2003

Calculations have not been made in some countries or parts of countries where data was incomplete

Economic performance of living areas in France and nine neighboring European nations

This map depicts the additional economic value created annually when workers live in increasingly more urbanized zones. From the viewpoint of employers (solution adopted in the present map), the creation of value is connected with the number of workers located less than an hour of travel away from the company plant, or more simply the center of the company's municipality (figures are based on the value of euros in the year 2000 per filled job).

In very rural zones, the number of workers within 1 hour travel is very low and their extra economic value is near zero. Similarly, workers base additional value on the number of jobs less than 1 hour away from home.

Areas where destination choices are very numerous have high added economic value and are represented in red. By contrast, very rural areas with few destination choices and modest added value are in blue.

Neighboring countries—northern Italy, Germany, Belgium/Holland, England—testify to the power of densely populated areas that are very well supplied by modern infrastructures.

A striking contrast can be observed between northern Europe, whose population density is 250 inhabitants per square kilometer, and France or Spain where the density is 100 inhabitants per square kilometer, or less.

In France, half of the country is organized with urban hubs connected by very efficient means of transportation. The economic vitality is coming from these zones. The other part of the country is composed of very low density rural zones.

Spain is witnessing the emergence of urban hubs that undergird its economic development. However, a number of rural areas that have very few people will likely remain fragile for the long term.

Data: NAVTEQ and Eurostat
© IGN (Institut Géographique National) 2003

Economic Performance of French Living Areas

Additional value created by workers annually
(based on the value of euros in the year 2000 per job occupied)

Value based on accessibility to workers located less than one hour away
(starting at the center of each municipality)

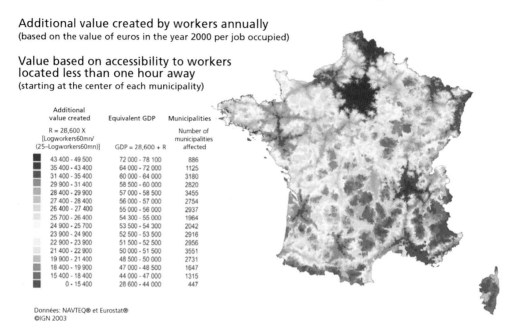

Additional value created	Equivalent GDP	Municipalities
R = 28,600 X [Logworkers60mn/ (25–Logworkers60mn)]	GDP = 28,600 + R	Number of municipalities affected
43 400 - 49 500	72 000 - 78 100	886
35 400 - 43 400	64 000 - 72 000	1125
31 400 - 35 400	60 000 - 64 000	3180
29 900 - 31 400	58 500 - 60 000	2820
28 400 - 29 900	57 000 - 58 500	3455
27 400 - 28 400	56 000 - 57 000	2754
26 400 - 27 400	55 000 - 56 000	2937
25 700 - 26 400	54 300 - 55 000	1964
24 900 - 25 700	53 500 - 54 300	2042
23 900 - 24 900	52 500 - 53 500	2916
22 900 - 23 900	51 500 - 52 500	2956
21 400 - 22 900	50 000 - 51 500	3551
19 900 - 21 400	48 500 - 50 000	2731
18 400 - 19 900	47 000 - 48 500	1647
15 400 - 18 400	44 000 - 47 000	1315
0 - 15 400	28 600 - 44 000	447

Données: NAVTEQ® et Eurostat®
©IGN 2003

Economic performance of living areas in France

This closer view of France clearly shows how inhabitants fall into two groups: Half the country consists of urban areas connected by high-performance transportation networks. The other half is sparsely populated, mostly oriented toward agricultural and tourist activities.

If France had adopted a strictly homogenous organization, its GNP would be about 45 percent lower. This structure has allowed France to remain competitive with its powerful neighbors to the north.

The map also illustrates the might of Île-de-France (north central red area), as well as Brittany (northwest peninsula), intersected by a very extensive transportation system.

Networks of towns with transportation links such as those found in the Pays de la Loire (red area southeast of Brittany), the Rhône-Alpes (east central red area) or the Provence-Côte d'Azur region (southeast red area) demonstrate their efficiency and beneficial economic effects.

Even rural areas near urban ones benefit by providing residents with a wider range of choices conducive to higher economic achievement. Only profoundly rural areas whose population densities are low do not benefit from this effect.

Data: NAVTEQ and Eurostat
© IGN (Institut Géographique National) 2003

In the Rhône-Alpes region, calculated economic performance stands at 145 billion euros; the performance obtained by INSEE is the same. A small divergence appears in two regions: Alsace, whose GDP is a little higher than the calculated performance, and Nord-Pas-de-Calais, where the GDP is a little lower than the calculated performance. All the other regions are in perfect consonance.

If instead of using the region as basis of comparison, one uses the department, the agreement seems somewhat less, but only apparently. In Île-de-France, we note a calculated value higher than the INSEE data in the departments of Seine-Saint-Denis and Val-de-Marne, and a lower calculated value in the departments of Hauts-de-Seine and Paris, while the correlation is perfect in all the other departments. This effect is probably due to the economic results of some firms' establishments being tied to the place where the business is headquartered. This would particularly benefit the departments of Hauts-de-Seine and Paris. On the other hand, the departments of Seine-Saint-Denis and Val-de-Marne would be shorn of the results from many "establissements" whose headquarters are located in la Défense or in Paris. So the completed calculations would be more rigorous than the uncorrected data published by INSEE, which makes even more evident the degree of pertinence of the evaluation of economic performance rates of living areas.

All observations and reconstructions confirm that the recommended evaluation method is robust.

Natural performance rates in the living areas of France reveal an equitable geographical spread

As in the case of economic performance rates, in order to evaluate natural spaces available within each living area accessible in 1 hour starting from the center of a municipality, we must first determine the list of municipalities whose center is accessible in 1 hour. The number is on the order of one hundred, if not more. Without affecting the quality of the results, we can decide that an entire municipality is included in—or excluded from—an accessible area depending on whether its center is—or is not—within this perimeter.

It remains to determine the number of ares of natural spaces identifiable in each of the municipalities of the area accessible in 1 hour. The most pertinent database for figuring out this identification is the "Corine land cover" base that covers all of Europe. This base, put together from space images, identifies about twenty attributes that can be grouped under three large headings regarding natural spaces: areas of water, forests, and agricultural land. The sum of these three groups constitutes a first approach that is enough at this stage of expertise for identifying the surface area of natural spaces. However, it is obvious that natural spaces don't all have the same value of pleasure and use. For example, coastal areas present a level of attraction that is clearly superior to that of agricultural areas. In a second evaluation phase, it would be necessary to take into consideration a qualitative factor to better characterize these specific areas. But it is best to not overestimate these differences too much. What residents appreciate above all is the possibility of access to open spaces in which they can find relaxation and renewal.

The logarithmic value of the surface area of natural spaces accessible in 1 hour expresses the value of using these spaces. We can, as we saw before, couple a monetary coefficient with this result—average value of 1 hour worked—divided by the constant coefficient a, which is independent of the standard of living of the residents of the area under consideration, or what economic orthodoxy recommends, a coefficient that takes into account this standard of living, that is to say, considers the cash value of the hour worked and not a national average value. In the first case, the strict effect of conditions for accessing natural spaces is emphasized. In the second case, the differences between zones are amplified. The result obtained must, of course, be multiplied by the number of annual trips in order to obtain an annual use figure.

What comes of the results of these calculations? Are we breathing freely in France or are there zones where the number of natural spaces is truly too limited?

What is most striking (a result that I had already noted in the sample towns that I previously studied) is that the natural performance rates of living areas in France are very much the same from one end of the country to the other. Agglomerations are not areas of decline, far from it. They even yield results slightly higher than the deepest rural areas. The paradox can be explained by the fact that urban planning has reserved within agglomerations large amounts of natural spaces (parks, forests, bodies of water, riverbanks) that are carefully protected. To take an example with which I am well acquainted, the new town of Marne-la-Vallée consists of 4,000 hectares of forests, numerous bodies of water, and 20 kilometers of laid out shores along la Marne. The Île-de-France region—population 11 million—includes in 12,000 km2 of surface area 7,200 km^2 of forests, bodies of water, and agricultural land. One would think, in such a small region (a scant 2 percent of the country) that the preservation of such extensive natural spaces would be impossible. But that is not the case. Comparable situations exist in the largest French cities. There is a second beneficial factor: transportation networks in large cities, while sized to move the considerable volume of traffic linked with daily economic activity, permit high levels of performance during off-peak hours. The quantity of natural spaces accessible in 1 hour in Île-de-France is definitely higher than that in rural areas served by local roadway networks. The same goes for the principal cities of France.

Overall, we observe that the natural performance rates of living areas in France lie in a very narrow range. The highest values only differ by 10 percent from the most moderate. We can consider that living areas of France have fairly satisfactory conditions of access to natural spaces.

The effect of transportation networks appears clearly. Maps depicting accessibility to natural spaces testify to the beneficial aspect of freeway interchanges for municipalities located near them.

When we take into account the standard of living of the areas studied, agglomerations sharply stand out, as they are the places of intense exchanges of expertise, the creative source of wealth.

These quantified results yield a picture that is rather different from the one commonly assumed.

A vision of European development: the urban phenomenon is at the heart of economic and natural vitality of living areas

A rather optimistic vision of matters flows from this analysis, at least in Europe. The living area would make it possible for people to organize mutual exchanges of expertise while still preserving a sufficient number of open spaces to allow renewal and relaxation. Isn't that too idyllic a vision?

I don't think it is. What I find most striking is how people organize themselves intelligently and reasonably, although they are too-often reproached for their rather erratic behavior.

As far as economic wealth is concerned, the phenomenon that is at work is the constitution of economic energy. The higher the number of workers there are in 1 hour of travel, the more human cooperative labor blossoms and the more produced wealth increases, without a rise in the effort required.

Europe, Germany, Austria, Benelux, the United Kingdom, and Northern Italy constitute the countries where economic energy is the highest. This is due to a high density of human occupation (on the order of 250 inhabitants per km2). In addition, high performance transportation systems serve and connect urbanization hubs that are both numerous and distributed rather homogenously.

In France, the country's low population density (100 inhabitants per km^2) has led to inhabitants grouping into metropolitan areas connected to powerful transportation systems. The occupation density of these areas is comparable to that of densely populated areas in Northern Europe. This organization has constituted the intelligent way in which the French have reacted in order to remain competitive with their neighbors to the north. The west of France, that is, Normandy, Brittany, the Pays de la Loire region, has become strongly urbanized and has constructed a high performance network of freeways. The Rhône corridor and the Riviera are also organized into clusters of urbanization that are well interconnected. Île-de-France is living on the fine infrastructures put in place over the course of 30 glorious years. With 11 million inhabitants, Île-de-France produces as much wealth as half the population of China, which stands at 1.3 billion. Based on the hour worked, productivity—strongly allied to workers' urban integration—is 60 times higher than that of the Chinese, whose country has remained largely rural in character. But urban growth is at work in China, with metropolises like Shanghai, Beijing, and many others becoming truly explosive economic centers. Consequently, the productivity gap is soon going to close. That is another reason for the Île-de-France region to once again pick up a reasonable rate of investment in high performing transportation infrastructures, particularly to serve large areas on the outskirts that are experiencing a growth spurt.

In Spain, population density of the country is also low, on the same order as in France. Here, too, economic vitality is being expressed in metropolitan areas such as Madrid, Barcelona, and the Basque region. Ambitious projects for freeways and bullet train connections between these metropolises will sustain this economic growth.

Before our eyes we can see the multipolar vision of Europe, the source of economic vitality. Of course, it is necessary to encourage the flourishing of this multipolar organization and not put obstacles in its way. From that viewpoint, the white paper published by the European Union in June 2002 includes some diagnostic errors. Fortunately, recent proposals by M. Van Miert depict more ambitious views.

And in the area of natural spaces, what vision of matters can we form here?

As far as natural performance of living areas is concerned, the phenomenon at work is that of spatial energy. The higher the number of ares of natural spaces accessible in 1 hour, the more renewal space increases and the higher well-being rises.

In Europe, it is France and Spain that offer the most spatial energy, taking into account their low population density. Half of France has an extremely low population density. Our country is the real oxygen lung not only of the French but of all Europeans. It is the same for Spain, though less easily accessible as a result of its relative distance from the most populated areas of Europe.

Outside of these vast areas set aside for agricultural and tourist purposes, there are areas of natural spaces carefully distributed throughout European countries. These spaces are closely associated with urban hubs and provide these with daily breathing space.

If one looks at the example of Holland, whose population density is the highest in the world, natural areas are distributed evenly over the entire country and give the impression of a verdant land in which nature is always present. One can also cite the case of Île-de-France, also densely populated, in which vast natural spaces have been preserved. These nearby natural spaces play a determining role in the general balance of urban living areas and explain the fine ergonomic performance rates of these areas.

Next to a multipolar Europe, source of economic vitality, we obtain a multispatial image of Europe, in which protected natural resources play an essential role in breathing space and well-being.

Notes

1. We can attempt to illustrate the formulation that expresses this phenomenon by making the following argument: Let's suppose that the salary paid annually to a worker in a given area is the sum of the salary paid to a worker active in a deeply rural area plus the economic benefit represented by the choice of a job among all the easily accessible jobs within the studied area. The annual economic benefit that the choice represents is proportional to the logarithm of E^{90}, proportional to the cost of the hour worked divided by six and proportional to the number of annual trips taken for work reasons. On the other hand, the cost of the hour worked is equal to that annual salary divided by 1,650 hours; the number of annual trips to get to—or return from—work is about 400. When all calculations are done, the economic benefit of a job choice, thus, is equal to the annual salary divided by 25, multiplied by the logarithm of E^{90}. It is this value, added to the salary of deeply rural areas, that makes it possible to find the salary paid within the area under study. Nevertheless, we note that the salary used for calculating the economic benefit of a job choice in a given area is the salary of that zone and not the salary of deeply rural areas.

So, in order to calculate the economic benefit of a job choice in a given area with the goal of taking into better account the salary of deeply rural areas, it is necessary to note that the salary within the area studied is *the sum of the salary in deeply rural areas* and of *the salary increase* between rural areas and the area studied. We obtain then the following result: the salary paid within the area studied is equal to the salary paid in deeply rural areas increased by a primary factor equal to *the salary of deeply rural areas* divided by 25 and multiplied by the logarithm of E^{90} and by a second factor equal to *the increase of salary* between deeply rural areas and the area studied, itself divided by 25 and multiplied by the logarithm of E^{90}.

We can follow the reasoning by observing that *the increase in salary* between rural areas and the area studied is equal to the salary paid in the area studied divided by 25 and multiplied by the logarithm of E^{90}. Since the salary within the area studied is the sum of the salary in deeply rural areas and of *the increase in salary* between the rural areas and the area studied, we obtain the following new result: the salary paid within the area studied is equal to the salary paid in deeply rural areas, increased by a primary factor equal to the *salary of deeply rural areas*, divided by 25 and multiplied by Log E^{90}, by a second factor equal to the *salary of deeply rural areas*, divided by $(25)^2$ and multiplied by $(\text{Log } E^{90})^2$ and by a third factor equal to *the increase in salary* between deeply rural areas and the area studied, itself divided by $(25)^2$ and multiplied by $(\text{Log } E^{90})^2$. This begins a development in series in which the factor "logarithm of E^{90} divided by 25" is raised to the square, then to the cube, and so on. The expression of net salary as a function of the number of accessible jobs in the area exceeded by no more than 10 percent of users is finally the following:

$$R = R_0 + R_0.\text{Log } E^{90}/25 + R_0.(\text{Log } E^{90}/25)^2 + R_0.(\text{Log } E^{90}/25)^3 + \ldots.$$
$$= R_0 + R_0 (\text{Log } E^{90}/25) / (1 - \text{Log } E^{90}/25)$$

If we adopt a decimal logarithm, the constant factor of the formula used becomes 11 (instead of 25). With a base two logarithm, the constant factor is 36.

This progression, which combines the effect of the choice of a job in a set, E^{90} and of the hourly salary, also linked to the choice of a job in a set, E^{90}, expresses with perfect agreement the rise of salaries in deeply rural areas and in the increasingly urbanized areas studied. The correlation is of very high quality.

2. How are salaries determined in these different agglomerations? The method is not direct since INSEE only publishes average salaries by department. How are the benefits of easily accessible work destinations determined?

For salaries, the following are subtracted from the net annual salaries published by INSEE in the department, including the agglomeration studied: all net salaries of the municipalities of the department, primarily rural, that do not belong to this agglomeration, assimilating those salaries with others of the rural municipalities in the region for which we know the average level. In the regions around Lyon and Île-de-France, this subtraction is done at the regional level. Thus we can obtain a very meaningful value of net average salary distributed in each of the agglomerations studied.

For economic benefits of travel to work, we use the results of transportation surveys conducted by the Center for Studies on Networks, Transportation, Urban Planning, and Public Facilities (Centre d'Etudes sur les Réseaux, les Transports, l'Urbanisme et les Constructions Publiques or CERTU), and in Île-de-France, by the Regional Administration of Public Works and Transportation. We can determine, in each agglomeration, the logarithmic value of the number of jobs established within the area delimited by isochronal 90, which is multiplied by the value of 1 hour worked, divided by the coefficient a (which makes it possible to transform this value into euros), as well as by the number of annual trips to work. We can thus evaluate the gross economic benefit of trips from home to work and back.

3. The expression of GDP, as a function of the number of accessible jobs in the area exceeded by no more than 10 percent of users is the following:

$$GDP = GDP_0 + GDP_0.\text{Log } E^{90}/25 + GDP_0.(\text{Log } E^{90}/25)^2 + GDP_0.(\text{Log } E^{90}/25)^3 + \ldots$$
$$= GDP_0 + GDP_0 (\text{Log } E^{90}/25) / (1 - \text{Log } E^{90}/25)$$

This expression makes it possible to reconstitute INSEE's published results with a great deal of precision. If we adopt a decimal logarithm, the constant factor of the formula used becomes 11 (instead of 25). With a base two logarithm, the constant factor is 36.

4. The formula of reference is expressed as follows:
$$U = GDP_0.(\text{Log } E^{90}/25 + (\text{Log } E^{90}/25)^2 + (\text{Log } E^{90}/25)^3 + \ldots)$$
$$= GDP_0.(\text{Log } E^{90}/25 - \text{Log } E^{90})) = GDP_0.(\text{Log}_{10} E^{90}/(11 - \text{Log}_{10} E^{90}))$$

5. The formula or reference is expressed as follows:

$$U = GDP_0.(Log\ T^{90}/25 + (Log\ T^{90}/25)^2 + (Log\ T^{90}/25)^3 + \ldots)$$
$$= GDP_0.(Log\ T^{90}/(25 - Log\ T^{90})) = GDP_0.(Log_{10}\ T^{90}/(11 - Log_{10}\ T^{90}))$$

6. Actually, 40,000, since the data for the former East Germany, Scotland, and Northern Ireland is incomplete. For the same reasons, Holland and Ireland have not been studied.

Part V

Negative impacts caused by humans

When I speak of negative impacts, I am always reminded of Jean, my namesake, an unmarried neighbor who lived near the house in the Campan Valley at the foot of the Tourmalet Pass where for several years I spent my summer vacations. I happened to see him again later, when I had already made progress on my studies and assumed a number of responsible positions. He was still single, and he hadn't found a wife because many young women in the valley had moved to town. He fantasized about my life as a townsman who had traveled and seen "folks," and consoled himself by periodically abandoning himself to drink—the bride of his solitude. Nonetheless, he had at his disposal a protected environment, some of the most beautiful countryside imaginable, and air that was extraordinarily pure. So, there you have it, a perfect environment doesn't necessarily make for happiness. A protected environment in a universe closed to others does not always lead to wisdom. You have to find a happy balance between the openness to others allowed by preserved mobility and the need to limit negative impacts incurred by this mobility. In fact, the vision I present of human activity in living areas is relatively optimistic. I am convinced it is compatible with a planet free from significant pollution sources.

From here on out, how can one explain that in the current societal debate on the environment there are many who question economic development? Isn't there a hidden error in my reasoning? Haven't I underestimated the weight of the negative impacts caused by humans?

I want to respond to this question as seriously as possible. I do not underestimate the weight of negative impacts caused by human activity. I was director general of the agency for saving energy at the moment of the second oil embargo from 1978 to 1981. During this period, I initiated the campaign "Chase Waste" that left its imprint on the French mind and made it clear that I expressed a true sensitivity to reasonable management of our wealth, especially our energy resources. But I was always moved by the desire not to commit involuntary misinterpretations in the name of generous, a priori coherent ideas. The best intentions sometimes bring with them tough perverse effects that only time can clearly identify. The economy as well as employment often suffers from these effects for long periods without anything in the human, animal, or plant kingdom feeling better for all that.

Actually, the question is to determine the minimum level of negative impacts tolerable, so that humans, as well as their plant and animal companions can develop a rational organization offering the totality of living species real possibilities for flourishing. The struggle for survival exists at every level of the biological scale. But there also exists, doubtless even more so, a cooperative activity between the members of different animal and plant species to develop on our planet. I do not share the approach of some thinkers who believe that humans are systematically opposing nature and that nature, imbued a priori with all the virtues, must be protected from their devouring, predatory activity. We belong to a living system that occupies our planet. We each must find our place in it. For many years, I have sought to evaluate the weight of the harmful effects engendered by humans in relation to the positive effects of human activities. Is it possible for humans to be masters of the negative impacts they create and keep them at a low level, or must they be bridled and restrained in their relationship with the living area in order to stop or reduce the negative impacts that they cause? In this relationship with our spatial environment, it is important to me to know, at least roughly, the weight of economic and ergonomic value created by travel providing access to the living area, as well as the weight of negative impacts incurred by travel activity.

Praiseworthy ambition, you will tell me. That's the realm of qualitative evaluations par excellence. Calculations will always be contested.

Doubtless, but I prefer an approximate calculation to none at all. Purely qualitative evaluations and analyses based on complex multiple criteria always end in confusion and paralysis of action.

How can we evaluate, even approximately, the weight of negative impacts in areas as complex as traffic accidents, traffic noise, and atmospheric pollution?

The primary method consists of determining the price that a resident is ready to pay for taking precautions against these negative impacts. For example, how much is the resident willing to invest to not have to put up with attacks from noise pollution? This is a very anthropocentric vision to be sure.

But without being animist, one can define criteria to appraise the damage inflicted on other animal and plant species sharing the same living area as humans.

It is thus possible to have a realistic vision of the actual harmful impact produced by human activity. Still, it is necessary not to take a too short-term view. We must realistically calculate what the situation will be in a few decades, that is, take the time factor into consideration. We must not limit ourselves to a snapshot of the existing situation, but introduce a cinematographic vision of the evolution of living areas.

First, I am going to give some information about pollution caused by humans today. I should have been able to limit myself to harmful effects linked to transportation activities alone, since these are the ones that create value through exchanges by making it possible for people to access the area that surrounds them and to contact their fellow human beings. All the same, I think it useful to recall in passing the nature of the main negative impacts incurred by humans in their basic activities in a given area—agricultural, industrial, residential[1]—if only to appraise the weight of what these negative impacts represent in relation to those linked to transportation.

I will then indicate, just for the one domain of creation of value linked to exchange, what this creation of value weighs, what transportation costs weigh, and what negative impacts incurred by travel weigh. An idea of the evolution of this triad over time will make it possible to appraise the critical or noncritical nature of the situation.

This analysis, which primarily concerns humans in their relation with their living area, will be followed by a chapter entirely devoted to plant and animal species in their mutual relationships, as well as with humans.

Pollution caused by agricultural, industrial, and residential activities

Soil pollution

In the agricultural arena, we often speak of the negative effects of pesticides and other products designed to eliminate parasites from cultivated plants. What exactly is at stake?

These products are, indeed, extremely effective in combating the invasion of parasites that can endanger a third of the harvest. But they also possess disadvantages that are now well known. Pesticides are classified according to the object of their application: herbicides for weeds, fungicides for undesirable fungi, insecticides for insects, acaricides for ticks and mites, and rodenticides for rodents. But their effect is far from amenable to precise application. Many pesticides are highly toxic to fish. Moreover, pesticides are by no means totally consumed by the pests for which they are destined. They accumulate in large amounts in the soil or are washed away and enter ground waters. Pesticides have harmful effects on human health. Ingested over the long term, even in very small quantities, they can have carcinogenic or mutagenic effects. At a minimum, it is necessary to ensure that pesticide residues do not contaminate products destined for human consumption. Of course, local public authorities must see to it that drinking water does not contain even trace amounts of such products.

One method that does not harm the environment is to promote the fight against parasites by introducing their natural enemies. We also can promote natural plant defenses, which are quite diverse. This method calls for a whole series of insecticides less toxic to the environment than artificial ones.

What about the world of industry? Very recently MetalEurop was in the news. An estimated 150 million euros would be needed to decontaminate the site of the factory that shareholders decided to close. Fortunately, a case of this size is rare. But it is true that sites linked with coking plants or the processing of petroleum or coal products have pockets of pollution that are often discovered decades after the closing down of the enterprises. This is how the Stadium of France came to be located on a piece of ground whose decontamination cost an additional 12 million euros not included in the initial estimates. Other examples can be cited, in particular in the large industrial basins such as those of the Ruhr region. All quarries that are no longer being worked are the object of a follow up by the Office of Geological and Mining Research. This entity keeps a database that includes detailed information on the nature of these sites, especially with regard to residual soil pollution that they cause or are likely to cause. Active industrial sites must dispose of the waste they produce. Certain waste products are highly toxic, for example, cyanides used in the surface treatment of steel, arsenic compounds for the processing of nonferrous metals, mercury residues from batteries and many other products. If possible, these waste products must be chemically neutralized before considering their storage in intermediate or final locations. These places constitute special dumping sites that require careful study into ways of making them leak-proof. In certain cases, the products are stored in high-security containers and kept in underground dumps that once were mines.

What about household waste? It is said that a human produces one kilo of waste per day. The quantity of household waste is increasing steadily. These wastes used to be burned in stoves; today they are stored in dumps or burned in incineration plants.

Sixty-five percent of household wastes are stored in dumps, which must be located on land that is naturally watertight. That would include clay or alluvial soil. If the opposite is the case, the soil must be made watertight in order to avoid contamination of the ground-water. Wastes thus stored undergo a series of chemical transformations, first aerobic, then anaerobic that finally produce methane, carbon dioxide, and a small amount of sulfur and nitrogen compounds.

The incineration plants now being developed burn wastes mixed with fuel oil or gas to aid combustion. The products of combustion must be carefully filtered so as to avoid creating air pollution that could reach high levels without treatment. Gases produced include sulfur oxides and nitrogen, heavy metals, as well as chlorides.

Selective separation of wastes makes their treatment more efficient and easy. This separation process is spreading in the country's main agglomerations.

Water pollution

Water is essential to life on earth. Vertebrates are made up of 90 percent water and 10 percent organic substances. So, drinking polluted water is particularly harmful to health. But how is it possible to test the level of pollution in water?

Testing polluted water is not easy. The solution that has emerged by experience consists of using living organisms to determine the way in which their behavior changes in situations of increasing pollution. Algae and bacteria often are used to test the toxicity of bodies of fresh water. These organisms consume oxygen at a rate that indicates maintenance or impairment of their metabolic process. So measuring the change in oxygen consumption can determine the toxicity rate of the tested water. One can also measure the change in biomass produced by the algae over the course of 10 days. Finally, measuring the change in biomass produced by bacteria can reveal the presence of organic pollutants. Other tests measure the rate of slowing in the growth of cultured bacteria in the presence of polluted water. How quickly organic products are breaking down can also be evaluated.

Measuring the death rate of water lice over 24 hours can indicate the presence of polluted water. The reference measurement is the concentration of pollutants that bring about the demise of half the test organisms.

Finally, there are tests that use fish. The highest concentration of pollutants that makes it possible to keep all the fish alive for 48 hours constitutes the primary criterion. The one that keeps none of them alive is the secondary criterion, and the one that keeps 50 percent of them alive is the reference median.

Water on planet earth presents many diverse aspects. What is there in common between the pollution that menaces stagnant waters of a mountain lake, river water loaded with sediment, subterranean groundwater, and ocean saltwater? Four strongly contrasted situations come to light: lakes with standing water, running water that carves out stream and river beds, oceans that constitute the natural outlet of these streams and rivers, and finally subterranean water.

Deep lakes are generally low in organic substances and have steady oxygen content. Lakes of medium or low depth are rich in nutrients and low in oxygen during the summertime, when these substances decompose.

Running water and underground water are the most exposed to all kinds of pollution. The toxic products they pick up along their route to the sea include salts, heavy metals, and biodegradable substances, with greatly varying rates of degradation. The salts come from potash mine scrubbings and water purification processes. The presence of increasing levels of salt produces a reduction in the diversity of animal species living in these waters. The biological demands on oxygen express a need to provide for the biological decomposition of the substances transported. Running water is usually broken down into four categories according to quality: water quality I, clear and oxygen saturated; quality II, slightly polluted, maintaining many species alive; quality III, highly polluted by organic substances, with a high demand for oxygen to sustain the oxidation processes initiated by bacteria; quality IV, extremely high concentration of organic products and complete absorption of oxygen by the microorganisms present.

Oceans receive the wastes from streams and rivers. Toxic products in the air also pollute them. Moreover, they receive the clean-out products of cargo carriers and oil tankers, entire oil cargoes when there are maritime accidents, and, lastly, the products that escape from oil drilling platforms installed in the marine subsoil. These types of pollution show up along the coastline, in the vicinity of towns, and around river estuaries.

Subterranean water plays an important role in the water cycle. In effect, it receives precipitation that is not retained by the soil and is, consequently, the first to receive the pollutants created by human activity.

What are typical pollutants that flow into ground waters?

In the *agricultural realm*, there are nitrates used as artificial fertilizers. Nitrates are not totally absorbed by the plants for which they are destined. The unabsorbed portion is carried away by run-off and ends up in the ground waters. Nitrates are not dangerous in themselves. They become dangerous as a result of the nitrites that are a product of decomposition in the organism. Nitrites oxidize hemoglobin and cause cyanosis and cardiac disturbances that can be fatal.

In the *industrial realm*, accidental pollutant spills are extremely serious. In 1986, the ground waters of the region of Basel and the Rhine were polluted by 30 metric tons of pesticides spilled in run-off waters as the result of an enormous fire. Fish in the Rhine were killed off up to 400 kilometers downstream from Basel.

In the *domestic realm*, groundwater pollution comes mainly from discharge of domestic wastes into soils that are not sufficiently watertight.

From these few examples, it becomes clear that water pollution is a vast topic that has not yet found satisfactory resolution. Taking a swim in the River Seine is not going to happen tomorrow, even if public authorities regularly announce this eventual possibility.

Atmospheric pollution

Atmospheric pollution has become a major preoccupation of our times. The widespread sentiment is that the situation is rapidly getting worse and that our industrial civilization is seriously threatening our planet.

I believe that the conquest of space has had, from that standpoint, a very beneficial effect. For the first time, planet earth appears in its global aspect with its thin and apparently fragile atmospheric layer. Humans realize that they belong to a complex system in which they are only one of the important agents, and that they cannot act without taking into consideration the consequences of their acts. Greenhouse gas emissions seem to be leading to a rise in the average temperature of our atmosphere. For the first time, humanity is discovering that it can have an impact at the planetary level. That doesn't mean that there should be a collective sense of guilt. Remember that for a long time nature has had a decisive influence on the chemical composition of our atmosphere. It is plant species that absorb carbon dioxide, fix carbon in their cells, and give off oxygen. What would be the current weight of the greenhouse effect on our planet if nature had not "invented" photosynthesis? I am convinced that over the course of several decades humans will be able to stabilize greenhouse gas emissions and also the average temperature of our atmosphere. That will probably require one or two hundred years. Some will say that this is a very long time, but it is a time span that is reasonable in the scale of geological time.

How is *atmospheric pollution* defined?

It is rather difficult. The substances that pollute the atmosphere are liquid or solid gases that substantially change the composition of the atmosphere, and that can have harmful consequences for life on earth. Pollutants occur in these forms: gases that only liquefy if the temperature drops; vapors that condense at ambient temperature; fog made up of fine droplets; smoke that is a mixture of solid particles and liquid droplets; and dust composed of solid particles. It is the chemical nature of these emissions that determines whether they are pollutants or not.

Are pollutants *exclusively the work of humans?*

No, there are natural pollutants. Flowering plants produce pollen that causes well-known allergies that are sometimes severe. Volcanoes send large quantities of ash into the air, going so far as to change the level of sunlight on entire continents when a large eruption like that of Mount St. Helens occurs. The planet is a living organism that sometimes displays its bad moods.

What are the *main pollutants resulting from human activity itself?*

Carbon monoxide (CO) is a pollutant that forms from the incomplete combustion of fossil fuels. Carbon monoxide is dangerous to humans and animals above a certain threshold, since it blocks the fixing of oxygen by blood hemoglobin. Large quantities of carbon monoxide are fixed by the soil and by microorganisms that break it down. The rest escapes into the upper atmosphere, which renders carbon monoxide not very dangerous at the global level.

Carbon dioxide (CO_2) is produced in large quantities and given off into the atmosphere through the burning of forests or fossil fuels. It is consumed in abundant quantities by plants as a part of photosynthesis. It is harmless except in confined spaces where it usurps the place of the oxygen necessary to animal respiration. Carbon dioxide allows short-wave solar radiation and absorbs longer-wave radiation reflected by the earth. The effect is a warming of the atmosphere, commonly called the greenhouse effect. Photosynthesis and the fixing of carbon dioxide by the oceans have a positive effect that does not seem to make up for the production of the gas during the burning of wood, notably in the Amazonian forest, or during the burning of fossil fuels. What is at stake is reducing these emissions while promoting alternatives to fossil fuels such as nuclear or solar energy.

Ozone (CO_3) is formed from oxygen through interaction with ultraviolet rays. The ozone concentrated in the stratosphere has a beneficial effect, since it intercepts a large portion of the ultraviolet rays emitted by the sun. When produced in the lower atmosphere, it is a pollutant because it causes serious eye irritation and pulmonary difficulties.

Sulfur dioxide (SO_2), oxides of nitrogen (NO_x), and hydrochloric acid (HCl) are pollutants that cause increasing acidity of the air. They harm plants and animals in the form of acid rain.

Other man-made chemical products such as Freon have destructive effects on the stratospheric ozone layer. Besides, they have been prohibited. Pesticides outside the range of their agricultural applications are dangerous.

What are the *main producers of atmospheric pollutants?*

Agriculture produces natural pollutants such as pollens that are a source of severe allergies. Television weather channels provide daily reports on the pollen index for different plants.

Pesticides dispensed by aerosol sprays can be carried by the wind over considerable distances, sometimes reaching several thousands of kilometers.

Chemical and petroleum industries are the source of the atmospheric pollutants sulfur oxide and hydrochloric acid. Increasingly restrictive regulation is leading to a noticeable reduction in emission rates due to installation of clean up devices at the source. But accidents, always possible, have repercussions that are often dramatic. Suffice to recall the 1984 Union Carbide factory accident in Bhopal, India, where the toxic cloud killed 5,000 people.

In the *domestic arena*, incineration plants that burn household waste can pollute if the treatment installations at the source of emissions are not of the best quality or have become obsolete. Here, too, regulation is becoming increasingly restrictive.

All sectors produce carbon dioxide as soon as they consume fossil fuels or use firewood. Techniques to improve energy output can lessen the rise in consumption rates, but stabilizing or lowering emissions depends on promoting alternative energy sources that do not produce carbon dioxide.

Negative impacts caused by transportation

The unsafe nature of transportation

There is a great deal of talk about highway safety since the president of the Republic has made it a national priority. Should the element of danger in the transportation system—and particularly on highways—feature in the list of harmful conditions?

As far as I am concerned, there is not the shadow of a doubt. Lack of safety in transportation, on the roads first of all, stands at the top of the list of negative impacts experienced in our society. When it sinks in that 8,000 people are killed every year (5,250 in the wake of spectacular campaigns launched by the government) and another 135,000 injured due to transportation-related accidents, the deep trauma that affects so many French families makes it clear that we're dealing with a genuine scourge that is repeated annually and that does not rest on simple hypotheses of potential danger.

What is striking in the area of highway safety, or lack thereof, is the still widespread idea that fatalities should be accepted as indissolubly linked to the freedom that comes with private transportation. People are responsible for the way they drive their vehicles. So they accept the consequences. In the case of other means of transportation such as air travel, companies responsible for the safety of their passengers spend 9 to 10 percent of their budget to provide safety through highly effective preventive measures. In the world of the automobile, on the other hand, the harmful effects of lack of safety mostly evoke curative measures. Insurance companies insure for damages but still engage in rather symbolic gestures in the area of prevention. The concept of prevention, so dear to ecologists, is beginning to seep into the minds of those responsible for private transportation. But in spite of recent efforts, there is still a long way to go.

The cost of highway dangers is estimated at 28 billion euros per year. To come up with this figure, we attribute to collisions the cash cost of repairs to be done, and to bodily injuries the cost of material repairs plus medical expenses. If there is a fatality, public authorities by convention fix a monetary amount that takes into account the next-of-kin's *pretium doloris* (i.e., payment for pain and suffering), as well as the economic and social loss of the community. The turnover of insurance companies is not much less than the global figure cited above. This turnover goes to remuneration of 36,000 insurance agents who write contracts and indemnify damages, 110,000 agents in the medical field and health professions who render services to the injured, and 110,000 auto repair agents who fix damaged vehicles. The economic loss attributed to fatalities, on a long-term cumulative basis, is equivalent to the disappearance of about 100,000 workers. It becomes clear why dangers on the highway top the list of negative impacts affecting our nation.

The recent campaign mounted by public authorities has yielded results. There has been a 30 percent decrease in bodily injuries and deaths. The authorities have taken action, focusing on respect for regulations in force, especially speed limits. It is well known that excessive speeds are the cause of the most serious accidents. But the campaigns in progress deserve to be complemented by preventive measures with a personal dimension designed to make drivers take more responsibility and to have them adopt the principles of safe driving. For these personalized measures, it is necessary to work more closely with insurance companies, so that they move from being companies that fix problems to ones that prevent them, thus respecting the principles of modern ecology.

What are the measures to be taken?

They focus on identifying drivers who keep committing repeated serious infractions. That comes back, for better or worse, to identifying drivers who have frequent negative points on their driving record. Nowadays, these drivers can redeem themselves and earn back points by taking driver's training courses that they pay for. The new way of going about matters would consist of having the insurance companies pay for these preventive training courses with the realization that the change in behavior observed as a result of the training will lead to avoiding many accidents and to reducing future damage costs, thus justifying the investment made by the company.

The training courses could be specially tailored with an option directed, for example, at alcohol abusers, one aimed at habitual speeders, one for young drivers, and one for owners of vehicles in poor mechanical condition. Doctors, who would have less work mending injuries after the fact, could spend part of their work time with preventive safety companies and conduct driver's education courses. In this way, a real policy of preventive safety could be developed, a course of action that would convert the primary harm observed in our nation into a field of exemplary citizen action.

Sound pollution

Surveys show that after highway accidents noise is the most dreaded nuisance. Sound pollution has a serious impact in the city. Sounds are immediately perceptible, and the nuisance they cause is incontestable. Noise is a disruptive sound that cannot only be characterized by its intensity. Intense sounds emitted by an orchestra can be perceived in an agreeable fashion, while traffic noises during sleeping hours can constitute a real nuisance. Sounds are characterized by their frequency, expressed in hertz; acoustic pressure, expressed in newtons per square meter; and intensity, expressed in watts per square meter. Sound level is expressed in decibels. Decibels are the logarithm of sound intensity. The famous logarithm turns up again as inherent to many biological laws. A doubling in sound intensity is expressed by an increase of 3 decibels in sound level.

The sound levels registered in daily life can be very different. They vary from 10 to 20 decibels for the simple rustling of paper to 160 decibels for an airplane engine. Between these two extremes, a conversation stands at 40 decibels and traffic noise from 65 to 80 decibels. At 90 decibels, intense noises are capable of damaging hearing.

How are the harmful effects of sound manifested?

Unwelcome noise makes conversations difficult, interferes with falling asleep, and causes untimely awakenings. It is the cause of chronic fatigue in those exposed to it. In large cities, more than 20 percent of inhabitants state that they are bothered by noise.

Traffic is the object of many complaints: it is the nuisance most difficult to tolerate. To measure the sound level to which a resident is exposed, machines called sonometers are installed 2 meters from the front of buildings. The cost of using this type of apparatus is fairly high. For this reason, efficient ways for simulating noise have been developed at very reasonable cost. Simulations use representations of the three-dimensional space under study, with the model of the terrain and exact visuals of the apartment buildings. Information about the level of traffic on neighborhood routes around the building makes it possible for the software to simulate traffic noise with great accuracy (within a decibel). The city of Paris recently had success in applying this method to all the apartment buildings in the capital. Prior to that, the method was applied by the Île-de-France regional Public Works and Transportation administration in various neighborhoods located near large circulation arteries. This tool is remarkable for establishing diagnostics and for evaluating afterward the effect of the protective measures put in place.

How can people protect themselves against traffic noise?

The best solution lies in conceiving new high-quality routes, or at least ones of optimal quality. The know-how is already available for constructing high volume roadways that have a low noise quotient. Techniques for partially covering roadways and installing acoustic barriers make it possible (without excessively increasing costs) to lower noise levels below 65 decibels and—most of the time—below 55 decibels, making it possible for residents to converse freely with their windows open. These new roads have the great advantage of relieving traditional traffic routes and have a very beneficial effect on the level of exposure of residents to the noise of streets and avenues, historically conceived for moderate traffic and not for the high volumes they are not equipped to handle. It's a question of acoustically "cleaning up" an entire neighborhood by installing new harm-free roads that are perfectly integrated.

Where roads have been built with insufficient sound-dampening qualities, they can be improved by installing acoustic barriers. These have proved very effective. The main problem encountered is visually integrating these elements into roadways whose profile cannot be modified.

Where roads cannot be improved, there remains the solution of soundproofing the facades of the apartment buildings themselves. This solution, while effective for attenuating traffic noise, poses restrictions on satisfactory aeration of the buildings.

What about nuisances linked with airports?

Harmful effects linked to air transportation are serious for those located in proximity to air traffic corridors. Measures, sometimes enacted by independent authorities such as at Roissy-Charles-de-Gaulle Airport, make it possible to appraise the evolution of sound pollution over time. Changes leading to improvements are developing. Modern airplanes are less noisy than older ones. Increased plane size on the most popular airlines allows a decrease in the number of take-offs and landings. On the other hand, air traffic is increasing quickly. The best solution for avoiding harm or negative impacts resulting from air traffic noise is to create airports far away from residential areas but at the same time easily accessible from the center of the metropolises they serve. The compromise position is difficult to achieve. Witness the recent debate about the third airport for Île-de-France. Noise exposure plans define the zones in which lower allowances for—or even prohibitions on—construction apply. For airports already in service, noise nuisance plans define laws that apply to indemnifying affected residents when soundproofing of apartment buildings is undertaken.

Whatever the case, noise remains one of the major preoccupations of people living in urban areas. We must pursue efforts to attenuate or eliminate the effects of this feared nuisance.

Effects on the landscape

Affected residents fiercely contest many new roadway construction projects in an urban environment due to their poor integration into the site where these residents live. And it is true that some projects completed over recent decades are not always successful in terms of their integration into the landscape. Overwhelming dividing effects mark entire neighborhoods. Improving such projects afterward is almost impossible—another reason to be especially attentive to the quality of integration of new projects. Rapid progress is being made in this area.

The ways in which projects are conceived have changed enormously. Building plans are now studied on three-dimensional computer mock-ups that faithfully describe, with accuracy down to the meter, the soil and its texture, the buildings and their facades, the green or open spaces, and the trees that make them up—along with precise identification of the species. In most cases, structures are unobtrusive, completed underground in the densest areas, in covered trenches, or in excavations where integration constraints are less demanding. In certain relief configurations, the choice is made to build in the air. Research has shown that these can be real artistic points of reference—hence their being called construction works of art. Look no further than the admiration evoked by the Millau Viaduct[2]. The area has been revitalized by the influx of tourists coming to see this technical and architectural marvel.

Every year France awards gold ribbon prizes for the most exemplary creations. Functionality and beauty go hand in hand when conception and completion are entrusted to talented project managers under the comprehensive authority of owners. The thousand-year-old example of the Pont du Gard Bridge is a noteworthy illustration of this fact.

Even if it is beautiful to behold, a construction work of art can never replace the intermediate green space or the neighborhood with its human aspect where residents go to run their daily errands.

It is for this reason that the conception of transportation construction should not allow forgetting about the neighborhoods into which the project is being placed, whether these neighborhoods are constructed or natural. It is necessary to jealously guard the reestablishment of pedestrian linkages making it possible to provide close interactions, as well as local thoroughfares assuring the continuity of urban functions. The coverings of new highways must become real living spaces in osmosis with the historical urban fabric. This is the price to be paid so that residents can recognize new infrastructures as pathways bringing services to the entire community without attacking local life.

The realization of such well-integrated roadways affords the advantage of removing from traditional streets and avenues all the traffic that doesn't belong there. These streets and avenues can, from now on, be handled in a spirit of creating living spaces for all recognized urban functions: public transportation in the immediate area, landscaped boulevards, bicycle paths, street furniture, integrated street lighting, and attractive plantings.

This is the way to create real urban planning projects that bring together functionality, pleasure, and aesthetics.

Atmospheric pollution linked to means of transportation; the case of carbon dioxide; the greenhouse effect

Air pollution linked to transportation is especially criticized. If surveys are to be believed, citizens are of the opinion that there is a continual worsening of air breathed in town and that this situation can no longer be tolerated.

The reality is rather different, however. Over the course of recent years, something positive has occurred: objective measurement of air pollution in principal French cities. Independent organizations are given the responsibility of identifying the principal pollutants and to publish the results obtained. So, in Île-de-France, the association AIRPARIF (Air Monitoring System in Île-de-France), bringing together representatives from the state and local authorities, has been measuring for 10 years air quality in the eight departments of the Île-de-France region. Other associations created later are putting in place similar measures in the principal agglomerations of France. The first year AIRPARIF was in operation was a revelation for the residents of Île-de-France. People talked about air pollution almost every day, creating a sense of a sudden worsening of the situation, and also of Île-de-France being an exception, a place where all the pollution in France was concentrated. In actuality, in the following years, other associations came up with results very similar to the ones from Île-de-France. What's more, out-of-the-ordinary pollution episodes proved to be fewer than expected, and continued to decrease. It is noteworthy that after several years of observation, air pollution is a phenomenon that does not have the level of gravity some people wanted to attribute to it. For example, driving on alternate days, a solution that I was in charge of applying in 1997, remained an isolated episode. All the surveys show that for more than 15 years air pollution in France has been in steady decline.

What are *the main pollutants linked with transportation*?

I will mention pollutants emitted by land transportation using internal combustion engines: passenger vehicles and heavy trucks. These are the most frequently used means. Air transportation that also relies on internal combustion engines emits pollutants of a similar nature. Rail transportation that uses nuclear-generated electrical traction does not emit atmospheric pollutants.

Until recently, engines emitted lead, which is now prohibited. Lead pollution no longer exists, as evidenced by the results of measures put in place. Nowadays, engines emit oxides of nitrogen, carbon dioxide, and unburned hydrocarbons. The highly restrictive regulations imposed on automobile manufacturers are leading to a rapid decrease in these pollutants that also is tied directly to taking the affected vehicles out of circulation. It is the introduction of catalytic converters that has made this evolution possible. The three-phase catalytic converter that relies on a porous ceramic body impregnated with a fine layer of precious metal makes it possible to transform oxides of nitrogen into atmospheric nitrogen, carbon dioxide into carbonic acid, and unburned hydrocarbons into carbon dioxide and water. Adjustments of the catalytic device must be very precise for the pollution control to be effective. But results are spectacular. One notes that a new vehicle today pollutes up to 20 times less than an old one. Only oxides of nitrogen are partially resistant. Pollution measures taken in Paris in locations that are particularly sensitive such as Victor Basch Square illustrate the evolution. From this example, it is once again evident that humans are able, thanks to their ingenuity and expertise, to master large-scale phenomena to some degree.

What happens when *episodes of pollution occur in connection with high temperatures*?

Under the influence of ultraviolet rays, the oxides of nitrogen emitted by internal combustion engines release oxygen made up of elementary atoms. This extremely reactive oxygen combines with normal oxygen to yield ozone gas. Ozone is an irritant. At sunset, oxides of nitrogen "recapture" the atoms of elementary oxygen released in the morning and bring the ozone rate back to a normal level. Paradoxically, it is above forests that ozone, lacking the oxides of nitrogen emitted by combustion engines that would reduce it, accumulates during the night. A different natural phenomenon occurs in the case of unburned hydrocarbons. Under the influence of ultraviolet rays, these combine with oxides of nitrogen to yield products that have an equally irritating effect. In very sunny areas of the United States, such as California, the phenomenon magnifies, giving rise to smog.

What about *particulate emissions?*

Diesel engines, which have the significant advantage of consuming 20 percent less energy than gasoline engines, emit very fine, unpleasant, and polluting particles. Automobile manufacturers have devoted enormous efforts to eliminating these emissions. The problem can now be considered resolved. Particulate filters are very efficient, and diesel-driven engines are a part of the entire range of automobiles available—a new example of human ingenuity for solving difficult problems.

And the problem of *carbon dioxide?*

Carbon dioxide gas is not a pollutant in itself. Indeed, it is indispensable to the process of photosynthesis. Plants are made up of it by retaining the carbon and recycling the oxygen. What poses a problem is the balance sheet between carbon dioxide production and consumption. Production results from natural phenomena such as volcanic activity or from human phenomena such as the combustion of fossil fuels. Consumption results from natural phenomena such as absorption by oceans or from living phenomena such as photosynthesis. It is not surprising that the account balance today has a surplus, if we note that human beings consume in a few hundred years the stock of fossil fuels produced by life on earth in the course of hundreds of millions of years. The ease with which humans do this can be only transitory. Thanks once again to their ingenuity, humans will have to rely on nonfossil energy sources—such as nuclear or solar energy—that they will produce for themselves year after year to meet their needs. The consumption of fossil fuels, even if it must last for decades to come, cannot be rational policy at the level of several generations. Starting right now, we have to think about promoting the use of hydrogen for driving automobile engines. Hydrogen, produced from nuclear electricity during off-peak hours and combined with atmospheric oxygen, yields water that condenses in the sea and can have no harmful effects. It will require decades for this evolution to take place. But it is, in my opinion, inescapable. The proof of that is evident in the enormous research efforts put forth by automobile manufacturers to perfect combustion reactors whose purpose is to consume hydrogen in place of fossil fuels. Instead of refineries we will have to construct and start running hydrogen production plants.

For air transportation, the promotion of hydrogen will be, I think too, the solution to advance over the course of several decades. Taking into account the lower density of hydrogen and the volume that fuel reservoirs hold, this type of solution cannot pretend to compete with the use of jet fuel, at least as long as petroleum can be extracted in large quantities from the substrate of our planet. But that cannot last forever.

If fossil fuels are consumed in lesser quantities—indeed, progressively eliminated over the course of several decades—and if the destruction of tropical forests (major consumers of carbon dioxide and emitters of oxygen) is finally brought under control, there is hope of achieving over this century an equilibrium between carbon dioxide emission and consumption, and stabilizing—then reducing—the greenhouse effect, which from all evidence seems to have a significant effect on our climate.

The relative weights of negative impacts and of economic and natural performance rates of living areas

The respective weights of negative impacts linked to travel activities and of economic and natural performance rates of living areas

I have just spent a long time describing the negative impacts caused by human activity, and in particular those linked to transportation infrastructures. As we have seen elsewhere, it is thanks to travel and transactions that creation of value becomes evident. But is the game worth it? Aren't the harmful consequences one day going to outweigh the services rendered?

In order to respond to this question, it is necessary to proceed to a difficult exercise: quantifying the "cost" of harm and nuisances, assigning value to what arises a priori from the qualitative. It is only at this price that one can imagine giving an initial response to the question.

I proceeded to that exercise for many years and turned for support to survey results I had at my disposal from 16 sample agglomerations that made it possible to evaluate the three factors: creation of value, travel generalized costs, and harm and nuisances.

To determine the benefits of easily accessible destinations, I have already explained how to proceed.

To evaluate the cost of negative impacts associated with trips (as travel from one place to another), it is enough to determine the number of kilometers covered annually in each agglomeration, relying on the results of surveys conducted at residents' homes. Having the information about these trips is also necessary to determine travel generalized costs, that is, the monetary expenditures and the worth of travel time.

Once the number of kilometers is determined, it is a matter of applying to them unit costs, expressing transportation danger cost per kilometer covered—mostly highway danger, noise pollution and, lastly, air pollution.

The calculations were done in 1990 in terms of French francs for that year. However, in order to facilitate a current reading, I have translated these results into 2000 euros by applying the following rules: multiplication of harm by the rise in standard of living between 1990 and 2000 (1.34), and by the increase in travel ranges (1.14), increase in travel generalized costs in relation to the rise in prices and the increase in ranges (1.20 x 1.14), and increase in creation of value in relation to the rise in the standard of living (1.34).

For *highway danger*, long practice makes it possible to determine the average cost of a collision, bodily injury, and—among the latter—the average cost where a fatality is incurred. In 2000 values, the level of road danger stands at about 8.17 cents of a euro per kilometer covered on traditional thoroughfares and 2.45 cents on freeways of optimal quality.

Three-quarters of these costs are covered by insurance policies, while public authorities finance the remaining one-quarter. This would include police costs.

As far as *noise pollution* is concerned, the procedure consists of determining the average kilometric costs as a function of the residential density of the neighborhoods covered and the nature of the thoroughfare under consideration. The basis of estimation is the amount it would be necessary to spend on soundproofing lodgings exposed to noise pollution in order to bring them up to approximately the same standard as lodgings not subject to noise. The average kilometric cost of noise pollution in the residential areas of French agglomerations is estimated at 1.84 cents when the route taken is a traditional one, and at 0.61 cents when the reference infrastructure is a high-quality highway. In the countryside, the residents' exposure to noise pollution is considered negligible.

Finally, in matters of *air pollution*, epidemiological studies on residents subjected to increasingly serious levels of exposure make it possible to ascertain a value of 2.25 cents per kilometer covered on traditional thoroughfares and 1.43 cents on urban freeways that have more favorable traffic conditions. In the countryside, the effects of air pollution are considered negligible, since the main emissions are diluted before they reach the areas where people reside.

What do the results of these calculations yield?

To clearly appraise the situation, it is necessary to give three figures at the same time: the value created annually by trips in the agglomeration studied, the *travel generalized cost* with its monetary portion and temporal value, and—lastly—the cost of *negative impacts and nuisances*. Even if the values relative to negative impacts are only orders of scale, there is no doubt that they make it possible to arrive at an initial judgment.

Thus, within the Parisian agglomeration, the creation of value linked to trips for *economic purposes* represents, in the year 2000, a resource of 44,530 euros per worker. The annual generalized travel costs needed to create this value amount to 10,760 euros, or about one quarter of the creation of wealth, and the negative impacts caused amount to 835 euros, or about 1.9 percent of the *creation of wealth*. Of this figure, 1.2 percent is linked to road danger, 0.3 percent to noise pollution, and 0.4 percent to air pollution. For Lyons, the figures are, respectively, EUR 30,840; EUR 6,380; and EUR 610. For Marseille, the figures are EUR 30,230; EUR 6,960; and EUR 722.

If we attempt to generalize at the national level, we find in 2000 euros a creation of value on the order of 622 billion euros per year, or 45 percent of the country's GDP. We also find a travel generalized cost for trips with economic purposes of 206 billion euros, of which 69 are equivalent to monetary expenditures and 138 billion to the value of time spent, or about 33 percent of the creation of value. Lastly, we find 19.2 billion euros in harm and nuisances. This includes 14.7 billion for road danger, 1.85 billion in noise pollution, and 2.65 billion for air pollution. This amounts to 3.10 percent of the creation of wealth, with

2.35 percent associated with road danger, 0.30 percent linked to noise pollution, and 0.45 percent linked to air pollution.

In light of these figures, it is clear that the creation of value is incomparably higher than the weight of travel generalized costs and even higher than that of negative impacts, harm, and nuisances. *It can hardly be a question of preventing creation of value in the name of harm and nuisances.*

Is the hierarchy of results maintained no matter what the *size of the metropolises* studied?

Some authorities in charge attempt intuitively to determine what would be the optimum size of an agglomeration. They realize that small agglomerations cannot render the services expected. They also believe that large metropolises have more disadvantages than advantages, and that there must be an optimum size between the two. Now, as far as I am concerned, I have not found an optimum size. The creation of value increases steadily as a function of the range of choices accessible in a given travel time. If high-performance infrastructures make it possible to efficiently serve large metropolises and to offer an increasing range of choices, the value added linked to this type of urbanization continues to rise. The rise in the value added is more rapid than that of travel generalized costs and, to be sure, that of harm and nuisances. It becomes clear to what degree arguments resting solely on resulting transportation costs and negative impacts can lead to erroneous conclusions.

The results obtained under the same conditions of calculation for trips to *open-air activities* confirm the hierarchy of values: service rendered has a value much higher than the travel generalized cost, and even higher than that of any harm caused. In 2000 euros, at the national level, the creation of "ergonomic" value amounts to 143 billion euros. Associated travel generalized costs are 36 billion euros, of which 12 represent monetary expenditures and 24 the value of the time spent, or one quarter of created "ergonomic" value. Harm caused stands at 3.4 billion euros, of which 2.6 billion are road dangers, 0.35 billion noise pollution, and 0.45 billion air pollution. That's 2.4 percent *of the created "ergonomic" wealth,* with 1.8 percent linked to road danger, 0.25 percent to noise pollution, and 0.35 percent to air pollution.

Directions in which to go when conducting a policy of harmonious development, respectful of future generations, are perhaps not those that many responsible authorities would consider in good faith.

The virtuous circle

What general conclusions can be drawn from these analyses?

My first conclusion is that in no case should human mobility be attacked. People must not be restrained in their spatial development for this is what makes it possible for them to progress both from the viewpoint of exchanges of expertise and the search for well-being.

My second conclusion is that there should be no hesitation—the creation of wealth being at the good level—about setting aside a significant portion of this wealth in order to build infrastructures and urban facilities of total quality—or at least optimal quality—and to eradicate in this way all the negative impacts, harm, and nuisances that can emerge.

My third conclusion is that there should be no fear of technological advances. It is via imagination and expertise that humans have been able to overcome obstacles on the road to progress.

My fourth conclusion is that life on our planet earth is a slow process of construction in which solidarity between different plant and animal species must be cultivated because it is from this solidarity that a lasting equilibrium has a chance to be born.

Some will doubtless say that this is the vision of someone who is overly optimistic. No doubt the path will be strewn with traps. Assuredly there will be difficulties to overcome. But it is the only path that gives meaning to our presence on our beautiful planet earth, while we await the opening, over time, of other horizons about which the conquest of space makes us dream.

Notes

1. I drew a great deal of inspiration for describing these negative impacts from the Atlas of Ecology by Dieter Heinrich and Manfred Hergt; original title: dtv Atlas zur Ökologie, 1990: Deutscher Taschenbuch Verlag, GmbH & Co. KB, München; 1993: Librairie Générale Française pour l'édition française.

2. The Millau Viaduct is a large cable-stayed road bridge spanning the Tarn River valley near Millau in southern France. It opened on December 14, 2004. Designed by English architect Norman Foster and French bridge engineer Michel Virlogeux, the Millau Viaduct is the tallest vehicular bridge in the world. One pier's summit soars 1,125 feet—slightly taller than the Eiffel Tower—and only 125 feet shorter than the Empire State Building.

Part VI

Attacks on the habitats of living species

November 2003: I'm in the Rue de la Convention, wandering through the stacks of a large bookstore that has a reputation for its works on ecology and the environment. My reflections on the relationships that humans establish with their living area lead me quite naturally to consider the relations that animals—and more generally plants and the totality of the living kingdom—establish with this same environment. Do the observations I have made on the behavior of *Homo sapiens* apply equally to other animal species? How do the natural spaces in which numerous animal, plant, and bacterial species flourish, and in which humans themselves renew their forces, change? Can harmonious relations be established among all these species? Is it possible for humans—who by their collective intelligence have profoundly modified the conditions of life on our planet—to limit the attacks to which they subject other species? Can they institute rules that make it possible for each one to find a reasonable place? That naturally leads me to better understand the relationships that exist between different living species, whether it is a question of microorganisms, plants, animals, or humans themselves, who comprise an integral part of the animal kingdom. Are these relations characterized by competition, domination, and submission—in a word—aggression? Or rather are they also regulated by principles of synergy and cooperation, making it possible for each one to find a place in our living space on earth? I am by nature more inclined to think that cooperation and synergy play a determining role. But my conviction needs to be backed up. How does life come to find a balance on our planet, and how do humans, dominant actors, bring a contribution to the flourishing of the totality of species? That means henceforth notably protecting and developing natural spaces exempt from artificial constructions, within which biodiversity can flourish and enrich our living heritage. If this worthy ambition is respected, humans will be able to flourish in spaces authorized for construction without harming other species.

I am drawn to several works that are going to provide me the enlightenment I seek. Three in particular answer my needs. They constitute the content of the pages that follow: Christian Lévêque and Jean-Claude Mounolou, *Biodiversity: Biological Dynamics and Conservation*; Hans-Jürgen Otto, *Woodland Ecology*; and Dieter Heinrich and Manfred Hergt, Atlas of Ecology, previously cited.

The introduction of Christian Lévêque and Jean-Claude Mounolou's book sets the stage well: "In less than a century, the way that Western societies perceive nature and the living world has changed profoundly. Scientists no longer use words such as 'predators' and 'pests,' whereas, new terms like biodiversity or bio-complexity are appearing. The will to master a nature that is apparently hostile has given way to an approach that is respectful of life through the search for a balance between the satisfaction of human needs and the necessity of preserving intact the diversity of the living world."

I totally share this point of view.

Humans are an integral part of the biosphere. They are as much dependent on it as they are one of the influential actors. It is indispensable that they have a clear consciousness of their place in the long procession of life in order to avoid disturbing the general equilibrium of species occupying our planet.

Life on our earth is, in effect, an enduring construction whose species make up interdependent links in the chain. What is most striking in this evolution, beyond its diversity, is its deep unity.

Research conducted for more than 100 years, as well as amazing studies in recent years to decrypt the genomes of principal species, reveal this grand unity of whatever lives on our earth. Life is a slow process that rests on three properties of organic macromolecules: organization by the formation of complex structures, nutrition by the capture of flux of matter and energy, and reproduction by duplication of elaborate structures. The saga of life for 3.5 billion years illustrates this long process.

As recent discoveries of molecular biology demonstrate, at the very beginning, structures called archeobacteria appear that possess the characteristics of living creatures. These are found today in hydrothermal springs on ocean floors, marine plankton, fresh water, and soils. Then bacteria proper appear that possess a chromosome consisting of one—or several thousand—genes within the DNA molecule. The chromosome is not enclosed in a membrane comprising a nucleus, but a membrane that delimits the bacterium itself.

In addition to its unique chromosome, the bacterium contains other—much smaller—DNA molecules—plasmids—that have a surprising property. They code proteins that lead the bacterium to stick to another bacterium. The plasmid can then migrate from one bacterium to another, carrying to the host bacterium a new piece of genetic information. Moreover, as it migrates, the plasmid can carry away a portion of the genes of the chromosome of the original bacterium.

This phenomenon explains the enormous genetic variability of bacteria and their surprising adaptability. Bacteria duplicate themselves by fissiparousness. In a nourishing environment, their numbers grow exponentially. Note that viruses—much smaller than bacteria—can only replicate by becoming parasites of a cell. In this they do not possess (considered in isolation) one of the important properties of life: reproductive ability. Today bacteria represent an important part of the earth's organic mass. They weigh as much as the totality of all plant species.

Cells more elaborate than bacteria appear 1.8 billion years ago, possessing a true nucleus delimited by a membrane. The nucleus contains several chromosomes. The cell also includes mitochondria and plasts that contain genetic information proper and produce enzymes. It is believed that these elements are of bacterial origin and result from fusion with a primitive cell. These evolved cells are going to live an independent life in the form of unicellular algae or protozoa. Later, some 1 billion years ago, they are going as well to live a much more complex life of cells grouped together to develop specialized tissues. An evolution toward multicellular algae or metazoa is noted in the period between 800 million and 600 million years ago.

About 500 million years ago, an explosion of animal life occurs, with numerous species, some of which survive today. Worms and mollusks appear. Several species live in the same territory, and predatory animals begin to attack their prey. Diversity is great, due no doubt to the least complex organisms appearing at that time in comparison with those that later evolve by specializing. The oceans occupy the large majority of the planet, but landmasses begin to emerge. Life is going to conquer dry land, which requires a massive effort of adaptation. The first plant forms come from green algae. They are closely related to present-day mosses. Then comes the period of ferns with roots and leaves. Ferns are going to invade the emerging landmasses. They are the origin of carbon sediments that date from the Paleozoic. At the boundary between the Paleozoic and Mesozoic, plants reproduce by ovules that detach and develop on the ground. Conifers come from that lineage. At the end of the Mesozoic, about 100 million years ago, flowering plants appear. Their reproduction takes place by pollination. Pollen that can travel large distances when carried by the wind fertilizes the ovule and bears a fruit that contains seeds. The flora of flowering plants is very diverse. This is the group that marks our planet today.

For animals, the conquest of the emerged landmasses begins about 400 million years ago with the appearance of myriapods and scorpions possessing a shell that protects them from ultraviolet rays. Aquatic arthropods are already armed with such a shell. Gills are replaced by terrestrial respiratory organs. Then come the insects, also provided with a shell that gives rise to an unprecedented proliferation thanks to the mobility conferred by their ability to fly. Another lineage of animals is going to develop a different structure, that of a vertebral column supporting their organs. The first vertebrates are fishes without mandibles that appear about 400 million years ago, followed by fish with cartilaginous mandibles (sharks) or bony mandibles that will diversify. Aquatic vertebrates develop feet to move in environments encumbered by plants and bushes. They progressively reach dry land. Amphibians and reptiles also appear in the period between 350 and 300 million years ago. These animals will remain for a long time near watery environments. Reproduction relies on an egg that makes it possible to detach from the watery environment. Reptiles give rise to dinosaurs—warm-blooded animals—250 million years ago. These disappear 56 million years ago. Mammals evolve from a line of reptiles 250 million years ago. Small in size, they occupy different ecological niches at the moment when dinosaurs disappear; they diversify and spread over all the landmasses.

Humans belong to a family of primates that has existed for 65 million years. Hominoid primates appear about 20 million years ago, but many families no longer exist today. In an extremely diversified evolution, hominids, including humans, appear. *Homo sapiens* cohabit with Neanderthal man between 40,000 and 30,000 years ago. Ever since, *Homo sapiens* is found on all the continents, and his population keeps on increasing.

There—in a few lines—is the grand adventure of life on earth. This description testifies simultaneously to a great unity and to a great diversity. Unity is linked to the unique support of life: organic macromolecules. Diversity is linked to the prodigious ability to adapt to situations in perpetual evolution, in particular to varying climatic conditions that have marked the 3.5 billion years of life on earth.

And undoubtedly evolution is not over! What's more, many researchers think that the experiment that has occurred on earth can reproduce itself perfectly in similar—but of course not identical—forms on other planets, since organic macromolecules with a carbon base are widely present all through the universe. The National Aeronautics and Space Administration (NASA) and the European Space Agency (ESA) are devoting significant efforts to the search for eventual traces of life on our neighbor Mars, at the time in a distant past when it had a denser atmosphere and abundant water. Fascinating!

In this context, humans cannot abandon a position of responsibility as soon as they attain a stage of development that shelters them from the life's basic needs: water, food, and reproduction. The attacks that people commit against the habitats of other species pose problems as soon as these aggressions threaten the equilibrium or the very existence of species to which they are intimately linked, even if they are not always totally aware of the fact.

So we have to study the following:

- Factors that characterize the habitats of living species, in particular evidence of territorial relations between these species.
- The nature of attacks that humans commit against the habitats of microorganisms, plant species, and animal species.

The habitats of living species

The notion of a living species; the appearance and extinction of species

Habitat is widely associated with the idea of living species. Thus, it is very important to carefully define what a species is, by making clear its place in the elements that make up life.

The base unit is the individual, with genes that make identification possible. The number of genes varies from about 1,000 for a bacterium to 30,000 for humans. The species is composed of individuals that can reproduce among themselves, that is, can exchange genetic information in creating descendants. Therefore, two different species cannot produce descendants between each other. The population of a species is composed of individuals living in a given environment. The species can occupy several separate environments and thus be composed of several populations. These populations can evolve toward separate species if they do not communicate among each other. Communities are the totality of the populations of different species living in the same environment. This is also called biocenosis. An ecosystem characterizes the relations between all species living in a given environment and the physical and chemical elements that compose this environment. At the planetary level, the totality of living species constitutes the biosphere.

Do we have any idea of the number of species living on our planet?

Paradoxically, while we speak of species disappearing, we do not know the exact number. It must be said that certain groups or subgroups of living individuals such as insects comprise a considerable number of species: 8 million estimated, 950,000 recorded. Viruses could comprise 500,000 species (4,000 recorded); bacteria, 1 million (4,000 recorded); mushrooms, 1.5 million (72,000 recorded); plants, 320,000 (270,000 recorded); invertebrate animals, including insects, 10 million (1,000,000 recorded); and vertebrate animals, 50,000 (47,000 recorded). In total, there would be 1,500,000 species recorded, with a potential for 14,000,000 observable species. It is obvious that the inventory of life is far from complete. However, knowledge of the species highest in the hierarchy of living creatures, such as the vertebrates, is very complete. So, the mammals have all been recorded (4,327), as well as birds (9,672). Amphibians and fish are known, with a possible error of 10 percent.

Species disappear—everyone is aware of that. But does the opposite exist? If yes, how is this possible?

In actuality, new species keep on appearing. The genetic heritage of species is modified under the influence of three phenomena: DNA molecules frequently change (mutate) when deteriorating chromosomes are repaired. Some persist because they are well adapted (selection occurs). Still others change randomly or even disappear (genetic drift occurs). The new chromosomes that result from these three phenomena give rise to new species that did not previously exist. These appearances can be produced by differentiation of a single species in separate environments that do not intercommunicate. It was recently discovered, notably in the lakes of East Africa, that new species also could appear in a single environment through differentiation of an original strain.

Thus, it can be observed that diversification of a living creature is a continuing process that has been at work since the beginning of time.

But it is, above all, disappearances that make an impression.

Extinction of a species is in fact a normal process of evolution. A species is born, lives, and dies just as an individual is born, lives, and dies. In the course of 3.5 billion years of the evolution of life on earth, major crises have been scattered along an irregular pathway with relatively intense periods of extinctions. The number of species currently in existence is estimated at 1 percent in relation to all those that have ever existed on earth.

Since the Cambrian, a period that saw the flourishing of many new species 500 million years ago, five major crises can be cited:

- Disappearance of 85 percent of species, 440 million years ago
- Disappearance of 75 percent of marine species, 360 million years ago, while continental species continued to develop
- Disappearance of 95 percent of marine species, 66 percent of insect species, and 70 percent of vertebrate species, probably linked to a significant climate change, 245 million years ago.
- Disappearance of 75 percent of marine species 215 million years ago.
- Disappearance of the dinosaurs 65 million years ago, along with a large part of earth's vegetation.

It is not easy to explain these large-scale phenomena. At any rate, they show that after the great Cambrian explosion 500 million years ago, major crises affected the evolution of life and probably created conditions suitable to the appearance of new species in environments subject to less-intense competition. We have witnessed successive decimations, with colonization of habitats by the lineages that survived and further diversified. But globally, the number of phyla has rather diminished. These large-scale phenomena show that we cannot draw irreversible consequences from short-term observations, which should not prevent us from being attentive and putting forth every effort to avoid the emergence of negative phenomena with serious consequences.

In the course of the last 100 years, what do we know about the balance sheet of species evolution in France?

If we limit our discussion to vertebrate species alone (fish, amphibians, reptiles, birds, mammals), the balance sheet is positive: 630 species in 2000 versus 609 in 1900. Ten species have disappeared; six have been discovered; 25 have been introduced. Growth in intercontinental exchanges is causing a diversification in animal and plant species. For plant species, large-scale intercontinental transfers have marked the course of the last 200 years: corn, manioc, potatoes, tomatoes, pumpkins, tobacco, strawberries, peppers, and beans have come to Europe from South American countries. Wheat, coffee, rice, cane sugar, soybeans, bananas, citrus fruits, and coconuts have reached the Americas from Europe, Africa, and Asia. In addition, cities and towns are sites of a new diversity with an environment that has a more temperate climate, more abundant food supplies and fewer predators. However, a situation that might generally appear satisfactory must be studied carefully, for the scale of changes due to human activity is creating imbalances in many countries, particularly at the level of plant species and ecosystems associated with them. We must pay close attention to the emergence of these imbalances.

Territorial relationships among living species

Living species have a very strong relationship with territory because they have an imperative need for matter and energy in order to develop and reproduce. To be sure, humans do not escape this imperative. In reality, it is in the relationships that living beings maintain with their living area that is found the key to the relationship of humans with other living species.

Organisms living in the same space mutually influence each other. Their relations have great complexity. Is it possible to derive some major tendencies that make it possible to understand the primary mechanisms at work?

Among these mechanisms, some have a *beneficial influence* on the life of an individual within a species or of a species within a community constituting a biocenosis. On the other hand, other mechanisms have a *negative influence*. Between the two, *neutral phenomena* emerge that indicate toleration between individuals within a species or toleration between species within a biocenosis

There are three *positive mechanisms*: the most favorable is called symbiosis, the next one probiotic, and the third positive collective interaction (just above toleration).

Symbiosis characterizes two or several individuals of different species that join their properties together in order to extract a benefit for both species from their close relationship.

Examples of symbiotic relationships include the following:

- Relationship between a tree and fungi. The mycelium replaces the rootlets of the tree. The fungus obtains substances that it can assimilate. The tree receives water, mineral salts, and is protected by substances produced by the fungus.
- Relationship between a legume and bacteria. The bacteria affix themselves to the roots and form nodules. The bacteria assimilate nitrogen from the air and provide it to their host; in exchange, they receive nutrients.
- Relationship between green algae and a fungus. This association gives rise to lichen. The green algae provide for the leaves' functioning, and the fungus takes care of the root. Lichens have colonized nearly all habitats, in particular those exposed to deep cold.

- Relationship between a man and a dog. The dog receives food and shelter. The man receives protection and companionship. Most domestic animals demonstrate symbiosis.

A *probiotic* relationship illustrates the fact that an individual of a given species that meets an individual of another species can obtain a benefit without the partner being allocated any advantage whatsoever.

Examples of probiotic relationships include the following:
- A partner uses the other to have itself carried from one place to another (dust mites by beetles).
- The beneficiary lives in the dwelling of the partner.

A *positive collective interaction* reveals the favorable influence that individuals of different species—or from the same species—can obtain from each others' proximity without having a connection to a precise partner.

Examples of positive collective interactions include the following:
- Trees in a forest: trees protect each other from violent winds and reinforce each other's root systems.
- Beneficial chemical influences: trees attacked by herbivores emit chemical substances to signal each other to create toxic products that permeate their leaves and thus drive off the predators.
- Members of an ant colony: division of labor and information exchanges allow long-term supplying of the community's needs.
- Members of an easily accessible human community: exchanges between members of the community augment global expertise and create added value.

Negative mechanisms are also three. From the least to the most aggressive, they include competition, allelopathy, and antagonism.

Competition occurs when individuals of the same species—or different species—attempt to appropriate energy and materials in a given habitat for their survival or development.

Examples of competition exist within a developing forest. The most vigorous trees absorb the maximum amount of light, while the less vigorous do not flourish, no longer bear fruit and very often disappear. Beneath the canopy of the tallest, full-grown trees, a hierarchy is also established between species of trees that use less light, bushes, and finally herbaceous plants. What is true for the crown of the trees is also at work for their root systems. The most vigorous trees send their roots down the deepest or the most extensively. When individual trees belonging to the same species have similar nutritional needs, the most vigorous take over, creating a more resistant species.

Examples of competition exist in coral reefs. Benthic fish have territories that they defend from fish of their own kind. On the other hand, pelagic fish that live on the high seas have no territory to defend and therefore do not adopt aggressive behaviors.

Allelopathy is characterized (above all in the plant and bacterial world) by the creation of substances that inhibit or destroy individuals of competing species. Trees often produce such substances, which they spread by way of their roots. These substances sometimes prevent the development of new individuals of the same species. In this way, they turn against their source.

In the microbial world, certain bacteria develop products that prevent competing bacteria from multiplying. These products are the bases of antibiotics used to eliminate pathogenic, or disease-causing, bacteria.

Antagonism, found mostly in the animal kingdom, represents the absorption of an individual of one species by an individual of another. The victim is devoured, eaten away or infected, depending on whether it's a matter of a predator, a parasite, or a pathogenic agent. The predator kills its victim in an instant, the parasite leaves it alive but absorbs any useful substances from it, and the pathogenic agent may leave the victim alive if its action is unsuccessful—or else kills it. Worldwide, pathogenic agents kill tens of millions of humans every year.

Between positive and negative mechanisms, there is an area of toleration. An example of an application of toleration mechanisms is that of old growth forests. These comprise individuals of different species that no longer compete with each other and that have found a sort of equilibrium, one might even say wisdom!

These few principles make it possible to understand how bacterial, plant, and animal species live and interact with each other in a given territory. Their interactions can have short-term effects, but also very long-term effects.

The territories of bacterial, plant, and animal species

What light can these principles shed on different species living on earth? For example, what about bacterial species that represent in weight the equivalent of the totality of all plant species, although this fact is not reiterated often enough?

Bacteria play *an absolutely central role* in the development of life. They fix nitrogen from the atmosphere and transmit it to plants. Thus, they complement nitrogen compounds that exist in the soil in relatively modest amounts quite insufficient for assuring the development of plants. Microorganisms fix 175 million tons of nitrogen annually, while nitrogen fertilizers contribute 40 million tons.

Bacteria also destroy compounds deposited in the soil after the death of living organisms and extract biochemical materials that will serve in the creation of new organic syntheses.

Bacteria in this type of activity often engage in symbiotic relationships with other organisms such as plants.

Unfortunately, bacteria also have *negative properties*, such as being pathogenic agents for plants and animals. Humans have been victims of great epidemics that, even today, decimate tens of millions of individuals worldwide.

Plant species constitute the most abundant organic mass of our planet. They absorb carbon dioxide and give off oxygen. They are, along with the oceans, the great regulator of the composition of the atmosphere. As fixed species, they establish numerous symbiotic relations or positive collective interactions. Thus, almost all dominant plants develop symbioses with microorganisms that supply them with nitrogen. They defend themselves against animal predators by putting to work efficient chemical processes that often make them unfit for consumption. Their roots secrete chemicals that prevent the growth of competing species. Thus, they use a broad range of solutions to protect themselves and to develop. They occupy a central place in the chain of life on earth.

Animal species are extremely diversified. Invertebrates comprise 10 million species, of which 8 million alone are insects. Some insects develop relationships of positive collective interactions in impressive intelligent structures. Vertebrates numbering 50,000 comprise 25,000 species of fish, 10,000 species of birds, and 5,000 species of mammals, most of which are herbivores. The relationships that unite herbivores are of the positive collective interactions type. At the top of the chain, carnivores establish relationships of opposition or antagonism. Humans, omnivores, and highly advanced social beings, establish positive collective interactions among the individuals of their species, symbiosis with certain animal species such as the dog and the horse, and relationships of antagonism with other animal species that they feed upon by hunting or raising them. Humans—in the process of developing a formidable industrial activity—are interfering more and more seriously with the totality of other species. Until recently, Homo sapiens was a species struggling for its own biological balance in face of multiple dangers. Now, humans are becoming aware of their responsibilities in regard to the totality of the biosphere.

Attacks on the habitats of living species

Attacks on habitats of microorganisms

Microorganisms play a decisive role in the maintenance and development of life on earth. Human action is not without impact on this life, which often is hidden.

Microorganisms form part of the great chain of production and destruction of organic matter on earth. Their value is often underestimated to the extent that their activity is less apparent than that of plant or animal species.

In order to appreciate how humans can disturb it, we must understand that in reality the cycle in which microorganisms play a part comprises *four major stages*:

- The production of biomass by plant species, the only one that has the property of creating organic matter from carbon dioxide and minerals by using the sun's energy via photosynthesis. The production of biomass results mainly from the activity of trees. It is also a function of smaller plant forms, but in much smaller quantities.
- The consumption of a portion of this biomass by animals that are herbivores or, at a second level, by carnivores that consume herbivores or each other. Humans are omnivores, that is to say, both herbivorous and carnivorous. They depend entirely—directly or indirectly—on plant species to obtain the organic matter they need to live.
- The breaking up and decomposition of live or mainly dead plant or animal species by small or very small animals living in the soil. These animals belong to the categories of macrofauna, such as, earthworms, moles, gastropods; mesofauna, such as, annelid worms and dipterous larvae; and microfauna, such as, amoeba or mites. These tiny animals feed notably on the wastes of plant species that litter the ground.
- The mineralization of products broken up and decomposed by fauna living in the soil thanks to the activity of microorganisms that include bacteria, fungi, and species that combine the characteristics of both bacteria and fungi. These microorganisms have the property of transforming organic remains into carbon dioxide, water, and mineral compounds suitable for reuse by plant species. Without microorganisms, the cycle of life cannot be carried out. The extent to which their activity is important is evident and ought not be put in danger.

To illustrate the relative value of these different sets of living species, take the case of a European forest: the respiration of all agents of destruction, decomposition, and mineralization represent a flow of 305 billion joules per hectare per year; plant species, 314 billion joules per hectare per year; herbivores, 8 billion joules per hectare per year; and carnivores, 1 billion joules per hectare per year.

Humans can disturb bacteria and microscopic fungi in performing their beneficial activities. This is how large quantities of *nitrates* favor the growth of bacteria that prefer or tolerate nitrogen at the expense of other types of bacteria. If at one time the need of plant species for nitrogen to develop favors tree growth, the next time around there will be fragility in the rootlets and nodules where bacteria and trees exist in symbiosis. This situation leads to a blocking of natural processes of regeneration and to the emergence of serious damage.

Chemical inhibitors such as phenols and antibiotics perceptibly alter the metabolism of microorganisms. This can seriously disturb them, albeit they react and develop mutant versions that are less and less sensitive to inhibitors.

Nonetheless, microorganisms do not possess beneficial properties alone. Bacteria are the source of *formidable epidemics* that have marked humanity.

Spanish flu raged between 1918 and 1919 and killed nearly 30 million people, more than the First World War. Malaria, yellow fever, and cholera decimate many populations. Malaria causes more than 2 million fatalities each year. It is perfectly legitimate for people to try to protect themselves against such scourges. They developed *antibiotics* that were expected to put an end to many human diseases. In actuality, antibiotics are natural products produced by bacteria to inhibit the activity of other competing bacteria. For many years, antibiotics have made it possible to control—if not to destroy—the pathogenic bacteria at the source of the gravest diseases. But the impressive ability of bacteria to mutate allow them to successfully resist antibiotics so that new variants have to be researched continually. In hospitals where numerous resistant germs reside, so-called nosocomial diseases develop and become a major problem.

It becomes clear that *humans are not this invincible predator* that overcomes all obstacles. They are caught short by the smallest little organisms that life has thought up: viruses and bacteria whose speed of adaptation is without equal. Humans are certainly a part of a living system in which it is appropriate for them to fit harmoniously by using weapons of cooperation, but also, when necessary, weapons of competition.

What can we say about the relations of humans with the *tiny—or even tiniest—animals* living in the soil and belonging to the categories of microfauna, mesofauna, and macrofauna? Although these are animal species, their dimension and manner of life in the soil really bring them much closer in function to microorganisms belonging to flora.

In effect, they play a role as important as that of microorganisms, since they break up and decompose plant wastes before their mineralization occurs. Pesticides have not-so-negligible effects on small animals living in the soil. This is how insecticides and fungicides not used up in the fight against plant parasites decimate earthworms essential to the oxygenation of the soil and the satisfactory process of oxidizing organic wastes. Used by humans to protect cultivated plants, these products also affect other animals. A great deal of attention must be paid to the toxicity of pesticides, herbicides, and other things employed to increase the yield of agricultural production destined for human consumption.

Attacks on habitats of plant species

There often is talk of the serious attack humans mount on tropical forests—considered the lungs of the planet. What exactly is going on here?

In order to judge the situation accurately, a backward glance would be useful. We know the history of plant species since the last Ice Age, 20,000 years ago (a split second in geological time) in Europe and across the entire planet. What do we discover? Twenty thousand years ago the average temperature in France was 4.5 degrees lower than today. A large ice cap covered England, the North Sea, Scandinavia, and Northern Russia. An ice floe connected England and Iceland. Sea level was 120 meters lower than it is currently. France and England were a single landmass. A single glacier covered the Alps. The same was true for the Pyrenees. France and Central Europe were occupied by tundra, Eastern Europe by steppes. Only the south of Spain, the south of Italy, and Greece were occupied by forests of broad-leaved trees and occasional conifers. Over the course of the 20,000 years following this glacial period, the plant landscape of Europe completely changed. Henceforth, the tundra occupies the northern part of Scandinavia, and conifers cover Sweden and the north of Russia, as well as the Alps and the Pyrenees. Broad-leaved trees and cultivated land are found all over western and central Europe, while Mediterranean vegetation covers Spain, Italy, and Greece. The oak, at the heart of the reclamation of all the spaces abandoned at the time of the Ice Age, spreads 500 meters per year between 13,000 and 6,000 years ago. This is an amazing result independent of humans who, over the course of this period, have not yet deployed any of the industrial means that constitute their power today. In fact, at the moment of glaciation, broad-leaved forests and conifers take refuge in more hospitable regions in Spain, Italy, and Greece. As soon as climatic conditions improve, plant species flourish and reclaim their rights in the habitats they had been forced to abandon. This description illustrates a key property of living organisms: adaptation.

If we now take a look at tropical forests, we discover a similar period of variations of equally large magnitude. In Africa 15,000 years ago, at the time of the last Ice Age, tropical rainforests blanket only limited territories. The savanna is ever-present at the level of the equator. Eastern Africa is occupied by a Mediterranean vegetation, and the Sahara is more extensive than today. In the course of the period following the Ice Age, the process of reclamation proceeds quickly. Around 8,000 years ago, the tropical rainforest spreads out on both sides of the equator, the savanna stretches out toward the north, grassy steppes occupy the north of the present-day Sahara as far as Algeria, and there are hardly any arid regions. This situation continues until 5,000 years ago. About 3,000 years ago, rainfall diminishes in central Africa. There is a reduction in the extent of tropical rainforests. The savanna moves farther south, and arid zones develop in the Sahara.

Over the past 1,000 years, an opposite movement seems to become apparent: a rise in rainfall and development of equatorial rainforests. In South America, a similar phenomenon is observable but with a time frame on the order of 4,000 years earlier than the situation that prevails in Africa.

It is obvious that the large-scale movements observed in the division of plant populations on the planet for 20,000 years have causes unconnected to the presence of humans. That is not a reason for ignoring the impact of present-day humans with their powerful tools that intervene in nature's course. Can they not be agents of change on a similar scale?

Yes, without a doubt. Demographic pressures are strong. In their relationship of competition or antagonism with other plant or animal species, humans are often in a dominant position. Only microorganisms are ahead of them. The fact is that human population is increasing rapidly: 2 billion in 1930, 4 billion in 1975, and probably 8 billion in 2020. In order to satisfy their needs, humans grow cultivated plants and raise domesticated animals. They also exploit forests. In Europe, all the spaces usually designated as natural are actually the result of human intervention. In agricultural areas, hedges make it possible to reconcile stock breeding, cultivation, and the presence of animal species. Forests are places where standard trees grow together. On a world-wide level, 20 percent of lands are used for cultivation and breeding. Hunting grounds or forest exploitation also account for about 20 percent. It is estimated that, globally, 40 percent of lands that have emerged have been transformed or controlled by humans. In these living areas, biological diversity is perceptibly reduced, priority being given to a few high-yield plant species.

Globally, areas covered with forests are on the decline. Exploitation of the tropical rainforest is taking place under conditions that are not always satisfactory. There is overexploitation of an asset that will require many decades to reconstitute.

In semi-arid zones, desertification is gaining on the terrain. It is impoverishment of biological diversity in these zones, which are subject to severe climate conditions, that explains the subsidence of plant species and the disappearance of means of subsistence for groups of people who must then migrate to more hospitable regions.

Nonetheless, in France, suffice to point out, is the opposite of what is happening globally: an increase in forest holdings. In the span of 40 years, the surface area of woodland has grown from 11.3 million hectares to 15 million, representing 25 percent of the total surface area of the country. The policy of the National Forest Office, created by public authorities in 1966, is doubtless the source of this result, which testifies to the effectiveness of public intervention when it corresponds to a strong political will.

Attacks on habitats of animal species

Finally, what of the evolution of animal species and the role played by humans in this evolution?

A return to the past here, too. In the course of the last 50,000 years, many terrestrial vertebrates belonging to large-sized species disappear on the Australian, American, and Eurasian continents without being replaced by other species, while a large variety of vertebrates belonging to very large species survive on the African continent. In the first cases, these disappearances correspond to colonization by humans. In the second, humans have been present for millions of years.

Humans colonize Australia about 55,000 years ago. All medium-sized and large mammals disappear about 50,000 years ago. Species larger than 100 kg, as well as 50 percent of species weighing between 10 kg and 100 kg, become extinct. North America is colonized 12,000 years ago. It contains a variety of large animals, a number greater than that observable in present-day Africa. Almost all of these large animals disappear 11,000 years ago. South America is colonized 11,000 years ago. Subsequently, the continent loses 80 percent of its large mammals. Eurasia, populated for long time, sees a large part of its cold-tolerant fauna become extinct 11,000 years ago. Africa, whose inhabitants date back to very ancient times, conserves a good portion of its large fauna.

What conclusions are to be drawn? It certainly looks like colonization has always been accompanied by a rapid disappearance of large species, doubtless as a result of hunting and the transmission of pathogenic agents by the new arrivals. On the other hand, a long tradition of occupation of the countries by ethnic peoples as in Africa makes possible their cohabitation with large species and introduces toleration. It is hoped that after a period of competition, not to say antagonism, humans will be able to initiate relationships of toleration, even cooperation or symbiosis.

Currently, however, erosion of biological diversity seems still to be at work. Some believe that too many species are becoming extinct.

The matter is probably not that simple. It is true that on many islands species extinction has been recorded. In marine environments, on the other hand, only 21 species extinctions have been recorded over the past 300 years, according to the Centre for Environment, Fisheries and Aquaculture Science at Lowestoft laboratory, Suffolk, United Kingdom, and the Pew Institute for Ocean Science in New York. Sixteen of these have occurred since 1972.

Worldwide, the Global Union for Nature has inventoried the extinction since the year 1600 of 584 plant species and 641 animal species, that is, an average of three extinctions per year. Undoubtedly, the reality is higher than this figure, since many species have not yet been recorded.

On the other hand, new species have not been registered even though it is known they exist. Thus, when humans create dams, they create isolated spaces that are going to give rise to new species of fish or batrachians.

When we do the balance sheet on the evolution of fauna numbers in France over the last 100 years, we note, as was previously pointed out, an increase in the number of vertebrate species: 609 in 1900, 630 in 2000, with 10 species extinct, 6 new and 25 introduced long-term from other countries.

Aren't humans overdoing their hunting of wild animal species, and are they not equally overdoing their exploitation of our ocean reserves?

This is a real question. Humans are endangering the species that they hunt, or have hunted too intensively. That is the case of the whale, the tiger, the rhinoceros, and many others, too. The implemented solution—of forbidding the hunting of these species—is the only one that currently makes possible preserving them from extinction.

In the domain of fishing, among the 200 species fished the most and that represent 75 percent of all fish caught, one-third are overexploited. Bringing their numbers back up is not assured.

So, humans must make progress if they want to preserve a harmonious balance between the different species living on our planet.

The need to demarcate and protect natural spaces, home to biodiversity

These analyses make it transparently clear that life on our planet is marked by a deep unity. All species, bacterial, plant, and animal, interact. Animal species only represent a tiny part of the biomass. They are dependent on conditions that promote the flourishing of the bacterial species, microorganisms, and plants that provide them energy in order to regulate their temperature and to move. They also are dependent on organic materials to build and repair their organism.

Humans, by their qualities of intelligence and expertise and by their ability to organize a highly effective cooperation between members, greatly influence the destiny of all the other species, whether it be their flourishing or their decline. They must not forget their deep dependence with regard to the entire chain of life.

Humans must systematically develop their abilities to establish relationships of cooperation with other living species and avoid making aggressiveness and antagonism their only behavior choice.

It is possible. A collective coming to awareness of human responsibilities with regard to balance in the biosphere is seeing the light.

International laws are being enacted to protect areas at risk. More attention is being given to the harms and nuisances caused by humans.

The very first thing that needs to be done is to clearly demarcate, in the urban planning documents that govern zoning laws for living areas, those spaces exempt from all residential or commercial construction. It is necessary to carefully demarcate these natural spaces within which the great diversity of life can express itself.

Laws such as the Coastline Law or the Mountain Law are designed to protect and develop spaces that favor biological diversity, as well as the well-being of human beings, who can renew themselves and wake up to their place in this beautiful adventure of life.

Urban planning documents therefore must be extremely attentive to carefully delimiting areas that are totally free of artificial construction. They must protect these spaces by force of law, for it is a matter of a common good—of all living species and, to be sure, of humans themselves. This demarcation must be placed in some hierarchical order. It should go from large forests and agricultural areas all the way to neighborhood squares, and include urban parks, the layout of riverbanks or lakesides, tree-lined avenues, paths, and walkways within urban spaces.

Having thus demarcated what must be protected, humans will be able to let blossom in the other spaces all the capacities for exchange of knowledge that constitute their power and originality.

Part VII

The dynamics of living areas occupied by humans

March 23, 2005: The deputy mayor of Lodève invites me to the restaurant of the National Assembly. He wants to discuss the work I have been doing for many years regarding living areas. The Ministry of Public Works, Transportation, and Spatial Planning has just given him the job of leading one of six working groups set up to prepare a colloquium on "The Living Areas" that will take place at the beginning of the summer. The subject he has to discuss is entitled "Transportation infrastructures and economic development." This is a vast topic that he experiences on a daily basis as mayor of Lodève and deputy of a district that is suffering the shock of rural exodus.

He describes to me his long years of political practice, his intimate acquaintance with the problems experienced by the inhabitants of his municipality and those of his district.

Lodève, prosperous during the Middle Ages, retains lively traces of this past, including a very lovely fortified cathedral. In the nineteenth century and at the beginning of the twentieth, the town owed its development to an active textile industry. The local industry was one of the main providers to the armed forces. Then the textile industry went into decline under the pressure of strong competition from areas with cheaper labor. Beginning in the 1960s, COGEMA (Compagnie Générale des Matières Nucléaires), one of the great forces of the French nuclear industry, exploited a large uranium mine. But in the face of commodities offered by other countries, the company gradually abandoned Lodève.

Today, Lodève survives on local and regional production activities and services. The town is subordinated to the influence of the chief town of the department, Montpellier, an agglomeration of 400,000 inhabitants that tends to monopolize departmental and regional development.

The deputy mayor explains his daily struggle with matters of employment, stabilizing the population, and his efforts to increase the town's attractiveness to tourists. He indicates that, for him, the opening of freeway A75, which links Clermont-Ferrand to Montpellier while serving Lodève, constitutes a wonderful development opportunity for his town. For many years, he has fought for the building of this infrastructure, so precious in his eyes.

"What is your opinion, M. Poulit, about the connection that can be established between infrastructures and economic development?"

"To properly understand this link, you have to make a clear distinction between the creation of wealth caused by the new infrastructure in the short term, and the much slower phenomena represented by setting up companies offering new jobs or building residences to house new workers. In the first case, there is an enriching of those companies and of workers already in place, in very short time frames on the order of a few months.

"In the second case, there is creation of new buildings, at a much slower pace, of course. From this point of view, the expression 'economic development' is a little ambiguous. It would be better to use two distinct expressions, one 'creation of economic or natural wealth' to characterize the first phenomenon, the other 'establishment of new industrial or residential buildings' to characterize the second phenomenon."

"So talk to me about the first phenomenon."

"First, I'm going to remind you of some survey results that are not well-known, even though they have been identified for several decades. The time that each person spends on traveling each day to work, shopping, taking care of business, entertainment, and running errands has not changed for decades. That is evidently what has happened with the opening of freeway A75, and even more recently with the opening of the Lodève loop. The users, regardless of their reasons, are taking advantage of greater travel access in order to seek out more pertinent destinations within an area that is expanding in an invariable travel time. Productivity per hour worked is rising, and there is collective enrichment."

"I was unaware of this phenomenon. But on reflection, that's exactly how I reason. I am interested in the job pool for workers and the worker pool for employers. For municipal services, I ask myself the question, how many residents are they going to serve? What range of services can I offer my inhabitants? Isn't it better to join forces with neighboring municipalities in order to offer better services?"

"When a new infrastructure is placed into service, it is necessary, first of all, to pay attention to the economic enrichment that it affords workers and residents in the areas served in the months following opening. That's what would need to be done for A75. In addition, it would be interesting to look into ways to increase the efficiency of this infrastructure. I am convinced that improving traffic flow at the outskirts of Montpellier would have extremely beneficial results, bearing in mind the density of jobs and workers that exists in the chief town of the department. Don't ever be afraid of your neighboring municipalities. The more numerous and effective the connections, the more abundant the wealth of the ensemble of players involved. It's not the same though for the establishment of residential or business buildings. The logic is a bit different there."

"Talk to me about the second phenomenon, that of establishing new buildings."

"First you have to identify a study perimeter that must be broad enough to reveal competition between areas of urbanization. Within this perimeter you have to predict population and employment over 10 or 20 years while taking into account the current birthrate and migrations of populations coming from other neighboring study perimeters. Having completed the predictions, you must determine how these new inhabitants or new workers, as well as these new jobs, are going to be distributed in the different competing living areas. What factors are going to come into play?

"The first factor—there's a link here with the preceding phenomenon—is the hope of economic or natural enrichment attainable by inhabitants interested in a given site. The higher the hope of enrichment, the more attractive the area will be, a priori. Yet, as decisive as it is, this factor is not the only one to consider. A second factor intervenes: the quality of the environment, or the lack thereof, that will affect the expectation of enrichment. Last, and this factor is often important, the cost of servicing the land for the new residence (or for the employer, the new business building) holds a great deal of weight on the balance sheet. It changes the value of the hoped-for enrichment. What drives development thus depends on these three terms. Thanks to use of a fairly simple formula applied to these factors, you can determine the trend of urbanization in a given area. New residents and jobs will be distributed over time in relation to these trends of urbanization. You note then that the creation of wealth is not the only factor that comes into play in the dynamics of establishing new buildings, although it is an important one. To be successful in creating a new urbanization, you have to simultaneously bring together the potential for wealth connected with excellent access, the care given to the local environment, and the low cost of servicing the site. All living areas compete with each other with regard to these criteria. So it won't simply be because the quality of access improves that the settlement rate will inevitably rise. You have to look carefully at the site environment and the cost of servicing the site, and tell yourself that if your neighbors are doing better from the perspective of these three criteria, it is they who will win the approval of new arrivals and attract new buildings. In order to sustain the least densely populated areas that represent, a priori, moderate potential for enrichment, it is necessary that public authorities not hesitate to subsidize the development of land susceptible to urbanization in the name of living area equity. In addition, you have to emphasize the welcoming of tourists via the establishment of high quality service facilities located in market towns, villages, and medium-sized towns in these moderate density areas."

"At any rate, you are confirming that even if opening things up is not a sufficient condition for accelerating new building starts, it is a necessary condition for it."

"Exactly. But make no mistake; the work of local authorities has only just begun. It is necessary to wage campaigns to improve the local environment and propose areas of land that don't cost very much to service. You have to find the best price-quality relationship, as well as the best relationship between the euro invested by the potential building start-up and the creation of wealth that can be anticipated in a quality environment. That's what urban development models want to identify in order to help local authorities in their decision making."

"Thank you, I have a better understanding of the difference between the aspects tied to the enrichment of current residents when they are served by new infrastructures, and the aspects tied to the start up of new buildings that are certainly linked to the preceding phenomenon, but that depend as much on other actions. We are in the midst of a discussion that has serious consequences and that will affect the lives of our fellow citizens for a very long time. That's a big job!"

"A big job that is a part of the long chain of responsibilities that falls to urban planners in our country and more generally on our planet."

For urbanization is a movement that has come a long way.

Humans, in the course of their evolution, passed from the stage of hunters to that of farmers and finally to that of urban dwellers.

At the beginning of their evolution, they are totally integrated into their natural environment. All we need to do is look at the people of the Amazon forest to be aware of this degree of integration. Living by hunting, fishing, and gathering, humans only remove from the natural environment those things that are strictly necessary, and can not at this stage be considered aggressors against other animal species, let alone plant species. Their ingenuity manifests in the use of handmade tools and in the controlled use of fire.

The next stage is that in which humans master the culture of grasses (cereals). From then on, they have at their disposal more abundant and less uncertain resources. They tame animals that are going to become their lifelong companions. Some of them, like the horse, improve human mobility and make it possible for them to reach new living areas. The great conquerors are associated with their faithful steeds, instruments of their conquests. Others, such as cattle and other animals bred for food, allow people to provide themselves with protein on a regular and dependable basis. The need to hunt diminishes. Humans situate themselves in places where they can practice agriculture, raise animals, exchange the goods they produce, and defend themselves collectively against the attacks of invaders from areas where the practice of farming and raising animals is less entrenched. Human communities begin to organize into market towns and villages, and—in certain locations—even larger towns that are privileged from the viewpoint of worship opportunities, as well as cultural, administrative, or commercial exchanges. The tools of mobility remained foot travel, riding horses, and, along the coasts, sailing.

Then the industrial era arrives. Humans master energy and multiply tenfold their ability to travel using steam-driven equipment and combustion or electric engines. Then follows the invention of trains, motorboats, cars, airplanes, and high-speed trains.

In the constant time devoted to travel, humans multiply their range of choices tenfold. They increase in extraordinary proportions their capacity of action, productivity, and the quantity of goods and services they can access. They find in urban organization the means of increasing the number of goods and services at their disposal. Towns of all sizes, from straggling villages to megalopolises, develop. The connections between these structures grow, thus creating networks of towns. At the same time, humans wish not to go too far away from the natural spaces that constitute their historical cradle and that are indispensable to them for relaxation and renewal. Collectively, they seek to protect them, realizing that, without this protection, this space for regeneration will be lost to them. They discover collectively their impact on other living species and begin to think about the value of cooperative work and not just about victory over their fellow living creatures.

This evolution is far from over. Humans, on all continents, live increasingly in urban spaces. The progress owed to communication technology and the instantaneous exchange of information that this technique makes possible have scarcely any influence on this evolution. Humanity continues on its way toward the era of megacities, of which China is providing us notable examples.

This phenomenon can be explained by the fact that humans belong to a gregarious species that extracts enormous advantage from the exchanges of abilities and knowledge that it can establish among its members. This exchange is essentially one of proximity. It occurs when words, gestures, and expressions play a decisive role. For example, even if prepared in isolation, a negotiation process is concluded in several face-to-face exchanges. It is the same for learning new practices and concepts. Work places are sites where teams form in order to reach objectives in a cooperative framework. Humans progress thanks to the specialization of the activities of members of the species. Increasingly extensive training is given to people who attain greater and greater managerial skills, and more advanced technical, economic, social, and legal competence. However, these multiple capacities can only be expressed and completed within groups that communicate and exchange their expertise primarily verbally. The daily physical proximity provided by transportation constitutes the means of rendering mutually complementary the specialized bodies of knowledge that would be useless without intense communication.

There lies the principal motive behind human presence in a living area, the one that largely determines physical establishment over the course of time, and that makes it possible to predict where the most serious conflicts of interest will be located in relation to other species living on our planet.

To be sure, that is not the only criterion, as we will see later on, since other factors play a role: quality of access to natural spaces, quality of the environment in the desired locale, and finally the efforts to embark upon servicing the site where it is anticipated that a resident will be located. But it remains overall the most important. This is the criterion that will largely shape the landscape of living areas occupied by humans and the way in which balance will be established with other species.

It is also necessary to be aware that the evolution of an area's occupation depends not only on multiple individual decisions optimizing the anticipated satisfactions of each resident, but equally on collective decisions made by the powers representing the community as a whole. These collective decisions are legal ones focused primarily on protecting certain spaces from all forms of urbanization or on reserving rights-of-way for establishing transportation networks to serve the whole living area. Such decisions are essential to the coherence of all human settlements and the harmonious cohabitation of different species living in the same area. They are, of course, integrated into urban planning models.

In this light, we are going to do the following:

- Present tools that make it possible to predict the location of humans over the course of decades to come. These tools are also known as simulation models for urban development.
- Comment on examples of recent urban planning projects that have relied on this type of approach.

Predicting the evolution of living areas: urban development simulations

Factors affecting the evolution of living areas: economic and natural performance rates, negative impacts, servicing costs

What are the factors that intervene in the propensity of humans to settle in one living area rather than another?

They can be classified in four categories:

- The hope of having access to more abundant choices of goods and services, including access to greater professional, social, or cultural advantages
- The hope of being able to access more natural spaces
- The hope of having a quality environment at their disposal
- The desire to spend the least amount possible on servicing the site where settlement is anticipated

The hope of having access to more abundant choices of goods and services, including access to greater professional, social, or cultural advantages is the main motive for the settlement. For example, thanks to this possibility of extended access to expertise humans can grow in ability to produce more sophisticated and more numerous goods.

The economic performance rates of living areas are nothing more than the translation into number values and monetary equivalents of this valorization of diverse types of expertise available within an easily accessible living area. Enterprise creates wealth by putting to work methods of producing goods and services. These methods are made good by the availability of the expertise necessary to apply them in a given place. The living area is all the richer in knowledge potential when the number of workers that can physically meet is high. Economic performance, as we have seen, is linked to the multiplying progression of the number of humans that can meet in a reasonable space of time—on the order of 1 hour—and this figure is in the form d.V^2, d representing the occupation density of the living area, and V^2, the square of the average travel speed designating the expanse of living area accessible in 1 hour. It is a question of the economic energy of the living area, that is, the intensity of exchanges of expertise among humans in a given area. The multiplying progression of this energy makes a linear progression possible in the collective performance of brains exchanging their knowledge by close communication. This is a powerful phenomenon. In the country overall, it represents about 45 percent of the GDP. All of that explains why humans, as soon as they have the chance, migrate toward connected living areas that provide high-level transportation services and the possibility of benefiting from more and more knowledge. It is the phenomenon of urbanization that is closely associated with economic progress. But urbanization does not automatically mean increasing density. What matters is making economic energy increase. This is done by increasing density, or yet again, by increasing human travel speed. If density rises, one can rely on means of transportation that offer high-frequency services although they are relatively slow door to door. If density is low, door-to-door transit must be much faster, which leads to opting for low-frequency transportation with high speeds. One of the reasons for urbanization is thus formulated as a result of the felt need of humans to benefit from the economic energy of a living area and to participate in its growth. Translated into a monetary equivalent, this is called the economic performance of a living area and its growth. For a given living area, net economic performance is obtained by subtracting from the gross economic performance the travel generalized cost issuing from this area.

Recently, a great deal of hope has been placed on telecommuting. Does it play a significant role in the economic performance of a living area?

Telecommuting is indeed possible thanks to the Internet. But it is apparent that it is far from taking on the importance that was predicted for it. This is quite simply because close physical interchange is of an intensity that no technology can replace. Information technologies complement physical exchange, but are not a substitute. Moreover, time spent on daily physical travel has not changed since the emergence and massive development of communication technologies, something that is reassuring when all is said and done.

The hope of being able to access natural spaces is certainly another essential factor in the interest paid to a living area. It is especially a means of attenuating the stress created by production and service activity.

People first of all are attracted by the possibilities for exchanges with their fellow human beings. But they do not wish to deprive themselves of nature and everything it brings them in terms of well-being and renewal. Easy access to parks, forests, and bodies of water affords humans relaxation, and they want to benefit from increasingly diverse destinations. As we have seen, the surface area of easily accessible natural spaces (expressed in the form $s.V^2$, where s represents the density of natural spaces per square kilometer and V^2 represents the square of the average travel speed) designates the expanse of living area accessible in an hour. This spatial or natural energy increases when travel speed rises, but also when the density of natural spaces s increases, that is, when the human occupation density of the living area, d, decreases. This phenomenon is observable in the most important metropolises. City-dwellers want to see economic energy increase; however, when travel speed improves, they arbitrate between a reasonable growth in economic energy and a reduction in the density of the living area that allows spatial energy to increase even more rapidly.

The multiplying progression of spatial energy corresponds to the linear progression in ergonomic satisfaction experienced, also called the natural performance of the living area. Net natural performance relative to a given site is obtained by subtracting transportation generalized costs from gross natural performance. It constitutes the second factor to which humans are sensitive when they look for a new area to settle.

The hope of having a quality environment available is a powerful factor of interest brought to bear on a site.

It is necessary to pay attention to existing—or potential—negative impacts about the projected site. There can be good accessibility to green spaces within 1 hour's time and, simultaneously, exposure to the negative impacts of noise or air pollution within the desired area. The value of negative impacts obtained by considering factors such as noise, air pollution, road danger, and dividing effects plays a negative role in the process of choosing. This nuisance value can be the object of evaluations expressed in monetary terms and compared subsequently with the value of economic and natural performance rates. But where performance rates act positively, "harms" and nuisances act negatively.

Finally, a site is less attractive in relation to *how high costs are for servicing it*. If it had to be, a terrain situated in a swampy area could lead to exorbitant outlays that would make it almost impossible to build on. To appraise the value of a site, the person who is looking attempts to evaluate expenses that must be incurred in order to set up the anticipated building. To establish a pertinent comparison between the value of the economic and natural performance rates from which benefit will come and negative impacts that will have to be borne, he must convert expenses for servicing the site into annual amortization costs and interest payable. This value is known as the servicing charge.

In sum, the petitioner is in a position to judge between different sites from which to choose once the following factors have been considered: positives, such as net economic and natural performance rates of the areas; and negatives, such as cost of negative impacts and servicing charges. There we have the principal factors that make it possible to forecast the behavior of new residents with regard to sites available for occupation.

Real estate costs, proof of the interest living areas hold

The development of urbanization gives rise to land transactions during which households or businesses that want to set up on empty land go to the owners of the sites to obtain use of the desired terrain. What happens?

The households or businesses that want a piece of land enter into negotiations with the landowner. They expect a benefit. Otherwise they would not negotiate and would not leave their current site.

Let's take the case of a household. The value that the household expects from its establishment on a new site is the sum of the positives and negatives that the desired terrain can bring. These advantages and disadvantages include the following:

- First, there is the economic performance the site will allow the household to share, that is, the creation of value linked to the possibility of accessing a larger job market, more varied businesses and services, and quality institutions of learning, versus a site that only has a low level of diverse activities and services. This creation of gross value, when cut by the generalized cost of travel, becomes creation of net value. It is the net value that must be considered here.

- Next is the spatial performance the site is going to allow the household to share, that is, the creation of ergonomic value linked to the possibility of accessing varied natural spaces, versus a site that does not have such possibilities. Reduced of travel generalized costs, the gross ergonomic value becomes the net ergonomic value.

- Finally, the negatives enter into consideration: the cost of negative impacts and the servicing charge expressed in terms of annual amortization of investments to be made. The sum of positive and negative values is designated "Global annual interest that the applicants attach to the desired site."

Of course, the site where the household currently lives also holds positive and negative value. It would be tempting to consider only the differences between the value of the current site and the value of the new one. In reality, if the move occurs, the land on the current site will be sold with account taken of its own enhanced value, and the product of this transaction entails the erasure of values previously attached to it. So the household takes into account the totality of positive and negative valorizations of the new site.

The landowner approached by the new arrival is going to seek to share the expected benefit of this location, that is to say, the cumulative and updated sum realized over time of the positive and negative annual valorizations of the site in question. In fact, the sale price of the land will be about half the cumulative and updated sum realized from these valorizations.

In this way, we discover the source of the strong relationship that exists between the price of lots in a living area that can be built upon and the economic and natural performance rates of these areas, balanced by the negative worth of harms and nuisances and that of servicing charges. Economic and natural performance rates are often the most important. Economic performance rates are more important in the center of towns where the range of choices of activity is the highest. This is also where prices of land are the highest. Authorities who base their reasoning solely on travel costs cannot arrive at such conclusions to the extent that the center of town has the most serious traffic jams. But where there is talk of traffic jams, there must also be talk of a high level of attractiveness, high gross creation of value, and high net creation of value. Prices of land definitely illustrate the attractiveness of different parts of a living area. They also confirm the pertinence of the notion of creation of value through access to numerous and varied goods and services.

Some may find it unfair that the landowner who does not have to put out any effort to take care of his piece of land draws a benefit from the collective efforts undertaken by the public to better serve a living area. But as much can be said of the resident who moves in order to take advantage of better employment and service options. There is enrichment in both cases.

Is it not the role of public authorities to assure through coherent initiatives the enrichment of all community members and to support activity? At any rate, there is creation of value when investment in transportation, for example, makes a living area's economic energy increase and allows the residential community, be they owners or tenants, to benefit from it. This is especially the case when the public finances transportation investments, not to mention when it partially assumes operation costs. It is a question of a political decision aimed at financing public services through taxation. The solution of financing through tolls is equally beneficial when selected short-return-of-investment operations make it possible for the entire community to use tolls to create a situation where value outweighs cost, without having recourse to the lean resources of taxation.

In the evolution of urban living areas, everyone gains as long as environmental conditions do not deteriorate so much that they wipe out the benefit contributed by improving economic and natural performance rates.

Urbanization trends: predictive models of urban development

Is it possible to predict the evolution of the physical occupation of a living area by homes, commercial buildings, or industrial buildings? Is the development of urbanization subject to prediction?

Major urbanization trends can in fact be determined on the basis of the four factors of evolution of living areas previously described.

First of all, the living area to which the forecast applies must be taken as point of reference. That can be the national area, a regional area, or a local area. The larger the area, the more difficult it is to make predictions. This type of study usually applies to local living areas such as urban communities, town communities, or municipal communities. Forecasts then address the way in which the different neighborhoods of these communities develop over a period of time, say 20 years.

The first element to take into consideration is the total volume of needs to be satisfied in the whole living area studied over this 20-year period. Needs are expressed in square meters of floor space to be constructed in order to satisfy residential, industrial, tertiary, commercial, and public facilities requirements. These requirements are of three kinds: those that result from the need to replace old buildings; from increased needs for comfort for current inhabitants and employees; and, lastly, from the need to house new people or new jobs. The new people or new jobs to be welcomed depend on basics such as the fertility of the households and the movements that take place between living areas in a region, between regions, or between countries. Forecasts can be made in the form of nested development models: local living areas, regional areas, and national areas.

Household fertility rates play a decisive role in the expression of urbanization requirements. Fertility depends on a number of factors: cultural, religious, and social. What is clear is that biological vitality almost always precedes economic vitality, since it is the cooperative labor of humans that is at the source of a large portion of the creation of wealth. Of course, if a local living area cannot be guaranteed satisfactory service conditions, human cooperative labor cannot be established. It takes large numbers of people all joined together to create abundant collective wealth.

In a given living area, after determining the total number of square meters of floor space to construct over 20 years, the question arises as to how this total requirement is going to be distributed among the different neighborhoods of the living area under study. How many square meters of floor space will be constructed in each of these neighborhoods?

The models used rely on an evaluation of (1) the supply of square meters of floor space construction authorized in each neighborhood in question, and (2) a factor known as the urbanization trend that expresses the rapidity of consumption of this supply of authorized construction.

The square meters authorized in a neighborhood result from provisions spelled out in the urban planning documents, the Local Urban Plan that recently replaced the Land Use Plan. The factor known as the urbanization trend is representative of the global interest that new arrivals bring to bear on this neighborhood. This interest is represented in annual values by the net benefit of accessible economic destinations, net benefit of accessible ergonomic destinations, minus the worth of the harms and nuisances of the site and the amortization of servicing charges. By analogy with the formulations adopted when there is a choice among several options (e.g., the formula of spatial distribution of trips, or the formula of distribution of traffic among competing itineraries), the urbanization trend is proportional to the exponential of the global interest that the applicants attach to the neighborhood studied.[1]

The result of multiplying square meters of authorized floor space by the "urbanization trend" factor expresses the number of square meters of floor space that will in fact be constructed in the neighborhood in question.

The portion of constructed floor space that the neighborhood in question will bring to the whole area will be in the form of supply of square meters of floor space authorized in the neighborhood multiplied by the urbanization trend of this neighborhood, related to the sum of supplies multiplied by the urbanization trends of all neighborhoods.

Neighborhoods that cannot be urbanized are taken into account by this type of approach. By definition, these neighborhoods do not include a supply of square meters of floor space since local urban plans make no provision for them. But the demarcation of neighborhoods not susceptible to construction implies a specific study that must integrate several considerations: the possibility of offering residents areas of relaxation and renewal, and also the possibility for plants and animals to benefit from places where their own biological balance is respected.

It is only at this price that it will be possible to establish harmony between human activities and the requirements of the plant and animal kingdoms. The connection with nature must be deep and lasting. Prohibition of construction—I keep repeating this—is the primordial act of urban planning. It is necessary to say where no construction will take place in order to preserve natural spaces and also to reserve rights of way of transportation infrastructures destined to serve the community. In such areas, the prediction model of urbanization indicates a supply of square meters of floor space equal to zero.

The model applies to the same conditions in residential neighborhoods and business zones or in commercial establishments. What will change is the value assumed by the factors contained in the definition of interest the applicant brings to bear to the neighborhood under consideration.

For residential neighborhoods, net economic performance represents the creation of value linked to the possibility of accessing jobs and services starting out from the residential area in question. The creation of net natural value represents the interest born to natural spaces starting out from this residential area. The nuisance coefficient represents the weight of negative impacts, in particular noise, that can become high, and the coefficient of serviceability—the annual cost to the applicant of servicing the site.

For commercial neighborhoods, net economic performance expresses the creation of value linked to the possibility offered to residents surrounding the commercial center project of easy access and especially of accessing on the rebound all the other commercial offers integrated into the center or adjacent to it. Commerce, it is well known, attracts commerce. The creation of net natural value illustrates the interest brought to bear by clients of the center to natural spaces in the vicinity (this interest is second). The nuisance coefficient represents the weight of local nuisances to which clients are moderately sensitive, while the coefficient of serviceability equals the annual servicing charges.

For business zones, net economic performance represents the creation of value linked to the possibility of business owners to access a significant pool of workers. The creation of net natural value represents the interest brought to bear by employers to the possibility of accessing nearby natural spaces, an interest that is manifested quite frequently. The nuisance coefficient represents the weight of negative impacts, a factor to which employees are increasingly sensitive, while the coefficient of serviceability represents the annual servicing charges.

By taking into account just the factors of accessibility and creation of associated value, a simulation executed for metropolitan Toulouse gave a correlation rate of 0.85, a value that is quite significant.

In this way one can have recourse to this type of simulation to determine urbanization trends and predict, with certain realism, the way in which a living area will be occupied by the human community in the course of coming decades, natural spaces for their part being protected by law.

Evaluation of the interest in an urbanization project in the present and in the future

I have just described the methods that can be employed to predict, at least in their large outlines, the trends of human occupation of living areas; how residential, business, and commercial areas develop and also how natural areas are preserved. These methods say nothing, on the other hand, about the interest or value that these spatial organizations can offer in the present and the future. Is there an improvement in the situation of humans, as well as animal and plant species with which we are supposed to live in harmony?

Methods for evaluating the development of a living area must not be confused with methods for appraising the value of such-and-such a spatial organization. The confusion is fairly frequent. Methods of evaluating economic and natural performance rates of living areas certainly belong to the category of methods for evaluating at a given time the interest an urban or rural organization can present at the economic or ergonomic level. On the contrary, that is not the role of instruments that focus on predicting how a spatial structure of occupying an area is going to evolve under the influence of different factors such as demographic development, servicing charges, or interest factors entering into the ensemble of evaluative criteria themselves, for example, the performance rates of living areas or the weight of negative impacts. When we evaluate, we are interested in the "why." When we predict a spatial evolution, we are interested in the "where."

But at the moment when an instrument predicting an organization's spatial evolution is put to work, it is fundamental to ask oneself the following question: What is the service that will be rendered tomorrow? To make the judgment, instruments intervene, making it possible to appreciate, for example, the economic and natural performance rates of areas, as well as the weight of nuisances now and over several years of change.

The great value of being able to associate methods of locating future urbanizations and methods of evaluating spatial organizations is making possible a fairly objective judgment on decisions taken by public authorities and agents in the economic or social sphere.

As an example, a model that predicts the evolution of the actual fabric and location of future urbanizations in an agglomeration indicates that the density of the central area is going to decrease and that urbanization on the outskirts is going to increase greatly. Certain authorities are troubled by the threat that looms regarding use of mass transit in the central area and think that this change is for the worse. In this case, it is absolutely indispensable to determine the economic and natural performances of the different neighborhoods in the agglomeration today and tomorrow—not just globally, but also by socioprofessional category and by means of transportation. It is probable that in the entirety of the urbanized area one will observe a growth in economic and natural performance rates, but that certain socioprofessional categories will see their situation regress, especially for accessing the center. The problem will therefore be posed in terms of equity between socioprofessional categories, and a political choice will have to be made.

We can also use this approach to determine if spatial changes observed over the course of past years have had beneficial or nonbeneficial effects. Those in charge in the political or economic realm often ask me if the maps of economic and natural performance rates that were established for nine European countries for the year 2000 can be established by adopting 1990 or 1980 as the point of reference in order to appraise the effectiveness of decisions made in the past. These maps can indeed be established by adopting as support the geographic databases existing at the time or bases reconstructed by eliminating the large infrastructures completed in the interim, especially for the most remote date, and taking as reference data from INSEE or Eurostat at that time. But this rather extensive work has not been taken up thus far. No doubt we would see the strong increase in economic performance in the regions of Brittany and Pays de la Loire under the joint effects of urbanization and the connection of these urban areas by powerful transportation infrastructures, included especially in the road plan for Brittany. We could also evaluate whether natural performance rates have increased or not. Strong growth that would be evidenced in natural performances would go against certain recognized ideas.

Examples of urbanization projects, of wealth and well-being from a viewpoint of sustainable development

The new town of Marne-la-Vallée in the context of the master plan for Île-de-France

Are the planning principles that I have just described to be found in Marne-la-Vallée, the vast development project east of Paris? I am well acquainted with the site since I was director general of the New Town Public Development Authority (l'Etablissement Public d'Aménagement de la Ville Nouvelle) for 10 years. In particular, I developed the Cité Descartes and the district of Val d'Europe where EuroDisney is located. Often a significant difference exists between theory and reality.

As a matter of fact, Marne-la-Vallée's development principles were fortunate to be perfectly defined in the town planning and development master plan for Île-de-France drawn up by Paul Delouvrier in 1965. These planning principles relied on concepts very close to those I have just presented. Paul Delouvrier incorporated in the master plan itself comprehensive directions that bring together economic performance and natural performance, factors of economic growth and factors for preserving nature.

In the period that preceded the elaboration of this extensive master plan, Île-de-France existed under the regime of general urban development plans that had raised to the level of a principle the maintenance of urbanization in the Île-de-France region within a limited space. This rule had led to a situation where there was an extreme dearth of land on which to build and a real blocking of development in Île-de-France. Paul Delouvrier decided, following a thorough diagnostic examination, to let the Parisian agglomeration breathe and to give it every opportunity for successful development both at the economic level and that of environmental protection.

At the level of the entire agglomeration, Paul Delouvrier's master plan affirms the principle of urbanization poles destined to structure the outskirts of Île-de-France. This is how five new towns are born: Cergy-Pontoise, Saint-Quentin-en-Yvelines, Evry, Melun-Sénart, and Marne-la-Vallée. These new towns intend to host more than half the new inhabitants of Île-de-France, a goal that will indeed be achieved. The new towns are complemented by powerful urbanization hubs in the small crescent that bring together numerous state services, including the prefectures of Nanterre, Bobigny, and Créteil.

Between the urbanization hubs, large areas of protected natural spaces are defined comprising notably woodlands as well known as the forests of Rambouillet, Fontainebleau, Ferrières, and Saint-Germain, as well as many others. Bodies of water are destined to host leisure activities. The banks of the Seine and the Marne rivers are fitted for pedestrian use. Regional natural parks are also planned.

To serve the totality of this regional agglomeration, a very extensive network of regional mass transit has been designed: the RER. An equally extensive network of freeways and expressways is also designed featuring high performance radial roads and several bypasses. The RER serves primarily the large urbanization hubs, and the freeways and expressways serve less-dense urban areas and recreational areas.

As these principles of town planning are stated, we recognize the importance of urban hubs served by high-quality infrastructures as a source of economic energy and performance and the importance of protected natural spaces as a source of well-being.

Paul Delouvrier's master plan is a fine reference when it comes to town planning.

This master plan reached its limits during the 1980s and became the object of a complete rewrite in 1994. I had the privilege of carrying out the establishment and the editing of the new master plan in my role of prefect, regional director of public works, transportation, and spatial planning for Île-de-France between 1991 and 1997. Of course, I confirmed and reinforced the options of Paul Delouvrier's master plan by giving it new breathing spaces, since the spaces that had been deemed suitable for building in 1965 had been, for the most part, used up.

What does the master plan say about Marne-la-Vallée?

At the level of the agglomeration of Marne-la-Vallée, it takes up again the town planning principles adopted at the regional level: in a living area that covers a surface area of 14,000 hectares, that is, one and a half times the size of Paris proper, there is an alternation of dense urban hubs and protected natural areas. For example, there are the following:

Four urban hubs: Porte de Paris, with a prospect of 1 million square meters of offices; Val Maubuée, with the scientific and university hub of the Cité Descartes; Val de Bussy; and last, Val d'Europe, host site for the EuroDisney project.

Three green channels: Forest of Champs sur Marne, Ru-de-la-Brosse, and Plaine de Jossigny. Each channel comprises a small stream punctuated by numerous bodies of water—30 in all. Protected forests cover a surface area of 4,000 hectares.

In this way, Marne-la-Vallée respects in every detail the principles of a plan simultaneously bringing together concern for economic performance rates via dense hubs served by high-quality transportation infrastructures, as well as concern for respecting nature via forests, bodies of water, and protected natural spaces. I had no difficulty being inspired by these principles in developing Marne-la-Vallée, for I had shared them for many years. Today, these principles have become a reality.

Putting into operation the planning principles embodied in the master plan for Île-de-France

How was a project as ambitious as the master plan for Île-de-France able to take on concrete form, and is it still being made a reality? Including a town planning project in a master plan is one thing, making it a reality is another.

The new towns, and Marne-la-Vallée in particular, have benefited from solid development organizations and priority financing of large infrastructures that explain the success of such complex projects. The New Town Development Public Authority (actually, in Marne-la-Vallée there are now two authorities, since the establishment of an authority specifically for developing the fourth district, Val d'Europe) offers the legal possibility of establishing what are called "urban development zones."

The constituent parts of urban development zones include the development program for an entire neighborhood, and detail the goals for establishing housing, offices, public facilities, and green space management. They also describe the entire network of projects that make it possible to service all the pieces of land that support these programs. They mention the large infrastructures completed and financed by public authorities such as the RER, the freeways and expressways, the primary thoroughfares, or those financed by providers of public services such as water, sanitation, electricity, gas, telecommunications, or public facilities administered by local authorities such as grade schools, middle schools, high schools, sports and cultural facilities, bodies of water, and managed natural spaces.

The services works completed by the New Town Development Public Authority are paid for with receipts from the property developers who complete housing, offices, and commercial centers. After approval of the urban development zone by the Board of Directors composed of state representatives and elected officials, the Development Public Authority can proceed to land acquisitions (by expropriation order if necessary), carry out the services works, and resell the lots to property developers who bring the construction programs to completion. This method is extraordinarily effective. It makes it possible to transform into concrete reality urban visions that would not leave the starting gate otherwise. In Marne-la-Vallée, the Public Authority initiated 60 urban development zones, all the while respecting the town planning directives that give coherence and unity to brand-new neighborhoods and, beyond these neighborhoods, all of the new town.

Several significant facts marked the birth and development of Marne-la-Vallée.

First of all, the establishment of powerful urban development hubs on a site that at its beginning did not appear destined to receive such developments. Today, Porte de Paris comprises 600,000 square meters of offices, a commercial center of regional importance adjacent to a parking lot of 5,000 stalls and numerous hotels and restaurants.

A little further east, on the fringes of Val-Maubuée, the Cité Descartes is host to 20,000 students and brings together on one site the fourteenth university campus of Île-de-France and about 10 prestigious higher education institutes. In the heart of Val-Maubuée, a large commercial center attracts residents from north of the Seine-et-Marne department.

Val de Bussy, currently in the midst of its development, is a premier center for hotels.

Finally, in the east, Val d'Europe attracts 15 million visitors per year thanks to EuroDisney Park and the total of 8,000 hotel rooms associated with the area. The "La Vallée" commercial center contains within its 800 meters luxury boutiques that even attract Parisians.

Twenty years ago, all of these sites were void of any kind of urban development. The last shepherd in Marne-la-Vallée could be seen from the land on which the Cité Descartes now stands.

What is equally significant is the scope of the transportation infrastructures that have been established to serve these urban development hubs and to create conditions favorable to development there. Line A of the RER serves the four urban development hubs, almost always with two stations, sometimes three. The neighborhood of Val d'Europe has a bullet train (TGV) station set up on the link route that runs east of the Île-de-France region. Thirty-two bullet trains stop daily at Marne-la-Vallée. London is 2 hours and 30 minutes away; Brussels is 1 hour and 10 minutes away; Lyon is 1 hour and 55 minutes away; and Bordeaux is 3 hours away, soon to be 2. The bullet train station is connected to the terminal station of the RER's A line. How many days did I spend designing this station shared by RER and TGV that is the key to the success of Marne-la-Vallée, and more especially its Val d'Europe district! The creation of value linked to the opening of this interchange complex is considerable. It stimulates an exceptional economic dynamic in the entire area north of the Seine-et-Marne department. La Seine-et-Marne is the French department whose development rate has been the most rapid in recent years.

Freeways also have developed at a sustained pace, at least over the course of the first 20 years that the new town has been in existence: freeway A4 is a radial highway, and the Francilienne is a bypass.

Airports are close by. Roissy-Charles-de-Gaulle is 15 minutes away by TGV and 20 minutes by freeway. Orly is 30 minutes away by freeway.

Marne-la-Vallée is becoming a place of economic energy and performance. Business owners make no mistake about it. They are flocking to this location that is so well served.

Finally, efforts to safeguard and manage natural spaces are noteworthy. The Public Authority itself administers 4,000 hectares of forest. Leisure centers in Vaires and Torcy, managed by the Île-de-France region, welcome many residents. Thirty bodies of water make it possible to regulate the run-off from streamlets in Marne-la-Vallée. Their banks are places to stroll. Many residents of the new town engage in fishing. The banks of the Marne are in good repair. Everything is done to lessen the stress of daily activity. In fact, the new town does not harbor a significant rate of urban violence. From all appearances, the calming presence of nature plays a role in this satisfying equilibrium.

On the basis of this real-life example, it becomes clear that respect for a few principles of spatial organization, coupled with a coherent policy of public and private transportation, makes it possible to bring true satisfaction to the resident population without attacking nature.

Notes

1. We get: $t = e^{b\,(I)} = e^{b\,(se + sn - x - v)}$ where:

t = urbanization trend within the neighborhood studied

I = Interest attached to the neighborhood studied by candidates for an establishment

$S^e = U^e - C^e$ = net annual economic performance of the neighborhood studied

$S^n = U^n - C^n$ = net annual natural performance of the neighborhood studied

X = annual worth of negative impacts in the neighborhood studied

V = annual amortization of the servicing charge of the neighborhood studied

b = the weighting factor of the interest attached to the neighborhood studied by candidates for an establishment. This factor takes into account the fact that a portion of the expected benefit is destined to be returned to the owner of the land.

Part VIII

Courses of action

At the end of this long reflection on our living earth, the earth of people and the earth of living species with which we share our beautiful blue planet, is it possible to make recommendations and sketch out some courses of action? Yes, absolutely.

We will do so with a strong conviction: humans can still master their future and establish intelligent acts of cooperation with all branches of life on earth. There are still vast areas of progress to be made in both the economic and the environmental spheres. The one should not be set in opposition to the other. They must both be emphasized.

In this context, we will suggest four types of recommendations that address the following:
- Embedding in town planning documents a magic trio composed of "space, humans, and exchanges"
- Protecting natural species and reducing negative impacts
- Welcoming humans in their residential function and their production activity
- Supporting mobility

These recommendations should make it possible to open up prospects of durable growth with an attitude of respect for our environment.

Space, people, and exchanges

Secure the balance between natural spaces, urban hubs, and transportation networks

What are the founding principles as far as organizing the occupation of space is concerned?

Occupying space must respect a balance between the imperatives of creating wealth and economic development on the one hand, and well-being and quality of life on the other. The creation of wealth implies more and more relationships between human beings in order to enhance the value of their knowledge, their training, and their acquired experiences. Well-being and quality of life imply protection of natural spaces, maintenance of harmony with plants and animals, and reduction of negative impacts created by humans in their economic or recreational activities. In order to respect this general balance, the organization of an area must pay attention to developing a close harmony among three types of spaces:

- Natural spaces, whether they be water, forests, or agricultural. These are places where wild plants and animals can flourish and where humans can experience renewal.
- Built-up spaces that host humans in their residential functions or those of producing goods and services.
- Transportation networks, public or private, whose function is to connect these different spaces in order to make it possible for them to express their potential for inducing well-being and stability, as well as to create goods and services. Transportation networks can only be established if rights-of-way, generally of a public nature, are set aside for them. They represent a specific need for space, modest in volume, but essential in functionality. No life without exchanges.

This spatial organization must be located at the level of each living area, at the level of a country, or, yet again, at the level of a whole continent such as Europe. There is a superposition of organizations. A natural space can be mainly represented by urban parks within an agglomeration or by forests within a regional area. A fabric of buildings can comprise zones of activity in proximity, or powerful tertiary hubs hosting headquarters of businesses branching out to vast areas. A transportation network can be composed of urban thoroughfares at the level of an urbanized area or of bullet trains at the national level. Depending on the extent of the area considered, one or another of the components will stand out. But the whole functions synergistically. Humans can move from daily activities in proximity when using urban transit, to exceptional commercial activities when occasionally making use of airplanes or bullet trains, for example. The main point is to find at the level of the area observed—local, regional, or national—the three components of natural spaces, built-up spaces, and rights-of-way harmoniously established. The injuries that come from societal existence often arise from abandoning one of these components, for example, the lack of green spaces or the absence of transportation corresponding to demand. Natural spaces are rather meant to occupy fairly extensive areas, within which the requirements of wild plants and animals are expressed, along with the needs of humans in their recreational activities. Built-up spaces occupy more concentrated areas within which human production and service activities are organized. That is why this type of organization is defined as "multispatial and multihub."

Natural spaces play a very important role, including in the life of urbanized areas. A quality urban plan must put a priority on determining spaces to be left free of all urban development. That is how natural life will be preserved and harmony developed between human activities and those of all the species that live on our earth and give evidence of the prodigious variety of life forms. One will preserve in this way—in areas that are predominantly rural—agricultural space, forests, and vast expanses of water. On the outskirts of urbanized areas one will preserve local forests, regional parks, and leisure centers, and in strongly urbanized areas, green swaths composed of urban parks, squares, or simply greenery along urban avenues. The important point is to consider carefully the need for spaces free from any urban development; this is the basis of balanced urban planning.

Humans need proximity in order to exchange their know-how. Economic energy feeds on exchanges between humans—the relationships that their minds can establish with each other. Physical proximity favors this intense exchange of knowledge. For this reason, economic activities preferably develop within urban hubs offering a large diversity of abilities and professional training. However, there is a limit to the concentration, namely nuisances connected with excessive proximity. Areas of activity—notably tertiary activity—tolerate great job densities. By contrast, residential areas are more sensitive to the effects of proximity and tend to reduce their density in order to integrate into the immediate environment a little of these green spaces to which humans are particularly sensitive.

Transportation networks must therefore satisfy multiple needs. To serve urban hubs and connect them inside large agglomerations, efficient—that is, rapid and frequent—public transportation is necessary. When density falls in the medium or large "crescents" surrounding urban metropolises or, to be sure, in rural areas, nonguided transportation able to go easily from door to door reclaims ascendancy. We rediscover the place of private transportation. For service to natural areas and the recreational spaces they contain, private transportation is well adapted. We see that a natural complementarity exists between public transportation and private, the former being primarily oriented toward serving strongly urbanized areas, the latter toward less densely populated areas with wide spaces for relaxation. Harmony once again!

Plan ahead: the role of town planning documents

As soon as space is to be organized, it is necessary to plan ahead. This is the role of town planning documents—an irreplaceable role, even if some people view such plans as having excessive constraints.

In actuality, in any communal life, the game has rules that must be respected. We cannot drive without applying the rules of the road. If there were no traffic lights at a very busy intersection, the intersection would become blocked and no vehicle at all would be able to get through. This example shows clearly that rules make it possible to optimize individual behavior and lead to reasonable collective behavior.

It is the same in the sphere of organizing a living area. The first goal of a global town-planning document, and of the more detailed plans that ensue from it, is to locate those spaces that will not be built upon. It is a matter of defining a legal rule: prohibition.

Some people who covet, for example, protected wooded areas for building homes can believe that the rule opposes legitimate ambitions, namely, allowing inhabitants to benefit from a pleasant location. But if everyone builds residences in wooded spaces, it is clear that these spaces will lose their character of collective goodness open to all and available for wild plants and animals to flourish. The well-being of all residents in the agglomeration will suffer as a result; plant and animal life will suffer too; there will be a global decrease of satisfaction at the level of the human community and even more so at the level of all living species. Besides, it is when rules of prohibition do not exist—or do not yet exist in certain countries—that "predatory" behaviors emerge, blameworthy with regard to natural spaces.

The law is equally indispensable for protecting rights-of-way of transportation infrastructures making it possible to connect humans with each other and to secure access to natural spaces. It is necessary to anticipate needs, define coherent networks of infrastructures with prospects of population and employment, choose public or private means of transportation making it possible to ensure these requirements for exchanges, and reserve ground rights-of-way in order to set up the projects at the right moment. These quite strategic rights-of-way also serve as support for the majority of networks that take care of transporting community goods: water, energy, and information. Without reserving rights-of-way, there is no possibility of easily making transportation infrastructures a reality. Instead, there is a need to rely on cumbersome seizure by expropriation order and acquisition of expensive real property, with all the ensuing litany of frustrations and suffering associated with giving up existing inheritances. Except in very rare cases, this is surely not the solution to recommend.

For residential and activity functions, on the other hand, I believe excessive constraints ought not be imposed. If natural spaces and rights-of-way for infrastructures are clearly protected by law, humans should be able to flourish in constructible spaces generously sized according to their needs. For calculating the amount of floor space to set aside, it is necessary to take into account the obsolete buildings to be replaced, new buildings designed to satisfy the comfort needs of the existing population, and, finally, constructions to plan for future new populations. According to the density goals set for each part of the living area, it will be possible to determine the surface areas of agricultural or natural spaces that need to be turned over to construction. The purpose of town planning documents is to periodically adjust these spaces without, of course, encroaching on natural spaces protected for the long term, or on rights-of-way for transportation infrastructures and exchanges. In constructible spaces, rules of law define maximum densities not to be exceeded that give rise to floor occupation coefficients and ground occupation coefficients. In this way, the maximum height of buildings can be set. So, inner Paris is characterized by town planning consisting of buildings whose height is generally limited to a ground floor and six upper floors. That yields a landscape of great compositional sharpness. In New York, the absence of such a rule leads to the appearance of skyscrapers in central areas that are very well serviced. Economic energy there is intense. Note that in the midst of this area of highly concentrated construction, law protects a space free of all construction: Central Park. What's more, as it is, rights-of-way of transportation infrastructures, primarily urban avenues, are rigorously defined and protected in the form of a grid of roads and avenues.

These town planning rules may appear fairly complex. However, their complexity need not be exaggerated if emphasis is placed on the considerable advantages that they bring to the community of humans living in a given area and to all the plants and animals destined to live in close harmony with that community. In France, two types of spatial planning instruments are available: collective plans for spatial guidelines and local urban plans. The former have taken the place of old local master plans and the latter replace land use plans. The collective plans for spatial guidelines define the large-scale aspects of planning in a local living area, and the local urban plans demarcate the spaces destined to residential and activity functions, to natural spaces, and to infrastructures. The local urban plans also specify construction rules such as the floor occupation coefficients. Elaboration procedures for these documents are the responsibility of the local authorities. Municipalities are grouped together to work out collective plans for spatial guidelines. They establish and directly approve the local urban plans that must be compatible with collective plans.

The State reserves important prerogatives, for it is guarantor of the coherence of national spatial planning. The State is involved with elaboration procedures for setting up the collective plans for spatial guidelines, as well as local urban plans. It can, via decisions that are its right, impose projects of general benefit to local authorities. These authorities are obliged to place them in their local town planning documents. Examples of general benefit projects include TGV (high-speed train) routes, strategic freeways, and structural facilities. The State can also draw up spatial planning directives whose extent is generally regional and that serve as a global framework for collective plans for spatial guidelines. These directives are mainly drawn up in sensitive areas such as coastal or mountain areas or yet again in areas with a great deal of potential such as urban metropolises. France is renowned for the diversity of its natural landscapes, the extent and variety of its forests and, with rare exceptions, for the quality of its urban development. It owes this reputation largely to its tradition of town planning relying on spatial planning documents. I believe we have to be delighted at that!

Protecting natural spaces and reducing negative impacts

Protecting natural spaces by law: the example of the master plan for Île-de-France
What recommendations can be put forward for the protection and value enhancement of natural spaces?

At first, protection by law.

I am going to take the example of the Île-de-France region that is subject of the urbanization pressure of a metropolis of more than 10 million inhabitants in an area that represents hardly 2 percent of national space. Despite its relatively small surface area, the Île-de-France region includes almost 80 percent natural spaces. Starting from the outskirts, these natural spaces consist of a yellow-and-green crescent, a green belt, and a green layout.

The yellow-and-green crescent, beyond a radius of 30 kilometers around the center of Paris, is primarily rural. It is made up of large agricultural entities such as le Gâtinais Français, la Beauce, la Plaine de Versailles, le Vexin, la Plaine de France, la Brie, as well as large wooded areas such as Fontainebleau, Rambouillet, les Trois Forêts, and Sénart. It is necessary to preserve there the economic vitality of agriculture that represents, in 2 percent of the national area, more than 5 percent of the country's production in cereals, truck farming, horticulture, and arboriculture. The farms in Île-de-France are at the top of their class nationwide in size. It is also necessary to preserve the wealth of wooded areas and agricultural spaces with a high aesthetic value. Last, it is necessary to protect the numerous wetlands that comprise multiple natural areas of interest for their ecology, flora and fauna, the famous Natural Zones of Animal and Plant Ecological Interest (Zones Naturelles d'Intérêt Écologique, Floristique et Faunistique or ZNIEFF).

The green belt, situated between 10 and 30 kilometers from the heart of Paris, is in contact with the urban bounds and therefore subject to strong pressures that tend to destabilize it. It is composed of public forests; woods; urban parks; public and private holdings that are planted but enclosed; sports facilities such as race courses, golf courses, and leisure centers; as well as forts and canals to be restored. The objectives to be pursued are those of a green belt composed of places of relaxation for the inhabitants of the nearby metropolis and places for local agriculture or family gardens. It is necessary to constitute a real network of green spaces and lively, diversified leisure areas.

The green layout is located within a radius of about 10 kilometers of the center of Paris. It is established in the heart of the dense urban area. It is made up of woods like the Bois de Boulogne and the Bois de Vincennes, urban parks like Parc André Citroën or Parc de Bercy, squares and canal banks like those along the Canal Saint-Denis and the Canal de l'Ourcq, planted urban avenues, and pedestrian walkways. It is necessary to carefully protect these precious spaces accessible to inhabitants of the most densely populated area.

How can legal protection of these spaces be ensured, from large wooded or agricultural spaces on the outskirts all the way to nearby squares?

The primary protection for the totality of these spaces is their inscription in the Île-de-France master plan in the form of spaces not subject to construction. The same measure applies for local master plans and land use plans (now known as collective plans for spatial guidelines and local urban plans) that transpose to the local level the directives of the regional master plan. The Île-de-France master plan clearly protects natural spaces of more than 2 hectares in the central area, of more than 4 hectares in the lesser crescent, and of more than 6 hectares in the greater crescent.

Other measures must be adopted.

For the most noteworthy forests there is the classification of protected forest. This is the procedure that was applied—or is in the process of being applied—in the case of Fontainebleau, Rambouillet, and Sénart. For the entirety of the woods and forests of more than 100 hectares, the Île-de-France master plan introduces the rule of prohibition (apart from urban sites already constituted) for all construction less than 50 meters from the edge of a forest. This is an efficient protective measure. Another rule requires that any area of forest that is put to another purpose must be compensated for by the creation of another adjoining forest area at least equal in size.

For agricultural spaces with a high landscape value, the master plan requires that the development of villages take place slowly, in a way that respects the environment and that matches buildings already in existence. The outlines of the plateaus and hillsides must remain visible, meaning there is no construction allowed. After long public inquiries, the most noteworthy sites are the object of classification in the form of Regional Natural Parks, with appertaining specifications. The following are proposed for inclusion in this classification: la Haute Vallée de la Chevreuse, le Vexin, le Gâtinais, and les Boucles de la Marne (Marne River Bends). In the urbanized area, modification of landscapes is allowed only if it does not impact the continuity of the green belt or the green layout. What is more, the portion that is turned over to another use must be compensated for by creation of like spaces with at least equivalent dimensions integrated into the network of existing green spaces.

For ordinary agricultural spaces that contribute to developing the construction front, the master plan delimits the area of spaces that can be authorized for construction until the year 2015 and leaves it up to local communities to designate, within the framework of local master plans, the areas that will actually be authorized for construction. These represent, in the greater crescent, 60 percent of potential spaces defined at the regional level and 80 percent in the lesser crescent. The development of villages in all agricultural spaces must be done in a moderated way that respects the environment and is in keeping with existing buildings.

For watercourses and wetlands representing numerous natural areas of interest for their ecology, flora, and fauna, the master plan ensures their protection by classifying them as natural spaces unavailable for building.

Thus, legal rules for protecting natural spaces are relatively numerous and already very effective. Nonetheless, it is necessary to complement them with measures that actively value them in order to give full impact to the policy of consolidating natural spaces, especially in areas subject to strong construction pressures.

Enhancing the value of natural spaces through active development policies

Protection through the legal system is not enough. Active policies for enhancing the worth of natural spaces must also be carried out. What are these policies of value enhancement? Are they truly effective in face of the deteriorations frequently spoken of?

Policies of valorization are truly effective if they are carried out with sufficient financing.

For example, for wooded areas, public authorities can proceed to the acquisition of private properties. The Marne-la-Vallée New Town Public Development Authority acquired several thousand hectares of woods and forests to beef up the green channels between the four development areas of the new town. In those sections of Île-de-France that are losing industry, it would be desirable that local authorities take the initiative in creating totally new green spaces in order to change the environment of these neighborhoods, and to create conditions favorable to a development of tertiary activities. It is equally useful, in the case of forests open to the public, to set up public welcoming facilities.

In rural areas that have sites of high landscape value, it is important that human activity, namely agriculture, occur in close harmony with the environment. Therefore, it is necessary to avoid legal protection measures that clash with human activity. Farmers must have freedom to choose the kind of crops they want to grow as well as their growing practices, and they must be allowed to build new buildings with the proviso that they respect the qualities of the site and the environment.

Within the agglomeration, valuing the green layout rests on multiple initiatives: creation of new green spaces in partially abandoned areas; agreement with owners of private parks to open these parks to the public and thus to allow a continuity of walking opportunities between public and private spaces; creation of green areas on the coverings of large infra-structures such as the garden zone on the TGV Atlantic route; creation of neighborhood squares; planting of green spots along broad avenues, along canals, streams, or rivers. The object is to bring into existence a coherent network of green spaces that makes it possible for a person on foot to cover large distances while remaining in a natural milieu or one that comes close to being natural.

As far as agricultural spaces are concerned, it is necessary to see to it that cultivation can remain a durable activity and to adopt measures favorable to making this objective a reality such as valuing the intangible nature of agricultural spaces within recognized natural boundaries and limiting uses other than agricultural, for example, by authorizing only those golf courses not linked to construction projects or public facilities of an intermunicipal nature. New transportation infrastructures must not make it difficult to access food-processing industry going or coming. Villages must continue to be able to develop, all the while respecting the criteria of moderation, respect for the environment, and matching construction style.

As far as watercourses, islands, and wetlands are concerned, there can be many initiatives that are particularly effective in the medium- and long-term.

The banks of streams and rivers generally ought to be developed, while seeing to it that they retain their natural character. Goals include restoration of plantings adapted to the environment, reconstruction of long sweeps of green, and reasonable stabilization of banks in order to preserve ecological balance. Leisure activities along these watercourses must be carefully located and integrated with a light touch that avoids overly significant encroachments. In densely populated areas, management can be more "mineral." Rehabilitation of former watercourses that have been turned into concrete channels or placed under stone slabs can be an opportunity to give back an aquatic presence to neighborhoods that have none.

Islands exist in diverse situations. Some, in densely populated areas, are entirely built up, like l'Île Saint-Louis; others are occupied by former industrial sites that are now lying fallow, such as l'Île Seguin; others are occupied by developed urban parks, like l'Île Saint-German; still others have been left in a state of abandon and can sometimes become places of large-scale illegal dumping. It is desirable that local authorities take the initiative to develop abandoned islands, or ones lying fallow, into places for ecological, landscape, or recreational use.

Finally, wetlands will not be an object of development. They are destined to remain in a natural state in order to welcome the greatest possible variety of plants and animals. However, some areas, such as backwaters and wetlands connected to watercourses, could be organized to serve as fish breeding areas.

Areas that once mined underground natural resources must be the object of careful rehabilitation. These areas often present scars that spoil entire sites. They should be landscaped. When this landscaping is done, and when the mining is being carried out, the site can look quite presentable. Certain quarries along rivers give rise to areas that have to be preserved with extremely interesting ecology, fauna, and flora.

Initiatives regarding value enhancement of natural spaces can be quite numerous and varied and make it possible for nature to flourish, even in those areas subject to strong construction pressures.

Reducing negative impacts

What can be done about reducing the negative impacts that are the object of so many discussions?

Remember that negative impacts are, for the majority of cases, strongly on the decrease, even in an extremely large metropolis like Île-de-France. Too much weight ought not to be given to this factor in relation to other elements of human life such as the creation of wealth or the protection of natural spaces required by plants and animals in order to flourish. But it is not because the situation has improved or is currently getting better that efforts shall be given up. Quite the contrary. The goal is total quality, or at least optimal quality. A significant portion of the wealth produced must be spent on actions that are favorable to reducing negative impacts. Besides, preservation of quality natural spaces will facilitate achievement of this objective.

First of all, there has to be rational management of water resources: fertilizers and pesticides must be prevented from becoming diffuse pollutants in groundwater; protective perimeters must be placed around catchments; deep drilling sites that have been abandoned must be under permanent surveillance so that pollution does not enter deep aquifers necessary for supplying water should there be a case of general accidental pollution.

Second, water resources must be mobilized by building new flood barriers—for example, in the case of Île-de-France—that will make it possible to ensure satisfactory flow capacity at low water levels, and by using resources that have not yet been exploited, such as the water in the Oise, the Eure, and the Iton rivers.

Further, the dependability of water supplies in rural areas must be improved by pursuing the interconnection of water distribution networks to meet any failure of the main system; this is already ensured in the urbanized portion of the region.

Finally, wastewater must be purified. In an agglomeration like Île-de-France, the problem is far from resolved, since the unitary networks (those that simultaneously carry wastewater and rainwater) are often defective. Untreated wastewater often spills back when it rains; there is an insufficient number of purification plants; wastewater treatment too often targets only carbon products, not nitrogen products; and rainwater emissions, frequently polluted, do not get appropriate treatment.

To eliminate these fairly serious types of pollution or to lessen the consequences, wastewater must be better purified by constructing new plants and fitting them with treatment systems that take care of carbon, nitrogen, and phosphate pollutants. Separate networks must be established for wastewater and rainwater in new urban areas, and action must be taken to reduce nonauthorized wastewater contributions. Dependability must be ensured by constructing additional reservoirs. Discharge points from large treatment plants should be distributed all along the river to avoid concentrating pollutants. At the same time, it is necessary to establish a serious program for removing pollution from rainwater. Rainwaters deposited directly into rivers by spillways during storms carry away with them many pollutants that accumulate in mixed main sewers—"rainwater, wastewater" at low water level. Specialized purification facilities need to be placed at the main overflow points of rainwater spillways.

The effects of accidental pollution must be reduced. The least serious accidents occur almost every day. The most serious can happen several times a year, entailing closure of drinking water production facilities. A reduction of the effects of these accidental pollutions can be obtained by putting in place retaining systems, deploying mobile dams to hold back surface pollution and using pumps and storage. The responsibility comes back to local authorities to set up these different facilities with the support of the Water Agency, the Regional Council, and departmental councils.

It is necessary to reduce the effects of floods. Floods in Île-de-France threaten about one quarter of the municipalities. To lessen the consequences, the free flowing of water must be preserved by prohibiting constructions that encroach on the riverbeds and, above all, by preserving the floodplains upstream from the urbanized area. It is also necessary to pursue the construction of water regulation areas in the basins of the Marne and Yonne rivers. The current stretches of water are notoriously lacking, since they only permit storage of a little less that 1 billion cubic meters, although 10 billion cubic meters pass through Paris when the rivers crest. In flood-prone areas, it is necessary to respect construction laws outlined in the regulations for flood prevention plans.

In areas that are in the process of becoming urbanized, it is necessary to limit the rate of flow of small streams to the level observed in the natural state. Waterproofing significantly increases rates of flow. Constructing retention basins can prevent this effect, and they also have the advantage of making the site more pleasant. So in Marne-la-Vallée, 30 stretches of water provide for the technical function of regulating water flow and at the same time provide amenities.

The treatment of wastes constitutes a problem that is increasingly difficult to deal with. Île-de-France, for example, produces 5 million metric tons of household waste per year, or about half a metric ton per inhabitant per year, to which must be added 2.5 million metric tons of ordinary industrial waste that can be mixed with household refuse. The volume to be treated increases 1 percent per year. Incineration plants, composting plants, and supervised dumps are saturated. To confront this situation, it is recommended that waste be reduced at the source and that the number of incineration plants fitted with high-performance equipment to remove pollution be increased. According to the law, all supervised dumps are supposed to be eliminated. As a result, there is a considerable amount of work to be done in constructing new incineration plants.

For specialized industrial wastes coming from specific industrial sites, hospitals, and purification plants in the form of residual sludge, it is necessary to rely on specialized burial sites, of which two are set up in Île-de-France.

Dealing with noise constitutes a large challenge. A differentiation is usually made between airplane noise and noise from land transportation.

Achieving reasonable objectives for airplane noise can be effected by two means: noise reduction at the source and prohibition of construction in the most seriously affected areas around airports. Airplanes are continually improving in their noise emission performance. The oldest models are no longer permitted at Orly and Roissy. Noise exposure plans determine the perimeters within which construction is prohibited or strictly limited.

For land transportation, the main negative impacts arise from road traffic. Setting up acoustic barriers can provide protection; this has proved effective. In Île-de-France, 50 kilometers of freeways and expressways are currently going to be the object of such a treatment, and probably another 100 will be retrofitted 15 years from now. It is imperative that new infrastructures be conceived so that they have no negative impact. It is possible. Examples such as the Parisian beltway in the western section demonstrate that is the case.

Rail transportation is also a source of negative impacts, notably in central areas. Eliminating these harms means developing protection against noise in the same way as for freeways.

The list of actions to carry out in order to reduce negative impacts is not complete. Notably, the course of action for limiting the greenhouse effect will be addressed in the pages dedicated to supporting mobility.

We can see in the wake of this enumeration that negative impacts, although numerous, can be the object of effective treatments at a reasonable cost.

Accommodation of humans in their residential function and production activity

Delimiting spaces subject to construction and instituting a multihub organization
What can be recommended for the other aspect of occupying a living area, the aspect that falls to humans in their residential role, as well as in their economic, social, and cultural spheres?

In this case, it is necessary to promote a spatial organization that favors increasing economic energy that results from putting into communication the maximum number of human beings within a travel time that does not vary. In the absence of all constraint, we would be led to accept a central hub with extremely high density of the type observed in Manhattan. However, several constraints must be respected for simple environmental reasons: maximum density in residential areas, and proximity of natural spaces. The only solution, then, is to develop a multihub organization that complements the multispatial organization put in place to delimit protected natural spaces.

It will therefore be necessary to develop hubs of different sizes providing points to focus human activities. These hubs will only develop over time. They will all have a history and will be shaped by the sites in which they are inserted. The oldest ones, or those that will have benefited from the best service conditions, will in general also be the most powerful. But new hubs, well serviced, gradually will be able to catch up with older hubs now wedged in and, hence, benefiting from less favorable developmental conditions. The dynamic created by service conditions is going to play a decisive role in the flourishing of this multihub organization. All the same, legal rules are also useful for accomplishing this natural dynamic and giving its full development.

Here, too, I will take the example of Île-de-France, which is not a uniform agglomeration of more than 10 million inhabitants—far from it. It comprises a whole series of differentiated hubs, from the heart of Paris all the way to the hyphenated towns in the largest crescent on the periphery. Île-de-France is a miniature France with all the variety of its sites, cultures, and activities. What I am going to say about Île-de-France will be valid not only in large established metropolises that are gradually developing multihub organizations but also in all of France. In this case, it is necessary to take into account as exchange infrastructures the rapid means of transportation represented by TGVs and airlines. Multihub and multispatial organizations constitute nested systems where each level is characterized by the performance rates of the transportation systems that link them together: from the pedestrian in a neighborhood to the TGV bullet train and the airplane at the level of a country or a continent.

Île-de-France comprises at its center Paris with its 2 million inhabitants and 1.8 million jobs, a world capital cradling 2,000 years of history. At its immediate periphery are the development areas of the lesser crescent. Industrial sites that have fallen into disuse will become large tertiary hubs in the future. La Défense in the northwest is the best-known example. But in the northeast, the Saint-Denis Plain around the Stadium of France is soon going to become a fine tertiary point of reference. Boulogne-Billancourt in the southwest will take over with the establishment of the historical site of Seguin Island, center of the Renault manufacturing plants. In the southeast, at the confluence of the Seine and the Marne, a large hub of industrial and tertiary activity will develop in Seine-Amont.

At the boundary between the lesser and greater crescents, powerful centers exist that are destined to host international companies with a European scope: Roissy in the northeast with the largest airport in Europe, Massy-Saclay in the southwest with its research centers of worldwide reputation, Marne-la-Vallée/Porte de Paris in the east with its prestigious higher education institutes and its university in the Cité Descartes. In the west, it is La Défense that unites the functions of a development area in the lesser crescent and that of a European-scope center. Perhaps it will be necessary one day that Montesson plays this role.

Forming the structure of the greater crescent, new towns have been home for 30 years to most of the new population of Île-de-France. In the northwest, Cergy-Pontoise; in the southwest, Saint-Quentin-en-Yveline; in the southeast, Evry and Sénart; in the east–northeast, Marne-la-Vallée and especially the Marne-la-Vallée/Val d'Europe hub that has become the largest center of tourism and premier conference center of France.

Beyond that, we find the historical towns of Mantes in the west, Meaux in the northeast, and Melun in the southeast. The two latter ones named have cathedrals and strong traditions marked by the land of Seine et Marne.

Even further away are towns that are smaller but equally marked by history, providing connections with the Parisian Basin. There are famous towns such as Fontainebleau, Provins, Rambouillet, and Étampes.

It is obvious the extent to which Île-de-France is made up of a broad diversity of hubs, with their specific characteristics and profiles. But these hubs exist in close synergy based on the powerful transportation systems that connect them and that allow them to exchange know-how, services, and products on a daily basis.

How is the spatial development of this network of hubs and towns comprising Île-de-France organized? These hubs and towns are composed of an existing urban fabric, along with spaces to be opened to urbanization—essentially agricultural spaces about which decisions must be made to change their purpose. The need for space follows directly from the amount of new floor space that must be constructed. It is a matter of responding to three housing and business demands: replacing obsolete buildings, satisfying comfort requirements that translate into more square meters per inhabitant or per worker, and providing residential or business accommodations for the new inhabitants of the region. It will be necessary to house or relocate 2,775,000 persons over the next 25 years, that is, more than twice the number of inhabitants resulting from demographic growth alone; to build 1,325,000 lodgings over this period, representing 116 million square meters of residential floor space; and to accommodate or relocate 2,060,000 jobs, or almost three times the net job growth, taking on the construction of 99 million square meters of business floor space. The main problem that arises at this point is deciding the portion of floor space construction to carry out within the existing fabric due to renovation operations or occupation of formerly abandoned spaces, versus construction within new spaces opened to urbanization. The debate is difficult. It pits two groups against each other: supporters of a tightly-drawn city that places the most emphasis on creation of energy through know-how—the source of economic, social progress, and liveliness—and, on the other hand, supporters of a less dense city emphasizing a better balance between the growth of economic energy and spatial energy—the source of relaxation and well-being.

In Île-de-France, the choice has been made to entrust to the existing fabric the responsibility of making room for a number of square meters of floor space equivalent to what is needed to renew obsolete buildings and space out current inhabitants. This is an ambitious goal. It consists of constructing 126 million square meters of floor space in 25 years in the existing fabric and 90 million in new urbanization sites. Experience shows that construction rates in the existing fabric are lower than the goals established and that, in contrast, rates in new urbanization sites are higher, confirming the strong priority given by inhabitants to the development of spatial energy—more accessible space—whenever it is not incompatible with a significant and simultaneous development of economic energy—more exchanges of expertise. The construction of 90 million square meters of floor space in new urbanization sites implies the opening up to construction of 44,000 hectares of agricultural spaces.

Legal measures, even if they are not the only ones capable of guiding a process of urbanization (transportation and establishment of large public facilities play an even more decisive role) constitute a valuable tool in new urbanizations and are an indispensable condition for new construction.

These measures in the existing urban fabric must favor the development of structuring hubs. This is how the following guiding principles are established in Île-de-France: more dense urbanization around the hubs, improvement of public transit service, clarity of urban and architectural composition, harmony between new structures and existing ones, coherent linkage between the parts of the local thoroughfares, excellent insertion of new large-scale infrastructures of regional extent in order to avoid physical or visual ruptures, restructuring of green spaces to ensure continuity and coherence, and establishment of plant species along the banks of waterways.

When urbanization is designed to spread out over new sites, legal guidelines fix the perimeters open to such development. Île-de-France distinguishes spaces authorized for urbanization before the establishment of a new regional master plan (with very rare exceptions, these spaces remain open to urbanization) and new spaces intended to be open to urbanization. The regional master plan sets aside large tracts, leaving to the local master plans the responsibility for determining the final dimensions: up to 60 percent of the boundaries fixed at the regional level for the greater crescent and 80 percent for the lesser crescent.

In addition, defined principles include moderated development for market towns, villages, and isolated hamlets where no strict delimitation of spaces open to urbanization exists. This method makes it possible to give precise instructions to owners of agricultural lands regarding their right to cultivate their properties permanently. Authorizations to open spaces to urbanization are accompanied by development codes that include extensions of continued preference with the existing urban fabric, clear separations between distinct urban hubs, harmonious incorporation into the environment and respect for the quality of the landscapes, clear structuring of space in the case of entirely new projects, and minimum density to ensure the vitality of nearby businesses and facilities. Densities, urban forms, and urbanization limits have to be defined in the local town planning documents.

In this way, legal guidelines play a fairly important role in the development of living spaces and business activity. But these rules are primarily for supervision purposes. They cannot constitute the mainspring for the urbanization, which is largely dominated by transportation infrastructures and large-scale facilities. Moreover, they must not hinder urban development. They must, on the contrary, be placed in the service of this development; their policing function remains primarily that of protecting natural spaces.

Conducting an active policy in favor of quality housing for all

Housing French citizens now and in the future is a high-priority goal. A roof is the first goal of any new household.

Even if the government cannot guarantee everyone a roof over their heads, it is clear that it has to do as much as possible to ensure the possibility. Housing is the first policy of solidarity in a country. Moreover, this is the reason why housing policy remains a prerogative of the state rather than local authorities.

When the new master plan was established in Île-de-France, the number of lodgings constructed annually rose to 48,000, representing 4,200,000 square meters of floor space. Despite a desire to provide reasonable development of the region around the capital, the demand is actually higher: 53,000 per year over 25 years. This conclusion is reached by taking into account the three well-known needs: the need to renew the most run down buildings; the need to space out current inhabitants who want more and more comfort, that is, more square meters per inhabitant; and finally the need to house inhabitants in response to the demographic growth of the region.

It is estimated that over 25 years the need to renew the stock of existing homes stands at 8 percent, that is, an annual renewal rate of 0.3 percent. That means that the total number is supposed to be renewed at the rate of once every 300 years, which does not seem excessive at first glance. Even so, 8 percent of the current population means finding new housing for 825,000 inhabitants of Île-de-France.

It is also estimated that over 25 years the need to lessen the density of the current population (because of a demand for more living space per household as well, as a larger number of households with a constant population due to a reduction in their size) will drive a building program to house 810,000 residents, that is, a program approximately equivalent to the one for renewing all aging buildings, that is, 8 percent of the current total.

Finally, there will be a need to house the 1,140,000 persons who correspond to the net demographic growth of Île-de-France during this period, about 11 percent of the current population.

In total, the population in need of housing or relocation will equal 2,775,000 persons, corresponding to 26 percent of today's population. It will be necessary to construct 1,325,000 lodgings over 25 years, which represents about 116 million square meters of floor space. The only program to renew aging stock and to satisfy the need for less-dense living conditions will lead to housing 1,635,000 persons, or 15 percent of the current population.

These building programs can take place within the existing urban fabric or in new areas of urbanization. The rather ambitious choice of the new master plan is an attempt to stabilize occupation density in the current urban fabric, which is tending to drop. According to the master plan, about 1,705,000 inhabitants should be housed—or provided new housing—in the current urban fabric, leading to a very slight net gain in population (70,000 or less than 1 percent increase over 25 years). For their part, the new areas of urbanization on the outskirts should absorb 1,070,000 inhabitants, or 70,000 short of the entire region's demographic growth.

As far as the type of housing is concerned, there are extremely varied needs: students, young workers, households with children, older people, all having diverse resources at their disposal.

It is necessary to see to it that financing is adapted to all the cases in question, with socially subsidized housing, intermediate housing, and free housing.

The size of the units also needs to be varied, from student rooms and studio apartments for young couples to single-family dwellings in the greater crescent for families with children.

Finally, a good balance must be ensured between housing constructed for home ownership and for leasing agreements. In Île-de-France, residential mobility is high, which entails a need for a higher number of lease properties than in other large French cities.

Housing, which represents more than half the square meters of floor space constructed, is one of the key factors in urban development. But being more sensitive to problems stemming from the environment and from density than business construction, housing by itself will not be able to sustain a policy of developing large radiating hubs—something indispensable to the success of the area's multihub organization. Only guidelines relative to tertiary jobs and facilities are capable of doing so.

Promoting business construction

It is, therefore, by means of employment that a multihub development can be established.

But not just any kind of job. Industrial jobs—or those directed toward logistics—are space-intensive and bring but little polarization. On the other hand, tertiary jobs permit greater grouping of companies, and favor the effects of synergy between humans. In my opinion, this is what explains why work converts to tertiary activity. Industrial and logistics jobs are relying increasingly on robots. People, in this context, can concentrate on design and marketing activities that require intense exchanges between those with diverse training, complementary sensibilities, and multiple experiences—all advantages that appear in the setting up of closely proximate offices where contacts between individuals (and not just between computers) increase. Economic energy reigns supreme. As for commercial enterprises, commercial centers operate in a similar fashion, as we will see later.

If I refer to the example of Île-de-France, our France in miniature, the master plan forecasts that in 25 years 2,060,000 jobs will have to be housed or relocated. Just as for residential housing, relocation of existing jobs—whether because the premises have become decrepit or in pursuit of better work comforts—will constitute the larger portion of building to be done. In effect, it is estimated that in 25 years it will be necessary to relocate 645,000 jobs that are currently in aging buildings, and that will need to be welcomed into new premises. In addition, 705,000 other jobs will need to be moved in order to free up space in current locations lacking work comfort, especially when the increasing volume of computer and business devices is taken into account. As for new jobs, there will be 709,000 representing almost one-third of the total jobs to be housed during this period. It is clear the extent to which transformation of the industrial fabric and introduction of new work methods, more oriented toward office automation, are capable of changing the buildings that house activities within an area. That also shows the plasticity of what is built, which evolves more quickly than is thought. Over 25 years, in order to respond to the goals of renewal, loosening up and net growth of jobs, it will be necessary to construct 99 million square meters of floor space. Of that, 33.5 million will be for industrial activities; 28.5 for offices; and 37 million for shops, facilities, and services, or about 4 million square meters per year.

The existing body of construction is destined to host a building program slightly higher (by 30,000 jobs) than that meeting the needs of renewal (replacing obsolete buildings) and spacing out (using more space in dwelling units or working places for comfort reasons). Newly established sites are sized to house a number of jobs (all but 30,000 units) equivalent to the net growth, which represents, must it be repeated, just a little more than one-third of jobs to house or relocate. This strategy is ambitious. It implies a tremendous effort to renovate current buildings while the natural tendency is toward a slight but steady decrease in the density of current urban fabric. New urbanization spaces will host 42 million square meters of business space compared with an overall building program of 99 million envisioned for the entire region.

What types of premises will be built in order to house all these jobs?

First of all, let's not forget, the premises designated for agricultural use and those for food industry associated with them. Then there are industrial premises and those that are home to logistics activities. Industry has changed over the last few decades. Many branches of industry make use of increasingly sophisticated machines and processes that depend less and less on an unskilled workforce. We have entered an era in which engineers conceive the process and controllers handle its functioning. But there is room, even in regions where the workforce is costly, for sustained industrial activity. Logistical activities are in the midst of an evolution. They are an integral part of the production chain and constitute the main link in the flow strategy that reduces the stock of fabricated goods by optimizing ordering, manufacture, and delivery conditions. Logistical activities take on a great deal of importance in Île-de-France. Mainly established along large bypass freeways or at the convergence of road, rail, and air transportation, they revitalize entire areas where employment had dropped. They rely on extremely advanced computer and robotic technologies.

Tertiary activities constitute the leading edge of employment today. These activities have the possibility of consolidating within powerful hubs and are thus a significant factor in polarizing activities in sites served by public transit and quality road infrastructures. In Île-de-France, tertiary establishments will make it possible to give heavy operations their due, for example, the Seine rive gauche in Paris. Tertiary activities have supported the operation of la Défense, which is a fine example of success in the lesser crescent west of the capital. They introduce a good level of economic vitality in the development area of suburbs in the north, the Plaine-Saint-Denis. They will soon take over in Boulogne-Billancourt and in the future at the confluence of the Seine and the Marne rivers. They are also present in hubs such as Roissy, Marne-la-Vallée/Porte de Paris, and Massy-Saclay. Finally, they provide the structure for the densest areas of the new towns of Cergy-Pontoise, Saint-Quentin-en-Yveline, and Marne-la-Vallée. The broadening of this creation of economic energy phenomenon, of which conversion to tertiary activity is one of the manifestations, is favorable to the constitution of strongly structured urban hubs. But tertiary activities are not the only ones to act in this way. Trade, public facilities, and services have similar and often even more powerful effects.

Supporting the establishment of facilities, stores, and services

There is no real policy of creating urbanization hubs if there are no facilities, stores, or services.

Public facilities and stores are places of intense exchanges favoring synergy among residents and creating true urban cultures. Trade attracts trade. This is perfectly true. Through proximity, one can use a single trip to take care of an entire series of problems, buy diverse goods, and access numerous services. The range of choices is at work and the creation of value appears.

A whole series of public facilities play a central role. Once again in the case of Île-de-France that is serving as our example, there are universities and their associated research tools. The Sorbonne is the oldest university in Paris. It is a symbol and a place of intense vitality in the heart of the Quartier Latin. Other universities leave their imprint on the capital: Jussieu, Dauphine, and Assas are among the best known. The master plan includes the principle of establishing a university in each new town. The Cité Descartes in Marne-la-Vallée is an example. This site, still occupied by the Haute-Maison farm 15 years ago, is frequented by 20,000 students today. The Cité Descartes comprises the fourteenth university in Île-de-France and is also home to a number of prestigious higher education institutes, including the National School of Bridges and Roads (France's oldest civil engineering institution), the National School of Geographic Sciences, the School of Electronic and Electrotechnical Engineers, the Louis Lumière School (which trains film and television engineers and, more generally, all kinds of audio-visual technicians), and one of the largest architecture schools in Île-de-France. A second university campus is about to be established in the heart of Val d'Europe, the easternmost hub of the new town, an event that will bring legitimacy and distinction to the area.

Research activities are closely linked to university activities. Establishments in the Saclay plateau area are the best known. Teams with international reputations in the field of nuclear research are concentrated there. In order to consolidate the most recent urban developments, the master plan for Île-de-France has anticipated establishment of large research teams in the development areas of Plaine-Saint-Denis (physical sciences), and Seine-Amont (life sciences and health), and in each of the new towns. Thus, Cergy-Pontoise will specialize in economics; Saint-Quentin-en-Yvelines in environmental science simulation; and Marne-la-Vallée in civil engineering sciences, town planning, and image management. All the establishments will have positive effects on the urban hubs that host them. Actions of the same type will be carried out in the main agglomerations of France.

Commerce is at the heart of the city. All companies have developed their urban buildings around a mercantile center, a sales location for goods produced by the community. The department stores in the center of Paris are famous throughout the world. The diversity of goods that one can obtain in these stores is impressive. But Paris itself no longer holds the monopoly on influential commercial enterprises. Commercial centers, often impressive in their size, have been established in the nerve centers of the suburbs: les Quatre Temps at la Défense, and Créteil Soleil in Créteil to cite only two of the best-known examples. The master plan recommends the establishment of influential commercial centers in the hubs that are in the process of being developed, notably in Sénart and in Marne-la-Vallée/Val d'Europe. All we have to do is visit these centers that have become a reality—Carré Sénart in Sénart, and La Vallée in Val d'Europe—to realize their considerable impact. In Marne-la-Vallée/Val d'Europe, Parisians can, if they so desire, acquire all the most prestigious brands offered by shops in Paris itself.

Centers for exhibitions, conferences, and hotels are also drawing points. In Paris, every French person is acquainted with the Exhibition Center of Porte de Versailles. The Villepinte center near the Roissy hub is taking over without detracting in the least from the attractiveness of the Porte de Versailles. For conferences, the Porte Maillot center has a very high reputation. The Marne-la-Vallée/EuroDisney center, remarkably well served by freeways, RER, and TGV, is of equal—if not higher—reputation. The number of days of conferences held at Marne-la-Vallée is actually higher than at Porte Maillot. The ensemble of hotels hosts business people and tourists. Paris offers a first-class choice of hotel capacity, but sites such as EuroDisney now constitute very large centers with a total of nearly 10,000 room units. All these establishments create important centers and are anchoring points for lasting hubs of activity.

It is also necessary to mention significant cultural facilities. Paris offers cultural facilities that have worldwide renown. Versailles is equally well known the world over. Saint-Germain en Laye and Fontainebleau constitute major cultural hubs. La Défense, Saint-Denis, and Marne-la-Vallée will have to take their place as hubs from here on out.

Finally, important hospital facilities must be mentioned. Paris is, of course, well known for its historic hospitals. In order to better distribute the services offered and to create important centers, a network of regional hospitals is to be promoted, especially within new towns.

The list is certainly not complete. But from these few examples, it is possible to appreciate the favorable impact that can be exercised on urban organization by the totality of facilities, stores, and services—locales of vitality par excellence.

Supporting mobility

Reserving rights-of-way for transportation infrastructures: foresight and coherence

What recommendations are to be made in the sphere of transportation and the exchanges that play such a crucial role?

First of all, do not impinge on mobility, this priceless good. Ensure a high level of mobility for everyone because curtailing mobility means leveling off, and even reducing, the range of travel in a transport time that remains invariable. Curtailing mobility leads to limiting the daily living area within which everyone can find a job corresponding to one's training, a purchase or service corresponding to one's expectations, or a natural space that allows relaxation and a sense of well-being. In fact, it is the attack on the creation of value allowed by a rise in meaningful choices, when these choices are permitted to flourish. In the final analysis, curtailment threatens employment. Limiting mobility creates perverse effects that have a negative impact on the community's economic and social life. Some officials believe that curtailing mobility can actually reduce negative impacts. This is not the case. Legitimate but unmet needs for a range of economic, social, or recreational destinations choices are then expressed in the form of motorized trips making use of ill-adapted traditional roadways. As a result, negative impacts are created on a scale much greater that those that would have resulted from satisfying those legitimate needs through well-integrated modern infrastructures. In reality, we must become part of a virtuous circle:

- Rigorously protect natural spaces by law, while permitting a great liberty of movement within spaces that can be urbanized. This will create fruitful contacts and value through exchange of expertise.
- Set aside a significant portion of the creation of value to design and create infrastructures that are of optimal—if not total—quality. This approach leads to satisfying travel needs that are expressed annually by additional kilometers covered, executed in constant time, that is, no increase in effort.

Taking the example of Île-de-France, the master plan envisions, over a period of 25 years stretching from 1990 to 2015, an increase of 55 percent in the kilometers covered by motorized means. This increase results from the coming together of three phenomena: a decrease in trips by foot in favor of motorized trips on the order of 0.5 percent per year (+13 percent in 25 years), a decrease explained by the fact that motorized trips offer a better range of choices than walking; increase in the range of motorized trips on the order of a little less than 1 percent per year (+22 percent over 25 years) resulting from improved performance of the transportation system in terms of travel speed; lastly, an increase of 0.8 percent per year (+20 percent in 25 years) in the number of trips and the kilometers covered associated with the arrival of a new population that will itself benefit from the carry-over coming from walking and improvement in trip ranges. It is claimed that 35 percent of the growth expected in kilometers covered (13 percent from transferring from foot travel and 22 percent from increase in travel ranges) is due to improvements in services rendered to the existing population, and 20 percent is due to services rendered to the new population. Not satisfying 22 percent of the needs linked to the opening up of accessible areas in a time that does not vary would come back to leveling off the economic growth of the region and make job conditions even more precarious.

Studies also show a leveling off of trips within Paris. Actually it is a slight reduction due to a slow but constant decrease in population and jobs, a moderate increase in kilometers covered on radial roads linked to a growth in ranges, and a very strong growth in trips from crescent to crescent, areas in which the three factors that cause an increase in kilometers covered come together (carryovers from walking, rise in travel ranges, and net increase in population).

On those bases, the infrastructures that make it possible to satisfy the needs in the long-term must be defined. Two criteria must prevail in this design effort: foresight and coherence. Foresight implies designing large-scale infrastructures in order to satisfy long-term requirements with a view to developing mobility, intended to create durable value and to sustain employment. Coherence implies avoiding redundancies of function, and thus selecting the infrastructures that make the most sense.

In broad strokes, what are these infrastructures that make the most sense? They are made up of two networks of complementary infrastructures: a network of freeways and expressways and a network of public transit. The first is primarily focused on travel in areas of medium to low density. The second deals with travel in densely populated areas, serving urban hubs in particular. In other words, freeways and expressways provide basic travel in all parts of the regional area, with limitations in dense or very dense areas. For its part, public transit complements these basic trips, particularly during rush hour, with effective services in areas of heavy or extremely heavy density. The two systems of transportation are thus perfectly complementary.

The network of roadways comprises three levels of infrastructures: one level consisting of powerful radial and circular freeways; a complementary level consisting of expressways that are not quite as wide; and, finally, a network of urban avenues and boulevards that structure the neighborhoods and can become, if well cared for, focal points for urbanization. The public transportation network also consists of three levels of infrastructures: one level contains RER (Réseau Express Régional), with the rail gauge of SNCF (Société des Chemins de Fer Français) long-distance lines; subway routes whose rail gauge is narrower; and, finally, trams and bus routes in their own lanes, traveling along the avenues and boulevards of the highway network.

All these infrastructures need to be protected by law. Roadway and public transportation infrastructures, useful in the long-term, even in the very long-term, are included in the master plan, by virtue of the principle of foresight. Inclusion in the master plan implies preservation of the linking function rather than the specific layout itself. It comes back to the local town planning documents to specify the layout and to reserve rights-of-way for the routing. This policy of reserving rights-of-way for large roadway and public transportation infrastructures constitutes a major act of town planning, since it makes possible ensuring the completion, at reasonable costs, of large-scale projects that shape the region. It is a guarantee of the will of public authorities to offer the region a good level of mobility over the short-, medium-, and long-term. Even then, it remains necessary that the will to bring these projects to completion be expressed by setting up a schedule that truly reflects the stated objectives.

Supporting the completion of roadway infrastructures that reflect optimal quality

Including the completion of roadway infrastructures among the first recommendations relative to the world of mobility may appear surprising at first in light of the recurrent criticisms leveled against this means of transportation. Actually, it is far from my intention to provoke a controversy of any kind or to defend a priori statements. I am simply attempting to remain consistent with the observations that have been carried out and the analyses that proceed from them. I would like the reader to be entirely convinced of the detachment with which I regard the ideas I am discussing. I want to be able to advance that reflection, quite objectively. Analysis of the situation leads to considering roadway infrastructures as the transportation system best adapted to serving rural areas and lightly populated residential areas on the outskirts of agglomerations. Now, these spaces cover most of the country. Such infrastructures therefore support residents' travel in the large majority of French municipalities, at least those that do not have a dense urbanization. As a result of their universal nature, these infrastructures render a great service to the large majority of our country's inhabitants. They constitute basic transportation that is well adapted to low-density areas, and gradually reach their limits in living areas of growing density. These infrastructures must be allowed to express their qualities, with the understanding, of course, that an irreproachable design and execution will limit as much as possible the negative impacts they can incur.

Some people in charge battle against roadway infrastructures, especially in urban environments; this is one of their flagship actions. They very often gain the support of area residents who fear that such infrastructures will bring with them extremely negative impacts. They base their arguments on the fact that, according to them, private transportation occupies a great deal of room, emits many pollutants, and constitutes a real intrusion into traditional urban neighborhoods that were not designed for cars. They point out that in urban environments completed road projects are almost always saturated when they are placed in service, which means that their usefulness is hardly proved. They recommend the massive promotion of public transit hoping thereby to stabilize automobile transportation and gain control over the negative impacts created.

To be sure, I am favorable to public transportation when their promotion is economically and ecologically justified. But I cannot turn away from a means of transportation that brings excellent service inside living areas of medium or low density, places where it cannot be replaced, as well as inside high-density living areas where its services and those of public transportation are totally complementary. The recurrent questions must always be kept in mind: What is the purpose of the trip? What does it contribute to me in terms of creation of value, usefulness, and increase in economic energy and spatial energy? Some think that we can penalize a means of transportation without there being anything but positive consequences for the community as far as the environment is concerned. That is not quite the case. If we severely penalize a means of transportation, we destroy a significant portion of economic and spatial value that this means of transportation contributes to the community. The consequences can be severe in terms of economic vitality and employment, for example. Now, remember that, in a transportation system serving a community of residents and workers, the creation of value linked to the possibility of reaching numerous economic and natural destinations is worth 100 when the travel generalized cost (valorization of time and money) for reaching these destinations is worth 33 and when travel negative impacts of all kinds are worth 3. In other words, it means that, when somebody travels, time and money expenditures reach only 33 percent of the creation of value he gets at his destination and the negative impacts of his travel reach still less: 3 percent of that creation of value.

We can't spurn the term 100 without taking great risks in the economic sphere and in that of well-being.

In order to understand what is taking place, perhaps it is necessary to recall, once again, the synthetic formulation of economic energy, $d.V^2$, that brings together human occupation density in a living area and travel speed within this area, and the synthetic formulation of spatial energy, $s.V^2$, that brings together the occupation density of natural spaces and this same travel speed. At every moment, residents are making value judgments between economic energy and spatial energy, between financial gain and personal renewal.

Nowadays, many urbanized living areas, including Île-de-France, have moderate occupation densities, in the order of 10 workers per hectare, while a historic site like Paris has a density that is 20 times higher: 200 workers per hectare. Natural spaces, bodies of water, everything that makes for pleasant surroundings in a medium- or low-density urbanization, are present in large numbers in these new urban living areas. Spatial energy is important there. In order that economic energy be equivalent to that observed in very high-density areas, it is necessary that travel speed door to door be much higher than in these densely populated urban areas. Only transportation that calls upon nonguided systems, that is, private transportation, makes it possible to achieve such a result. In Marne-la-Vallée, as I already pointed out, average travel speed, door to door, by car is four times higher than a trip made by subway in downtown Paris, and the living area covered in a given time is 16 times higher. Even if the density of jobs is 20 times lower, economic energy is consequently at a level barely more moderate than in Paris. The level of economic energy afforded by surface public transportation in Marne-la-Vallée outside the sphere of influence of the RER (which unfortunately can only satisfy a part of the population) is clearly a less favorable option because of the technical difficulty of picking up many users in an area that is only moderately populated. I therefore see absolutely no objective reason to deprive myself of the service rendered by private transportation in areas of light to moderate density, except to contradict the in-depth analyses that I have undertaken. What's more, the behavior of users testifies to their belief in this conclusion. Many white-collar workers, technicians, workers, and young people daily thank their community for the possibility of using their vehicle to go to work, take care of purchases, or relax in these medium-density areas.

We have to rid ourselves of these false arguments that bring about perverse effects that sometimes have severe consequences. For example, one of the perverse effects of refusing to complete infrastructures adapted to the transportation needs of individuals is that traditional streets and avenues not designed to deal with such traffic flows are overburdened in ways that are unacceptable. Negative impacts of noise, pollution, and danger become more serious, whereas the original intent was to reduce them. In reality, in low-density neighborhoods, private transportation carries over very little to public transit because the place of residence or of work of the car user practically makes it impossible for him to give up this means of transportation, unless he accepts a considerable reduction in the living area that can be accessed in a given travel time and a loss of creation of value and well-being.

I believe that in these conditions it is infinitely preferable to provide these neighborhoods with functional infrastructures destined to offer quality service to those who do not currently have other means of travel and will not have such in the future. It is necessary to complete these infrastructures with all the quality of integration desired, without dividing effects and ill consequences of noise, which is totally possible, and equip the streets and avenues thus freed with an eye to urban integration. It is a matter of doing a clean-up job. Everyone stands to gain. Car drivers see improvement in the creation of value of which they are both authors and beneficiaries in low-density areas. Area residents along streets and avenues see the negative impacts, of which they are victims, drop significantly.

The utility of the new infrastructure appears clearly as much from the viewpoint of creation of wealth as from the reduction of negative impacts. In the traditional approach, *not* taking in consideration the creation of value, in invariable travel time, when travel speed increases at the moment a new road opens, leaves out an essential piece of data from the argument. That leads to expectations of a transfer toward public transportation that actually remains marginal, and of a reduction in negative impacts on streets and avenues that does not jibe with the facts. I sincerely believe that by constructing large infrastructures that are totally integrated, respond to the needs of users, do not contribute negative impacts, include corresponding fitting out of streets and avenues, afford people who do not drive but who live or work in areas of low density efficient transportation on demand, and ensure promotion of efficient public transportation in high-density areas, we will be on the path to a real improvement in the environment while, at the same time, creating value.

If I look at the example of Île-de-France, I note that the master plan anticipates a coherent network of roadway infrastructures functioning in perfect harmony with the public transportation network. The roadway infrastructures are primarily oriented toward taking care of bypass traffic, without forgetting important radial roads, while public transportation is primarily oriented toward radial travel, without forgetting to gradually include bypass travel. Three levels of service are anticipated: very large freeways, expressways that are not quite wide, and streets and avenues.

In the first category, there are two circular freeways that complete the Parisian beltway and that carry every day the same number of people as route A of the RER: A86 freeway in the lesser and greater crescents, and the Francilienne freeway in the greater crescent (that should need widening here and now). There are also about ten large radial freeways that are connected to these circular ones and to the Parisian beltway. One of these radial freeways is still to be completed. Most of them need widening.

In the second category, there are intermediate expressways such as Parisis Boulevard that connects municipalities in the north, and the connector A6 RN6 in the south. These expressways have an essential role in managing traffic flow in their respective areas.

Finally, the network of streets and avenues is made up of traditional national routes, department highways, and large municipal thoroughfares. These roads are destined to be landscaped and to welcome pedestrians, cyclists, and local public transportation. All the large infrastructures must be completed within norms of total quality, particularly as far as noise is concerned.

The freeways and the expressways of Île-de-France and the thoroughfares connected with them will carry two-thirds of the travel growth anticipated in the region over the course of the next 25 years, whether or not all the networks included in the master plan are completed. If the projects completed are fewer than the needs to be satisfied, it is the local road system that will bear the difference and negative impacts will increase. Overflow to public transportation will remain minimal.

If we compare the annual creation of economic and ergonomic value resulting from putting these projects into service with their cost, average rates are on the order of 40 percent. The return on investment comes in under three years. This testifies to the worth of such projects at the economic level and at the environmental level. This explains why they cannot just be kept on the drawing board for too long.

Giving the streets and avenues back to the town

What is to be made of the urban rehabilitation of streets and avenues?

The infrastructures that serve a living area have no other purpose than to make a harmonious communal life possible, with the opportunity of creating economic and social value and to experience renewal through contact with protected nature. Communal life is expressed in motorized exchanges. It is also expressed via exchanges in proximity, resting to a large extent on trips on foot. Now, the principal streets and avenues today are the locus of usage conflicts that make life in the neighborhood difficult. Motorized traffic that uses these roadways because there are no proper infrastructures severely disturbs local life. If large-scale regional thoroughfares are completed, it will be necessary to immediately adjust the use of these freed streets and avenues and give them the character of local thoroughfares that ensure traditional service functions to a neighborhood. That is when the coherence of the action becomes apparent.

I recommend that, each time a large transportation infrastructure is completed, we should anticipate a simultaneous rehabilitation of the principal streets and avenues affected by this infrastructure. A significant portion of the redevelopment budget should even be included in the original estimates of the project. That might represent about 10 percent of the cost.

An avenue that is rehabilitated within an urban framework must respect some simple principles. For example, the portion of the right-of-way expended on pavement open to motorized traffic ought not exceed one-third. Two-thirds will hence be spent on verges that will consist of trees lining the road, finished sidewalks, and if necessary, bicycle paths. If public transportation routes are projected for the area, a specific study will be conducted in order to carefully locate the lanes for it. Public transportation lanes will not become an obstacle but rather an integral part of the urban structure.

Traditionally, national highways have rights-of-way of 30 meters that allow the design of verges 10 meters wide. Such dimensions make it possible to plan for quality landscaping as well as accommodating pedestrians and cyclists.

Ambitious projects for environmental rehabilitation have been designed in Île-de-France. A project recognized for its quality is the rehabilitation of national highway 86 in Seine-Saint-Denis. When the northern part of A86 freeway was completed, national highway 86 was entirely remodeled. A tramway was created in the central part, plantings were done and bicycle-friendly adjustments put in place. This example perfectly illustrates what can be contributed by the insertion of a well-integrated large-scale freeway project (since this one is mostly concealed by coverings) when its completion is linked with urban rehabilitation of the original national highway.

Other examples that could be cited are freeway coverings like the one on the A1 in the department of Seine-Saint-Denis between Porte de la Chapelle and the Stadium of France, or the one on l'avenue de Neuilly where the A14 begins. In the first case, the landscaped and rehabilitated covering makes an urban look possible that the freeway in its initial design did not allow. In the second case, local life, terribly disturbed by the intense traffic flow on the avenue, is able to be restored.

Other projects have not seen the light of day due to the fact that the relieving of congested freeways has not been completed.

More examples that can be mentioned are national route 16 and national route 1 whose rehabilitations are linked with the completion of A16 freeway. Rehabilitation is composed of quality plantings, bicycle paths, and—in the central part—a bus on its one lanes and then a tramway. A final example is national highway 184 whose rehabilitation is linked with the placing in service of Francilienne West freeway between Cergy-Pontoise and Orgeval.

All of these rehabilitations, completed or projected, are perfect illustrations of the goal of transportation infrastructures: to create exchanges, an urban fabric, and amicable social relations.

Implementing a toll in built-up areas for completion of quality roadway infrastructures and urban rehabilitation of streets and avenues

We have just seen that roadway infrastructures are not to be underestimated. Without being truly in competition with public transportation, they bring, in areas of low or medium density, possibilities for exchanges that other means of transportation can scarcely offer.

What's more, research on spatial comfort leads to a reasonable but steady loosening of urbanized areas both in France and in other countries. Historical centers see their population and their jobs leveling off, even decreasing. Population is henceforth located in the middle or greater crescent of urban agglomerations. And it is in these areas that private transportation finds its greatest pertinence.

Of course, a whole range of inhabitants without motorized transportation ought not to be excluded from efficient transportation. For that reason, in areas of low and medium density, it is necessary to design flexible, efficient public transportation on demand, so that everyone can benefit from quality mobility. I will come back to this point later.

It is also necessary to promote on the outskirts dense urban hubs, generators of economic energy and performance in terms of creation of wealth, social life, and access to diversified services. Within these dense hubs—and between them—efficient public transportation must find a place.

It remains nonetheless true that requirements for private travel remain very high in the intermediate—and greater—urban crescents. For example, in Île-de-France over the next 20 years, two-thirds of new trips will be completed by private transportation and one-third by public transportation. It is therefore necessary to invest in total quality roadway infrastructures in order to sustain economic and natural development of the living areas and to combat negative impacts incurred by traffic using traditional thoroughfares unsuited to its volume. These infrastructures are made up of new circular freeways or expressways connecting radial ones. They also include the renovation of infrastructures already completed and insufficiently integrated, with establishment of generous sound protection. Lastly, they comprise rehabilitation of local thoroughfares freed to give them back the urban characteristics that have too often disappeared.

How is all of this to be financed?

In order to be concrete, I am going to use the example of Île-de-France. Estimates will be expressed in terms of 2005 euros, even if they apply to earlier references, in particular 1995, that was supposed to see the start of the project (a period of 15 to 20 years would be anticipated if the decision to complete the project would be taken). Freeway investments to be made over the period of implementation of the new master plan (1990 to 2015), that is, over the course of 25 years, represent 26 billion euros, including 19 billion for new infrastructures and 7 billion for enlargements of freeways currently in service. In addition, another 2.2 billion euros must be included for repairing existing freeways and expressways and environmental improvements of these infrastructures, including a vast soundproofing program. Lastly, urban rehabilitation of traditional thoroughfares implies an investment on the order of 1.9 billion euros. To conclude, 0.7 billion euros are projected for repurchase of very old concessions so there can be a coherent toll-free network. In total, the investment program stands at 30.8 billion euros. Now, at the rate observed in 1995, increased by 1 percent per year, and taking account of financing already committed for 1990 to 1995, public authorities have already invested—or are about to invest—16.1 billion euros over the period from 1990–2015. The amount is 14.8 billion euros short of what is required. Moreover, if we consider costs for maintenance and exploitation, these are expected to increase from 3.2 billion euros to 4.1 billion, meaning an additional financing of 0.8 billion, bringing to 15.6 billion the unmet amount over the period.

This amount can, at first glance, seem large. In fact, compared with the number of vehicles in circulation, it is fairly modest. The total of automobiles in Île-de-France is, in effect, 4.5 million for the year 1995, to which it is necessary to add 780,000 commercial vehicles, 615,000 utility vehicles weighing less than 3.5 metric tons, and 42,000 trucks weighing more than 3.5 metric tons. In fact, 15.6 billion euros could be raised in 20 years by providing an annual contribution of 110 euros per automobile or commercial vehicle in 1995, 220 euros per light utility vehicle, and finally 440 euros per truck.

This contribution is expected to increase by 2 percent per year in constant euros, that is, at the same rate as the GDP, in the course of the next 20 years. That represents in 2015 (still in 2005 euros) 165 euros for a car and a commercial vehicle, 330 euros for a light utility vehicle, and 585 euros for a truck.

For a car, an annual investment of 110 euros in 1995 represents 2.5 percent of the amount spent annually on operating and amortizing of this vehicle. A simple insurance policy represents on average of 640 euros per year. Supplementary resources to mobilize in order to satisfy the infrastructure needs appear relatively modest, which greatly reduces the accuracy of arguments put forward by those who point to the high costs of roadway infrastructures in order to recommend decreasing investment in them.

The solution that seems the most natural and acceptable to users for mobilizing such a resource is to institute an annual, monthly, or weekly subscription card giving access to the current or future urban freeway network (this card could be named the Emerald Card in the same vein as the Orange Card for public transportation). As far as the current network is concerned, the card would allow access to additional lanes resulting from the network enlargement projects (clearly indicated by special markings) while lanes already in service would continue to be accessible to all. The financial elements relative to this type of subscription can thus be summarized, remembering that the study carried out in 1995 bears on the period from 1995-2015. At the beginning of the period, in 1995, the subscription amount is on average 110 euros per year for a user of Île-de-France. This subscription can be modulated depending on the engine rating of the vehicle, which introduces an objective criterion for equity. Users not from Île-de-France are charged a toll of 3 euros at the inter-urban freeway tollbooths, established on the boundary of the Île-de-France; this amount allows them free access to Île-de-France for a week.

Moreover, it seems judicious to have this type of subscription handled by the employer when the vehicle is used to come to work, in the same way that half of the cost of the Orange Card for users of public transportation is collected (550 euros of the 1,100 euros). Indeed, the contribution of these new infrastructures has a rapid effect on the economic performance rates of the areas in question. Bearing in mind the high economic efficiency of this type of investment (return on investment in three years), the 110 euros—invested annually—create, at the end of three years, 110 euros of additional wealth per year. At the end of 10 years, it is 365 euros, and at the end of 20 years, 730 euros—that is, an average of 365 euros per year over a reference period of 20 years against 110 euros per year in outlay. The business enterprise that has the possibility to capture 40 percent of this produced wealth, as well as its salaried employees (in net value), or 150 euros, stands to gain.

Public authorities (public communities and social partners) also stand to gain since of the 365 euros of value created annually registered over a period of 20 years, they recoup 220 euros in the form of social contributions and taxes, including 55 euros benefiting the State. Thus, this action is particularly virtuous.

For its implementation, it would probably be necessary to entrust the concession of such a project to an organization with a council comprised of State representatives, and representatives from the region, departments, and affected local authorities. Clerks who already handle parking vouchers could issue subscription tolls.

If we wanted to make the process really sophisticated, drivers could be supplied with an on-board device like "Fast Track," akin to those on vehicles that today do not want to stop at tollbooths and which receive a personalized bill on a monthly basis. Another possibility is a device integrating GPS (to become Galileo), making it possible to ascertain how many miles have been covered on toll roads and, in this way, making it possible to issue a monthly bill.

Financing quality road and freeway infrastructures in urban environments, improving existing infrastructures especially while eliminating noise pollution, participating in rehabilitation of streets and avenues freed up of useless traffic and establishing bicycle paths, local public transportation, and plantings—all of this is perfectly possible in satisfactory economic conditions, by means of a concession, without relying on taxation, which constitutes a decisive advantage when the public deficit must be held in check.

And everyone would benefit: the community, business enterprises, users, and local residents.

Promoting public transportation on demand on the outskirts of urbanized areas in order to provide mobility for residents without vehicles

Attention must be paid to persons in low-density areas who do not have vehicles. Leaving them without means of transportation is tantamount to excluding them from economic, social, and recreational life. How can we deal with this problem?

This is a difficult subject that must be approached with determination. In low-density areas traditional public transportation finds its limitations. Regular routes serve only those homes within walking distance of the stations where the buses stop. When density is low, the number of users involved is modest and the use of the route suffers from that fact. During off-peak hours, buses are often empty. The financial balance of the routes is difficult to maintain and the service rendered to residents is mediocre.

The only solution is to call upon minibuses that are not limited to following predetermined routes, and are able to make detours to pick up a resident. The resident calls the minibus from a landline or mobile phone and indicates where he or she is located. A call center system optimizes the route the vehicle takes in order to serve residents as quickly as possible. The appearance on the market of mobile telephones equipped with GPS should make possible improved efficiency of the service. In effect, the minibus driver will know exactly where the caller is located and will be able to transmit this information automatically to the call center. The call center will then optimize the itinerary of the vehicle. The service offered by such a system is better than that offered by regular routes. The number of persons who can be served in an hour of travel is much higher than in the case of regular routes.

Experiments like that conducted in Saint-Quentin-en-Yvelines testify to the worth of the approach.

In order to encourage this type of solution, it would be necessary, for example, to add to the Emerald Card project, if it should come to fruition, an additional possibility for minibus service in low and medium density areas. A fixed subsidy could be attributed to the company entrusted with providing such an on-demand transportation service. On first reflection, there could be an increase in the cost of the Emerald Card on the order of 27.50 euros per year, which would bring the yearly subscription rate up to 137.50 euros.

In areas of average density, public transportation service becomes much more efficient and must be encouraged, especially when rehabilitations are being made to streets and avenues that are being freed up of superfluous traffic in the wake of completing new infrastructures.

In the case of Île-de-France, for example, a bypass of surface public transportation is recommended for implementation at the boundary of the first and second crescents. This bypass is expected to have dedicated transit lanes. Some sections use buses, others tramways. The usage expected for this type of route is quite reasonable in the wake of completion of a close linkage, including connection with radial bus routes.

So, by designing a service system by minibuses on demand in the large crescent and a network of interlocking routes in the middle crescent, the functioning of public transportation in low and medium density areas can be optimized and quality services can be offered to residents without vehicles. No one is left at the side of the road. The living area is accessible to all.

Promoting mass public transportation to serve densely populated areas of large cities and ensure connections between urbanization hubs

What role should public transportation play in its traditional form, that is to say, in the form of fixed route transportation with very high passenger occupancy?

Fixed route public transportation has a decisive role to play in serving the historical centers of large cities. What would Paris be without the metro or the RER? These fixed route transit systems are equally essential for ensuring service to densely populated hubs that have been restructured, e.g., strategic sites in Île-de-France (la Défense, la Plaine-St-Denis, Bologne-Billancourt, Seine-Amont), or entirely new hubs such as the new towns. They provide concrete examples of multihub organization of urban spaces.

Economic energy, which is primarily at work in dense areas where it creates wealth, is, as we know, in the form $d.V^2$. It brings together the density of human occupation of the living area served and the travel speed within this area. In a multihub organization, it is necessary to clearly distinguish the economic energy attached to the internal servicing of the historical center or of each of the dense, clearly identifiable urban hubs, and the energy associated with bringing humans together between hubs that are sometimes quite distant when we consider that protected natural spaces lie between them.

Multihub organization only takes on its real meaning within living areas comprising 500,000 inhabitants or more. In agglomerations of less than 500,000 inhabitants, we may figure that there is a historical entity, on the outskirts of which urbanization has developed because of proximity. Above 500,000 we can begin to envisage creation of new densely populated hubs, separated from the historical center by protected natural spaces.

In order to ensure service to the historical center or to each of the clearly identifiable urban hubs taken separately, it is necessary to provide closely-knit public surface transportation, able to offer the best service possible, using dedicated lanes that emerge as—and when—traffic increases. When the size of the agglomeration rises, taking into account space constraints that accompany density, we are led to envisage public transportation routes with dedicated lanes that give rise in this manner to tramways installed locally underground, or actual subway lines with reduced clearance. The most successful example is the network of the traditional Paris subway, also called the "Bienvenüe" metro by the name of its originator. The routes comprise stations every 400 meters and are closely interconnected. The urbanization density served is extremely high: 200 jobs per hectare. Travel speed door to door is not important (on the order of 9 km/h, with trains that move at 24 km/h on average), but the economic energy is excellent (2,500,000 jobs accessible in an hour).

Improvement projects for the Paris subway network in years to come focus on extending the routes by a few kilometers in order to serve very dense areas on the close outskirts of the capital. These projects also include creation of a circular metro route that will link together the terminal stations of the radial routes. Beyond that, it is the bus with dedicated bus lanes or the tramway that take over. The second bypass, built about 4 kilometers beyond the first, relies on a system of routes featuring buses with dedicated bus lanes or tramways.

As—and when—urbanization density decreases, the use rate of the routes drops. So it is necessary to be less ambitious regarding use rate specifications while paying attention to travel speeds.

In dense hubs on the outskirts, it is primarily bus routes with their own bus lanes that handle internal service, often with central stations built underground due to the occupation density of the space. The total number of trips handled by public transportation must not exclude trips by private vehicle when these are unavoidable: usually we don't use the metro or the bus when we go to buy a refrigerator, a television, or a dressing table. There is indeed mutual give and take.

As far as transportation goes, public transportation is the equivalent of gas turbines feeding the electric grid in the energy sector. Gas turbines multiply by two or three times the power of the electric grid that basically runs on nuclear energy. They make it possible to respond to spikes in energy use. The power is multiplied, the running time is shorter, but the operation costs are of course higher.

The same applies to public transportation: usage increases, with rush hour traffic representing about 25 percent of the daily total while 8 to 10 percent is the rate for private transportation. Operating costs are obviously higher due to driver salary costs incurred throughout the day. Viewed in this way, public transportation constitutes an efficient transportation system that allows high densities, generates economic energy and is opened to all socioprofessional categories. The subsidies that public authorities grant public transportation come from a desire to develop high-quality town planning, the heart of a robust urban life.

For exchanges between hubs, particularly for exchanges between peripheral hubs and the central historical hub, it is necessary to design high capacity rapid public transportation. The sample solution that must be implemented is that of the RER operating in Île-de-France. It is a matter of trains offering average commercial speeds of 60 km/h, with stations one to 2 kilometers apart. Within the hubs, the stations are built in the center of the urban area to facilitate terminal trips on foot, and are interconnected with the metro stations or the local transportation systems with their dedicated lanes. Whenever space permits, particularly outside the hubs, stations have parking lots where users arriving from low-density peripheral areas can leave their cars. Average speed door to door is 25 to 30 km/h.

To take an actual example, line A of the RER serves Île-de-France from west to east over a distance of nearly 80 kilometers. In the west it serves the new town of Cergy-Pontoise with several stations, links the main activity hubs in Paris, and in the east reaches Marne-la-Vallée, which it serves efficiently with eight stations. The last station is Marne-la-Vallée/Val d'Europe whose station is adjacent to the transit connection for the Île-de-France TGV bullet train. Exceptional openness is the result of this communication junction, in the direction of the main economic hubs of the Île-de-France region and the rest of the nation. It explains the success of Val d'Europe, considering that 15 years ago this site was void of any urbanization. These high capacity rapid public transportation systems handle large numbers of passengers in relatively short times. Total daily traffic hardly exceeds four to five times the traffic during rush hours. These routes complement the network of freeways handling traffic flows that stretch out much more over time (12 to 15 times that of rush hour traffic). There is a great synergy between the two systems, the network of freeways providing the basis for travel and rapid public transportation supplying the indispensable complement to the economic and social vitality of urban hubs.

Is it necessary or possible to develop high-flow connections between peripheral hubs themselves, that is, while bypassing the historical center?

This goal is rather difficult to achieve, for traffic between the peripheral hubs is not always sufficient to justify the type of heavy investments implied by rapid public transportation with dedicated tracks. The economically sensible answer thus depends on the strength of the peripheral hubs. In Île-de-France, the master plan provides for railroads running tangentially and linking the new towns together, but they have not yet seen the light of day, because of low profitability. In countries where the occupation density of the living areas is very high, e.g., Holland, Germany, or southern England, trains that connect urban hubs function well. The response has to be nuanced for it truly depends on the strength of the hubs to be connected and on their distance from each other. If necessary, some peripheral connections can be handled by dedicated lanes on urban avenues. What should be completed are projects that contribute a genuine additional service in relation to traditional private solutions.

From these few examples, it becomes clear that public and private transportation ought not be set in opposition. Rather, solutions must be found that make best use of each means with a global objective of multihub, multispatial organization of the living areas, the source of economic and environmental progress.

Developing interregional transportation: the case of the bullet train—TGV—and airport services

Living areas must also be linked with each other by means of transportation that place them in synergy on the national level, and even on the continental level. What recommendations can be made regarding this matter?

France, as we have seen, is a low-density country: on average one inhabitant and a little less than 0.5 jobs per hectare. Spain has a similar density. Benelux, Germany, and the United Kingdom, on the other hand, are much denser in population: on the order of 2.5 times more dense.

A density of 0.5 jobs per hectare represents a level 20 times lower than that of 10 jobs per hectare noted in Marne-la-Vallée—a new town with large green spaces—that itself offers a density 20 times lower than that of 200 jobs per hectare observed in Paris.

The economic energy of Paris, some 2.5 million jobs accessible in an hour, is achieved with a metro that offers an average travel speed door to door of 9 km/h. A comparable energy, though lower, is achieved in Marne-la-Vallée with transportation systems, particularly private vehicles, that offer door to door a speed on the order of 36 km/h, four times higher than that of the metro, making it possible to cover in 1 hour a living area 16 times larger, thus compensating for a job density that is 20 times less.

Job density being 20 times less at the national level than in Marne-la-Vallée, it is necessary, in order to achieve comparable levels of economic energy, to design a transportation system offering average door to door speeds that are four times higher. For that, it is necessary to attain average speeds door to door on the order of 150 km/h, which implies (including terminal trips) commercial speeds on the order of 300 km/h. The bullet train (TGV—train á grande vitesse) corresponds precisely to this objective. It represents a mode of transportation perfectly adapted to a low-density country like France. This is what explains its success. Spain could also benefit from equipping itself with TGVs in order to compensate in speed for the low density of its area. On the other hand, countries two or three times as dense like Benelux, Germany, and England are logically less sensitive to great speeds. They can achieve results equivalent to those of France with speeds door to door of 100 km/h, accessible to cars moving at 130 km/h on interurban freeways or on railroad systems that would offer, considering terminal trips, commercial speeds between stations on the order of 200 km/h.

The network of high-speed trains is thus an efficient transportation system that unifies the French country. In the long run, all main French metropolises will be linked to the capital. They will also be linked with each other. So, Lille is 1 hour from Paris, Lyon is 2 hours, and Marseille 3 hours. Bordeaux soon will be 2 hours from Paris, as will Strasbourg. The interconnection TGV route running east of Île-de-France makes direct links with Lille, Lyon, and Marseille possible, and also links between Lille and Bordeaux.

For its part, Spain is equipping itself quickly. Madrid is linked to Saragossa and to Barcelona. Soon the capital will be linked to Valencia and Bilbao. Connections between France and Spain will make possible bringing together regions currently separated by the Pyrenees. That is how the link between Montpellier and Barcelona is planned, as well as connection between Bordeaux and the Basque Country, via Irun. Thought should be given to appraising the conditions under which a connection of less than 2 hours could be established between Bordeaux and Saragossa, Toulouse and Saragossa, three agglomerations with almost a million inhabitants each. Such a solution without excessive outlays is perfectly thinkable using, along a short section of 30 kilometers, the historical one-track link between Oloron and Jaca via the Somport tunnel and Canfranc station, the access to the Marches of Pyrenees being provided by high-speed routes from Bordeaux and Toulouse on the French side, and from Saragossa on the Spanish side. We see a network emerging that not only gives unity to each of the countries, but also offers a broadly European perspective.

Airlines can provide equivalent services. Besides, TGVs and airplanes are in competition. The airplane goes more quickly at commercial speed but is penalized by the difficulties of terminal trips. The negative impacts of noise incurred by airports lead to building them farther and farther away, which increases the length of travel door to door. What matters, in reality, is the number of workers accessible in a given time starting from home. Trips by TGV or by airplane are part of the range of 2 or 3 hours of travel. They only represent less than 1 percent of daily trips of which (remember) 50 percent exceed 30 minutes, 10 percent exceed 1 hour, and 2 percent 1.5 hours. On a trip of 2 hours, if the sum of terminal trips exceeds 1 hour, the average speed is divided by two. If it reaches 1 hour and a half, 45 minutes at the start and 45 at the destination, the average speed is divided by four. It falls at around 200 km/h and hardly represents benefits compared with the TGV whose stations are established in the heart of urbanized areas. It becomes clear to what extent conditions of access to airports play a crucial role.

Today, on connections like Paris-Lyon that take 2 hours by TGV, the TGV handles 80 percent of the trips and the airplane 20 percent. On connections like Paris-Marseille that take 3 hours by TGV, the TGV handles 40 percent of the trips and the plane 60 percent.

At the level of international relations, the airplane becomes unbeatable because its extremely high commercial speed of 800 km/h makes it possible to cover in a few hours areas that no other means of transportation can service in the same time frame. The existence of international airports is an asset for cities thus equipped. This is especially the case in Île-de-France that has in Roissy an exceptional airport, as much for its capacity as for its service quality. However, problems with noise pollution are becoming increasingly sensitive. This factor will be the one that will probably limit the capacity of the airport, incurring the need for a new airport, a subject that raises a great deal of passion, as has been witnessed.

In order to function harmoniously, a living area also needs infrastructures to handle exchanges of products, goods, and services. These requirements are linked to the economic activities practiced by people. Freight, for example, constitutes one of the links in the structure of production of goods and services. Efficient transportation reduces warehousing costs and improves productivity. The vitality of a living area depends significantly on the quality of its networks of production and energy transport—electricity, gas, petroleum products—or on telecommunication networks, with the increasingly imperious need for high-capacity networks. All these infrastructures complete those that ensure the physical mobility of humans. They afford them accompanying services that increase their performance. But the guiding principle of economy—its basis—remains the exchange of know-how between human beings.

Combating the greenhouse effect: promoting vehicles that rely on hydrogen and fuel cells

Many of the transportation means I have mentioned produce greenhouse gases. Now, my recommendation is that mobility be allowed to flourish to make it possible for people to exchange their skills, and create more economic energy, the source of wealth and employment. I also propose that people have access to more natural spaces to renew themselves. However, the consequences of the greenhouse effect are becoming noticeable. It seems that the rise in average temperature observed on our planet for decades is indeed the result of human activity. Isn't there a profound contradiction in these propositions? How can the Kyoto Accords be respected under these conditions?

This is a real question. Besides, it is at the heart of the arguments raised by those who recommend that mobility be restrained. These officials point out that transportation is responsible for about one-third of greenhouse gases; that if we want to reduce these emissions, there is no other choice than to level off and reduce this kind of travel.

I have a different response. As I have shown, when the weight of the creation of value due to the possibility of reaching numerous economic and natural destinations (and then exchanging know-how or appreciating natural spaces) is 100, the weight of traveling time and expenditures in order to reach these destinations is 33 and that of negative impacts incurred by traveling is 3. One can justly point out that if the greenhouse effect unleashes climatic phenomena that profoundly disturb the life of plant and animal communities on our earth, the comparisons that I am presenting rapidly lose their significance. Now, it is probably *not* true because humans just like animal and plant species in general, have impressive abilities to adapt and react. I am totally convinced that humans are perfectly capable of stabilizing greenhouse gasses, especially those linked with transportation, then reducing them to the point where they more or less disappear without impacting travel, which is so useful for exchanges of know-how.

The solution is to be found in the promotion of hydrogen use each time electricity cannot be used directly. Hydrogen combined with oxygen yields water. Water is not a pollutant and does not create a greenhouse effect. Hydrogen can be produced in quantity. It is indeed the most abundant element in the universe. It is at the heart of the nuclear fusion that takes place within stars and even now provides us with the radiant energy that most plants use so well through photosynthesis to create organic molecules necessary to their development.

Large quantities of hydrogen can be produced on earth without emitting greenhouse gases by using electricity created from nuclear energy to decompose water into its two base constituents. If humans continue to produce wealth, they will have the capacity to construct nuclear plants whose electricity will be used to provide this hydrogen production. Current technological evolution, born of human ingenuity, will make it possible to adapt this means of energy to most means of transportation, present or future. The production of greenhouse gases will be stabilized and then reduced. What remains for us to do, of course, is to make policy decisions to adopt hydrogen as the energy standard for transportation and to organize the progressive relinquishing of carbon energy such as gasoline.

After all, the adaptation of hydrogen to different means of transportation has been the focus of considerable experimentation over the past few years.

Efforts are particularly important in the sphere of automobiles, buses, and trucks, the dominant means of transportation. Manufacturers are spending large amounts of money developing viable solutions.

The technology is difficult to perfect given the problems posed by hydrogen storage. But undeniable progress has been made. There is more and more talk of fuel cells that produce electricity from sources such as hydrogen. This technique is used in particular in space stations. The physical phenomenon at work in a fuel cell is the reverse of the one employed for producing hydrogen and oxygen from water through use of electricity. In a cell, the combination of hydrogen and oxygen yields water and produces electricity, usable in electric traction motors of vehicles.

Several buses fitted with fuel cells are currently running without incident in the United States.

If the technique can be considered mastered, the financial returns are still out of reach. There is still progress to be made in this area. But it is only a question of time.

As for air transportation, the idea of using hydrogen instead of carbon fuels also has been mentioned. The tanks would be much bigger than in the case of traditional airplanes and would have to be kept at very low temperatures, but the balance sheet with regard to weight and performance would not be unfavorable. Hydrogen combined with oxygen causes a reaction that produces a great deal of energy. Aerodynamics would still work. A stock of planes of this type could make viable commercial sense. It would be necessary, of course, to organize a hydrogen distribution network that does not currently exist and that could come to fruition if a political decision were taken to promote hydrogen on the global level.

The path has been traced out and the installation of hydrogen as fuel in different forms of transportation will be progressively introduced into our way of life. The "hydrogen society" will probably characterize the second half of the century.

In the area of rail travel, trains—especially high-speed trains—depend on electricity for their motion. Eighty-five percent of their energy source is nuclear, so no greenhouse gases are emitted. It is one of the virtues of a transportation system that also provides for high commercial speeds and serves the core of urbanized areas.

Public rail services inside urbanized areas are also using electricity from now on. Like the TGVs, they rely indirectly on a significant amount of nuclear energy that does not produce greenhouse gases.

Based on these facts, can we be confident about conquering the greenhouse effect?

In the long term, yes. On the technical level, solutions exist or are being designed. On the political level, that will require courageous decisions in order to change energy consumption habits. Investments also will be important, in particular for constructing hydrogen production plants and establishing distribution grids for this energy within airports, along roadway and freeway networks, or in industrial enterprises. But the solution is in sight. It will be a new and exciting challenge for humanity.

Growth prospects from a viewpoint of respect for our environment

Promoting mobility, sustaining human cooperative labor, and facilitating access to nature

How shall I summarize my reflection on living areas, their operating logic, and all the benefit that the totality of plant and animal species as well as humans stands to gain?

Our beautiful blue planet, when seen from space, presents a magnificent sight that is at the same time fragile. The atmosphere constitutes a thin gaseous layer and we understand the intimate connections that it has with the earth that gave rise to it.

Life has taken four billion years to develop in this exceptional environment. It presents a great unity and, at the same time, a prodigious diversity. Humans, even if they tend to forget, are profoundly connected to the totality of living species that surround them. They are connected as much to microorganisms as to the plants or animals that make up the chain of being. They are also connected to the most complex organisms that, in the framework of evolution, have acquired very high-level functions. Humans are in solidarity with the extraordinarily varied totality in which aggressive relations—but also many cooperative relations—play out.

The first goal to pursue, if we are interested in what is to become of the planet and our living areas, is therefore to protect this long chain of being and allow it the possibility of flourishing in all its diversity. From this fact it follows that natural spaces must be forcefully protected, for they are what make it possible for the phenomena of life to develop most fully. This must be done through the legal system. Humans must self-regulate in order to leave room for all other plant and animal species. By so doing, they will preserve their own future since they are totally dependent on other living species for their biological development.

Moreover, humans must enhance the worth of natural spaces through active development policies for developing wooded areas, maintaining endangered crops, rehabilitating streams and bodies of water, and landscaping spaces that have been deteriorated.

This policy of preserving and valuing nature bears fruit when it is carried out with perseverance. It suffices to take the example of French forestry policy. The surface area of forests today is noticeably higher than 20 years ago, even while the human population of France has increased in the meantime. In these preserved spaces, plants and animals are developing with great vitality. It is necessary, obviously, to pursue and broaden the policy of setting aside protected natural spaces free of all urban activity with a double objective: to allow all species the possibility of flourishing without major conflicts with humans, and to allow humans to maintain contact with the natural environment, which is necessary for their own balance and well-being.

However, the ambition of preserving the living space of other species must not lead humans to overly constrain themselves. They must define and manage the spaces where they themselves can flourish in their own specific ways such as designing and producing goods, developing services, improving know-how, developing knowledge, and engaging in social, cultural, and religious relationships. It is therefore necessary that spaces destined to accommodate housing, business activity, and service be harmoniously demarcated, with care given to leaving to everybody the place he needs. Useless constraints imposed on spaces that can be urbanized can only lead to undesirable effects such as the emergence of scarcities and discomforts that ought not to be. Experience shows that, even in extremely populated areas such as Holland, a harmonious organization of natural spaces, as well as those that can be urbanized, yields a feeling of great respect for nature and—simultaneously—a great freedom of movement in residential and business areas. Respect for nature does not have to be opposed to the search for a comfortable life—quite the contrary.

Like all animal species, humans have a special privilege: they are mobile. They take advantage of their exceptional ingenuity to acquire the means of going from one place to another that multiply tenfold their capacity for exchange. They know how to move on earth, the sea, and the air in conditions hard to imagine just 100 years ago. In invariable travel time, that is, without expending more effort than their ancestors did while moving on foot, they can access ever-larger areas daily, and diversify the economic and leisure destinations among which they make a choice. Increasing the extent of choices means increasing the relevance of the choice made. In the economic sphere, it means creating more goods and services by mobilizing increasingly numerous skills. In the area of well-being and renewal, it means accessing more natural spaces and sharing the resources of our planet "Earth" with other plants and animals.

Mobility is a phenomenal amplifier of economic and ergonomic choices. It is not to be constrained, even less cut off. It must simply be provided with the help of well integrated means of transportation without negative impacts. With their intelligence and know-how, humans can achieve this result.

What's more, the wealth they will create based on their mobility will allow them to conquer the negative impacts that they are likely to produce. It shouldn't be forgotten that almost half the wealth produced by a country like France comes from the ability to mobilize skills in areas of daily life. Of course, it is essential to preserve this possibility of accessing diversified skills—a possibility that constitutes the power of humans linked to their living area. Affecting mobility means constricting the extent of easily accessible living spaces, and interfering with the diversity of contacts that can be established with fellow human beings whose temperaments, skills, and aspirations are as diverse as life itself. We need to keep in mind the notion of an area's economic energy, which links its occupation density with the travel speed of the people who live and work there. Immobile human beings do not produce wealth. A few isolated individuals moving very quickly do not produce any more beyond that. What we need are many humans and—at the same time—travel speed to create exchanges of know-how favorable to the creation of goods and services. We cannot think of bridling mobility without considering the destruction of value incurred by such a policy. The consequences are often pushed under a cloak of silence, hence the surprises after a few years when serious negative effects appear. These effects include economic sluggishness or a rise in unemployment, phenomena that we are seeing right now. No doubt, since it is certainly one of the reasons for it, we have not done enough over the course of past decades to ensure that mobility receives support in metropolitan areas.

Humans, due to their mobility, also can go out and enjoy the benefits of nature and spend time in proximity to an increasing number of forests, landscapes, and bodies of water. They can renew themselves, rediscover the "fundamentals" of life, and relate to the totality of the living world. When they go walking or hiking, they can preserve the conditions of well-being that come from being in close contact with nature. There, too, we need to keep in mind the notion of spatial or natural energy that links the density of natural spaces to the travel speed of the humans who wish to access them. Neither nonaccessible natural spaces nor rapid travel in living areas without natural spaces yields the desired well-being or relaxation. We need abundant spaces free of all urban encroachment, diverse in nature and high in quality, and—at the same time—the speed to access this diversity. This form of energy, in my opinion, is as essential as economic energy. We need to preserve and increase it. To do that, we need to avoid interfering with the rapidity of leisure travel. On the contrary, we need to support it to allow everyone to find renewal in easily accessible spaces. The contact of humans with nature presents many positive aspects. It increases peaceful relationships between species. The complementary nature of their needs and their positive synergies emerge. It is up to humans to honor them.

Placing technology in service of the battle against negative impacts

These visions are certainly reassuring. But what can be said about the negative impacts that are the object of so many current debates?

It cannot be denied that humans incur negative impacts when they produce goods or offer services, when they mobilize energy resources to assist them in their activities, when they build and put into service increasingly sophisticated means of transportation for the purpose of meeting fellow human beings and exchanging skills and know-how. These negative impacts are connected, for example, with agricultural production, with the use of fertilizers and herbicides that can be dangerous. Ill effects are linked to industrial production with the use of chemicals, of which certain compounds have serious effects on the development of plants and animals. Negative impacts come with transportation, the source of pollution that raises the most sustained criticism. But at the moment of passing judgment, we must draw the distinction between the urge to criticize and the reality. Are the negative impacts that lead certain people in responsible positions to recommend reducing mobility so serious that we must interfere with this priceless good? Or is it rather to be hoped that thanks to human know-how and intelligence, we will progressively overcome negative impacts and take advantage of mobility without suffering its disadvantages? All the observations in which I have engaged over the course of these many years of reflecting on the topic lead me to this alternative, that is to say, an optimistic vision of overcoming negative impacts in a world that can continue to progress economically and ecologically…

If we take, for example, the case of air pollution linked to transportation, the situation, as we have seen, is continually improving. Lead has completely disappeared. Vehicles no longer emit it. Regulation has made a pollutant disappear without interfering with mobility. A technical adaptation took place. Emissions of sulfur oxides are also decreasing due to an improvement in fuels that contain fewer and fewer sulfur impurities. Carbon monoxide, nitrogen oxides, and unburned hydrocarbons are changed into carbon dioxide and atmospheric nitrogen in three-stroke catalytic converters that are now required on all vehicles. Nitrogen oxides are the ones that are most resistant but there is a significant decrease. Technical progress is once again at work. As for particulates emitted by diesel engines, the new filters installed in this type of engine considerably reduce them. The enumeration of this long list of technical improvement reveals how a phenomenon that public opinion perceives as serious is actually in the process of being solved. Mobility has not been affected in order to resolve the problem. Technical progress has simply been mobilized in order to find solutions.

One emission that is not, properly speaking, a pollutant—carbon dioxide—cannot be reduced significantly as long as we continue to depend on fossil fuels to power our vehicles. Carbon dioxide contributes to the greenhouse effect. First of all, emission levels will have to be stabilized and then steadily reduced. There, too, technical progress will find the solution. It is hydrogen the clean fuel par excellence that will gradually provide the solution.

To be sure, a strong political will is going to be necessary, and significant legal and financial means will be required to attain resolution. But there is no doubt that the solution exists and, to reiterate, that it does not imply reducing mobility. Humans will have lived for one or two centuries on the fossil fuel accumulated by life over the course of millions of years. After this period of relative ease, they will have to produce a type of energy that is clean over the long term, thanks to their intelligence and their unique know-how. No doubt they will achieve the goal, for research already being conducted is showing the way.

If we look at the topic of noise as a negative impact connected with transportation, there, too, progress is considerable. New infrastructures are designed with noise emission levels far lower than what was observable just a few years ago. In urban environments, many roads are covered. The coverings are used for parks, sports complexes, and places to walk. Traditional roadways freed of all kinds of nonlocal traffic become streets and avenues that welcome pedestrians and cyclists. It is obvious that exposure to noise is on the decline.

Road danger will probably remain the most serious of the negative impacts connected with travel. The fatalities and injuries recorded every year are real and represent too many heart-rending stories. But there, too, progress is possible if the political will exists. The installation of automatic speed controls has caused the number of fatalities and injuries to decrease by almost one-third. It is interesting to note once again that it is technology that has made it possible to significantly reduce the impact of an undesirable effect of transportation.

In adding up the balance sheet of negative impacts incurred by transportation, I see no objective reason that could make me lean toward a limitation of mobility. Even if the calculations are short of perfect, the calculated economic value of all negative impacts incurred by transportation only represents a moderate percentage of travel generalized cost, which itself represents only a third, at most, of the creation of value connected with these trips. Reducing mobility would have negative consequences, in terms of economic and natural performance rates, that would be disproportionate in relation to the goal of reducing negative impacts. For me, the solution is clear. It is necessary to allocate a significant portion of the wealth produced toward combating these negative impacts, to design infrastructures that are optimally, even totally, adapted, and to effectively improve the quality of life of inhabitants. In contrast, it cannot be a question of interfering with mobility in the name of combating negative impacts, for that is tantamount to agreeing to significantly amputate the creation of economic and ergonomic wealth and to tighten the job market without contributing any real improvement to the quality of life. Rather, to the contrary.

Is it possible to definitively reconcile economic progress, development of well-being, and preservation of our planet? Yes, absolutely. That will require large-scale individual and collective efforts. But humans are able to take up this challenge and to place all the resources of their intelligence in the service of this worthy ambition.

Conclusion

An optimistic vision of our future

It is evident from all I have said that the future awaiting us on the beautiful blue planet which houses us is not as dark as people want to say.

However, everything I hear on a daily basis gives me the opposite impression. People talk to me about human overpopulation, extinction of species, destruction of rainforests in the Amazon, pollution of the oceans, the greenhouse effect, global warming, releasing of methane in the Siberian tundra, increases in the level of oceans, and destructive hurricanes.

What should we think of all this?

I am not a wide-eyed optimist, but a realist who is attempting to form an overall picture about the way that life has been developing for millions and billions of years, whether in our oceans, on our continents, or within our earth's atmosphere.

What strikes me first of all is the extraordinary diversity of the forms of life and the way in which species adapt to changing environments. Hundreds of millions of years ago, our atmosphere did not contain oxygen. It is life itself that introduced this very powerful oxidizing agent after having "invented" photosynthesis. Nature fixed huge quantities of carbon in the biomass and released oxygen. Today, oxygen is considered as creator of life—a wonderful adaptation to a change of much greater dimensions than the greenhouse effect we talk about so much nowadays.

Entire species are born, develop, and die, just as individual living organisms—obviously at a much faster rate—are born, attain maturity, decline, then die. The species currently living on our planet only represent about 1 percent of those that have existed on the earth for billions of years. The development of life has never been a long, quiet stream but has known periods of great growth spurts followed by great crises. Since the Cambrian period, 500 million years ago, five great crises covering several millions of years have taken place. At the time of each crisis more than half the species became extinct; others appeared and occupied the ecosystems they colonized. Many new species regularly appeared on our planet. It seems that a certain contraction in the number of species was at work after the Cambrian period, and at the same time, increasingly evolved species emerged. All that shows that the earth is indeed alive and that the species it hosts must forever adapt.

As a result, I believe that human beings today must, like their ancestors, adapt to the evolutions of the earth, evolutions connected with cosmic events, or evolutions caused by humans themselves, in the same way plants did when they "invented" photosynthesis and introduced oxygen into an atmosphere that had none.

Moreover, humans are one element in a long chain of life that comprises numerous microorganisms whose biomass is widely dominant, as well as very diverse plant species and equally diverse animal species. Without this chain mankind cannot live on our planet. Humans are in solidarity with the living species that surround them, and with which it is indispensable to institute broad cooperative relations rather than just predatory ones—thus the respect for nature that they must include in their grand ambitions.

At the end of the day, humans are social beings endowed with a great intelligence who manufacture goods and produce diverse services. They complement their natural locomotion with the assistance of powerful means of transportation, giving them opportunities to meet many fellow human beings daily, exchange all kinds of expertise, and access vast natural spaces in which they can be renewed. As a result, humans have access to living areas that grow wider and wider and open economic and ergonomic horizons that are always new. To be sure, they incur negative impacts that are linked to this activity and that can affect the entire planet when, for example, they transform the atmosphere through greenhouse gases. However, I strongly believe that individual and collective intelligence demonstrated by humans throughout their development can make it possible for them to create technologies that will reduce, even eliminate, the negative impacts they have caused.

Based on the evidence we have seen, reining humans back in their creative energy and limiting them in their interactions cannot be a solution. They must be allowed the possibility of organizing, reacting, and finding solutions to the different problems that they confront along with other species that share with them the same planet—while awaiting maybe the day when they will have to explore other horizons, other planets that will enlarge their living realm.

Background notes

The research works cited in this book began when I was director of the urban division of Freeway and Highway Technical Studies Department (Service d'Études Techniques des Routes et Autoroutes or SETRA) from 1972 to 1975. These works resulted in publication of working notes and later global documents. Author: Jean Poulit.

January 8, 1973—Working note: Accessibility Criteria: indexes of user choice and indexes of satisfaction.

April 26, 1973—Working note: Indexes of Urban Development: relationships with user indexes of satisfaction, costs of urbanization and environmental factors.

November 1973—Global document: Economic Approach of Accessibility. 36 pages.

September 20, 1974—Global document : "Town Planning and Transportation: criteria for accessibility and urban development." 55 pages.

September 1, 1994—Report addressed to the Council General of Bridges and Roadways (Conseil Général des Ponts et Chaussées), entitled "Evaluation of the economic and environmental efficiency of transportation infrastructures. Influence of the size of agglomerations." 36 pages, 4 appendixes and graphic illustrations. This publication cites research works conducted during three years in 16 reference agglomerations—from Guéret to the Paris metropolitan area, when I was prefect, regional director of Public Works and Transportation for Île-de-France (préfect directeur régional de l'Équipment d'Île-de-France).

June 19 and 20, 1996—The minister of Public Works and Transportation (ministre de l'Equipement et des Transports) entrusts me, along with the president of the economic affairs section of the Council General of Bridges and Roadways, with the organization and implementation of a colloquium on "The stakes of urban mobility," for the benefit of all national, regional, and departmental ministry officials. The minister of Public Works and the secretary of state for Transportation participate in this colloquium. The proceedings of the colloquium are published.

During the years 2002 and 2003, as general director of the National Institute of Geography (Institut Géographique National) (1997–2002), then as member of the Council General of Bridges and Roadways (2002–2003), I proceed with economic and natural performance evaluations of the different living areas of France, and—as well—economic performance evaluations of the different living areas of nine countries neighboring France.

April 28, 2003—A global note sums up these works, accompanied by numerous cartographic illustrations of these performance evaluations.

November 7, 2003—The president of the economic affairs section of the Council General of Bridges and Roadways signs a directive to the research director of the ministry of Public Works and Transportation as well as to the director of the Center for Studies on Networks, Transportation, Urban Planning, and Public Facilities (Centre d'Études sur les Réseaux, les Transports, l'Urbanisme et les Constructions Publiques) and to the directors of the Centers for Technical Studies of Public Works and Transportation (Centres d'Études Techniques de l'Équipement), the contents of which I established.

March 25, 2004—The minister of Public Works and Transportation signs the global directive on the evaluation of large-scale transportation infrastructure projects. This directive introduces the concept of the creation of value. The compiling of appendix 2, dedicated to methods for determining this value, is entrusted to me.

In the course of the years 1973 and 1974, I am actively supported by Jean Gérard Koenig, civil engineer (Ingénieur des Ponts et Chaussées), in the urban division of SETRA.

Jean Gérard Koenig publishes, in June 1974, in the *General Journal of Roads (Revue Générale des Routes)*, an article entitled, "The Theory of Urban Accessibility, a new tool for city planners."

In April 1976, Koenig publishes a second article in the same journal entitled, "Indicators of Accessibility in urban studies: from theory to practice."

I collaborate once again with Jean Gérard Koenig over a 7-year period—from 1991 to 1997—while at the head of the Île-de-France Regional Public Works and Transportation Administration as prefect, regional director charged notably with revising the master plan for Île-de-France. At that time, Jean Gérard Koenig is director of the division of Infrastructures and Transport, an important division in charge of road infrastructures, public transport, and strategic transportation studies.